MACRAMÈ:

---

3 Books In 1:

Everything You Can Learn About Macrame. Knots, Patterns and Step By Step High Definition Images To Create Your Homemade Bohemian Projects

---

EMILY SENRA

THIS BOOK INCLUDES:

BOOK 1:
MODERN MACRAMÉ:

Easy Step-By-Step Macramé Projects And Patterns For All Levels To Make Your Unique Handmade Home And Garden Décor. Embellish, Make Gifts, Sell.

BOOK 2:
MACRAME FOR BEGINNERS

An Easy Step-By-Step Guide To Macramé. Projects For Beginners And Intermediate Learners With High-Quality Images For A Much Better Experience.

BOOK 3:
MACRAMÉ PATTERNS:

The Easy Beginner's And Intermediate Guide To The Ancient Art Of Macramé. Including Step-By-Step Projects For All Levels And High-Quality Images.

© Copyright 2020 - All rights reserved.

MODERN MACRAMÉ:

Easy Step-By-Step Macramé Projects And Patterns For All Levels To Make Your Unique Handmade Home And Garden Décor. Embellish, Make Gifts, Sell.

EMILY SENRA

Table Of Contents

Introduction

In old times Knots and knot lore were closely associated with magic, medication, religious views for much of history. Knots also acted as bases for mathematical structures (for example, by the Mayans), before writing skills were introduced; and string games and other alternate uses were and are still numerous, of course. With these things have been carried out in one way or another and by all cultures since ancient times. They are even being taught all over the world nowadays. Additionally, it is safe to say that it will continue to follow until the day comes that humankind no longer exists.

Macramé as a part of enhancing ties pervades almost every culture, except inside those cultures, it can show in various ways. The carefully braided strings, with the assistance of a needle-like tool, became the item for shaping fishnets. Their purpose in the fashion world has been incredible and well-known among the generation today in making sandals, shoes, jewelry, etc. It is now used also with other products to fashion all kinds of beautiful works of art.

Macramé is closely associated with the trendy youth due to its rapid growth, quick adaptability, and extensive uses. Concerning its use for fashion items, macramé practiced in the materials turned into a basic spotlight on the making of each beautifying garment, especially on the edges of each tent, dress, and towel. In this, macramé became a synonym for hanging planter. In its traditional forms, Macramé (is an Italian name given in Genoa-its home and place of birth) became one of the most common textile techniques.

Knots are used for the passage of time for several practical, mnemonic and superstitious reasons. The Peruvian Incas used a Quip, made from mnemonic knot (Basically, overhand knots) to help them record and convey information. In the early Egyptians and Greek times,' Hercules ' knot (square knot) was used on clothes, jewelry, and pottery, which had a spiritual or religious meaning.

As a product of the artistic intervention of scholarly artisans, this human intellectual accomplishment became necessary to incorporate modern architecture requiring the use of other materials for trendy artifacts. While macramé art has been created and used for onward creation in most cultures aimed at achieving both practical and artistic appeal, their end products vary from one culture to the next. These innovations, however, are, by definition, integral parts of cultural growth and are the results of the macramé artisans ' revolutionary accomplishments over the years. The use of adornment knotting distinguishes early cultures and reflected intelligence creation. It is an art that fits all ages and abilities. Today, macramé is experiencing a Revival of the 20th century.

Both men and women transition to work with their hands and build not just utilitarian pieces but also decorative ones.

Macramé has also proven to be an excellent natural treatment for those undergoing recovery procedures and helps to restore memories once again, making it a unique experience for all.

Macramé has the added benefit of embracing the self-expression cycle by establishing the underlying purpose concealed within.

CHAPTER 1:

Different Knotting Techniques

Many Macramé tasks are easy to finish. Each job has a great deal of models to create it your own. At any time, you feel used to knotting, you are inclined to be in a position to produce your routines and make some genuinely exceptional cloths. Consider ways you can change a number of these Subsequent Macramé ideas:

- Wall-hangings
- Planters
- Crucial chains
- Hanging chairs
- Belts
- Antiques

Fringe on special fabrics

Button square knots: begin out with three square knots then keep onto screw pliers by the back amid the horn cables before their original. Publish a rectangle under the bottom of this button to finish.

Cosmetic Dentistry: used making jewelry or to get Special knots such as Celtic and Chinese. These two approaches go perfectly with handmade jewelry and precious stones, for example semi-precious stones, crystals, or pearls. These Macramé knots usually are intricate and could have a while to know.

Double-hitch knot: that Macramé knot is created by Generating two half hitch knots you afterward a second. Yank on the knots attentively. Half Hitch knot: place Inch cable through your job Area (pin therefore that the cable will not proceed). At the finish of the cable that's been hauled across, the unmoving cable is drawn under the cable and pulled the loop which has been shaped. Half knot: One of the normal Macramé knots to create. A fifty% knot is an ordinary knot; you start with four strings. Put it using this loop produced by the center cable together with your hand cable. Tug to Fasten the knot. Overhand knot: Just one of the Most Often used knots in Macramé. Start with developing a loop by way of one's cable. Pull the knot carefully. Square knots: construct out of this fifty-five percent knot to produce the square knot. Take your righthand cable behind the center strings and then send it about the left-handed cable. Only choose the left-handed cable and place it throughout the ideal hand by simply moving the middle strings and pull. You wanted to be able to make your bracelets & designer handbag, but did not comprehend just how or did not have the appropriate resources? You have probably experienced such a difficulty. Macramé design is exactly what the physician ordered. Macramé is just a sort of fabric which works by using knotting. Materials that are utilized from the macramé process comprise jute, linen, strings got out of cotton twine, yarn, and hemp. It's a procedure for knotting ropes codes or strings collectively with one another to check something. This item might be described as a necklace jewelry, necklace, etc. Macramé designs can be made complicated if different knots have been united to produce one layout or complicated.

A macramé bracelet can be made under:

Desired materials a Razor-blade, a pencil or polyurethane Plank, or t-pin, a hemp cable, and sometimes some series of somebody else's taste.

Guidelines

Step 1: Measure Inch that the circumference of the wrist will probably soon be Measured. Afterward, cut two bits of this hemp rope together with the assistance of the scissors. The bits cut needs to be two times the magnitude of this wrist or the circumference measured initially. As an instance, when the dimension got was 5 inches, two strands measuring 15 inches per needs to be trimmed.

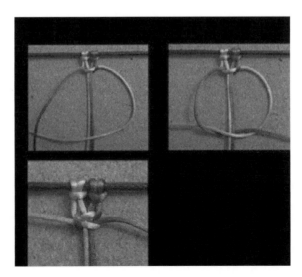

Step 2: Measure 2 strand is folded to around 30 minutes. Holding The pencil at a flat place, the strand is likely to probably be reverted onto the pen's cone to possess a loop just on the leading portion of stand, also, to guarantee loose finishes do hang. These ends ought to be passed via the loop and closely pulled. This procedure ought to be replicated with yet another strand too.. Mentally, you might label these strands from side to left side, only 1 2. It's likely to work with whatever tagging procedure you locate easily.

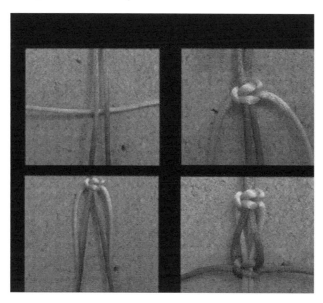

Step 3: Measure 3 strand Inch ought to be obtained, on the other hand, significantly more than just two strands 2 and strand 3 (that in personality will be stranded at the center), and then below strand 4.

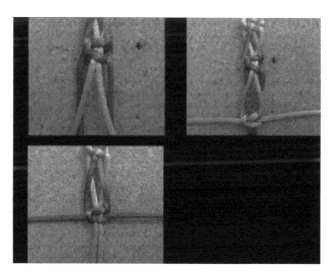

Step 4: in This Time select strand 4 supporting the two Strands 3 and 2, throughout the loop that strand inch did form. To be certain a half square rectangle is achieved, carefully pull strand 1 and strand 4.

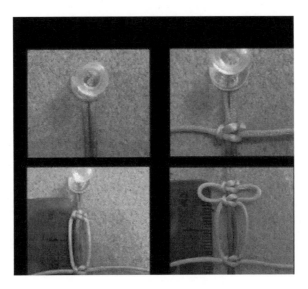

Step 5: now you need to know a strand Constituting process. Take with this particular strand crossing process until fundamentally the bracelet accomplishes this particular period which you can so desire. Spirals will probably be formed in both square knots because you carry on working out.

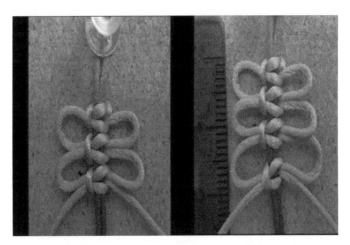

Step 6: the loops have been slid off the pen. After that, pull strand 2 and strand 3 to have the ability to lower the magnitude in these loops shaped only a small bit. Each of those four strands may then hold together along with two knots attached like a way of procuring the job. These

knots are crucial. Those strings which you side-by-side should subsequently be trimmed, and this also should attentively be performed since close those knots as you possibly can.

Step 7 in the time you have obtained the bracelet set on your wrist. The-knot needs to be passed via the fold, therefore to keep up the bracelet onto your wrist.

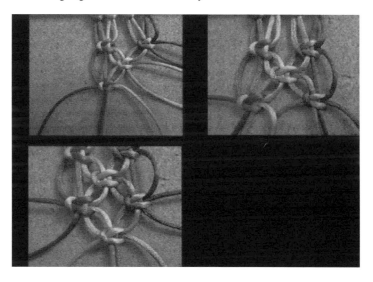

The measures above will allow you to design a Straight-forward macramé bracelet. This macramé approach uses knotting instead of weaving or knitting process. You may utilize beads to craft a beaded macramé necklace. You'll design distinguishing forms of decorations with macramé strategy. This is dependent upon you personally.

Fantasy catchers have gotten Remarkably Popular and so they're extended in an enormous variety of styles and layouts. It's likely to uncover crotchet, woven or knotted dream-catchers. Macramé is a material making procedure which is based on knotting in the place of knitting or weaving. It's a French saying that ostensibly means knot since it's on the list of very first art-forms there is. The main knots within this procedure are square knots and hitching types that may be twice or entire feasibility.

Macramé is a technique that's been used for its Maximum period to decorate and craft numerous goods. You'll detect magnificent among a sort macramé handbag, wall-hangings, fantasy catchers, and a good deal of longer. It isn't too complicated to produce your macramé dream house particularly the moment you have a couple of guides to take you through these knots. At any time, you have mastered the knotting, you're getting to be astounded by just how creative you can acquire.

The Strings

The strings are the most significant things you Are likely to have to generate your piece. Cotton twine strings would be one of the most common due to the complete appearance they furnish and you're getting to be in a posture to select unique colors to generate a design that fits with your taste. Besides cotton, then it's very likely to choose many substances for example cotton, linen, silk, and jute determined by the kind of structure that you would like to realize. Numerous those cable chemicals are a ton easier for cosmetic purposes on the fantasy catcher than they truly are correct in creating a comprehensive slice.

Cord structure may potentially be 3-ply value it Consists of three different spans of fiber to produce a robust and superbly shaped fantasy catcher.

The Rings

Macramé fantasy catchers can be accomplished with just wooden joints nevertheless in some specific scenarios you could like to consider account a dowel determined by the dimensions of one's own thing. A decorative or metallic dowel may conduct the task well in offering you a fantastic surface to disperse a large number of strings and that means that you may readily control them to accomplish your favorite design in the very long haul. If you'd like to produce smaller sized ones, a push board, maybe whatever you need to begin on work.

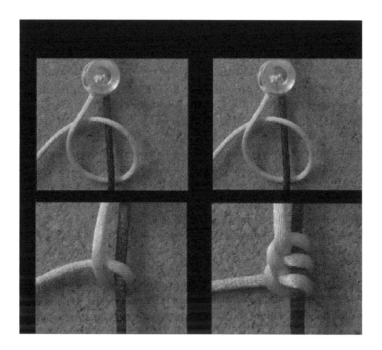

Decorations

Despite macramé fantasy catchers, it's extremely potential that you simply incorporate jewelry along with other cosmetic capabilities in the own piece. You're able to tie the ribbons using Different strand colors or maybe you include different necklaces, beads, and Cubes to make points of interest inside your design. It's likely to utilize right Hooks, u-pins or upholstery to preserve the decorations and strings put up. If You Would like to use beads as Well as another accessory, then you should pick strand thickness attentively; preferably thick strand can Not provide this alluring appearance using attachments. Thinner strings make it to Be potential for the decorations to stick out from elegance.

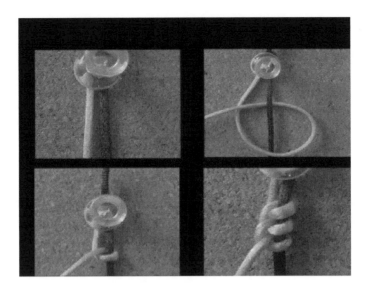

Mix and Match Knots to Create All Kinds of Patterns

The Square Knot and Square Knot Variations

Each knot is made using two steps and needs a minimum of three cords. Two cords are needed for tying the knots and a further cord is needed to knot around.

Beads can be added to the knotting cords as you tie. They can also be threaded onto the central cords and then the knotting cords can be carried around them. For very large holed beads all the cords can be passed through the beads. The square knot can be tied individually or in sennets. Using two different colored cords will produce a simple pattern through the sennet. This knot can also be tied in various formations to achieve decorative and more complex looking patterns for jewelry making and other items. This guide contains photographs showing how to tie a basic square knot and then illustrates four further ways in which square knots can be used.

 These steps can now be repeated to create as many knots as desired.

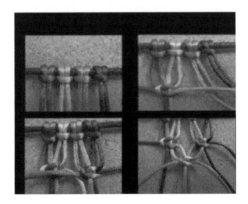

The Half Hitch Knot and Half Hitch Variations

The half hitch knot is another very common and versatile knot that is used in macramé. Like the square knot it is fairly easy to learn and can be used to create a variety of designs. Beads and other items can easily be added to either the central or knotting cords to embellish your designs.

Half hitch knots can be tied in two different ways. The knotting cord can be tied either over-under-over the holding cord or alternately it can be tied under-over-under the holding cord. I have included photographs showing both on the following pages. Either of these half hitch knots can be used to tie a variety of formations and I have included step by step photographs for four of these in the following part.

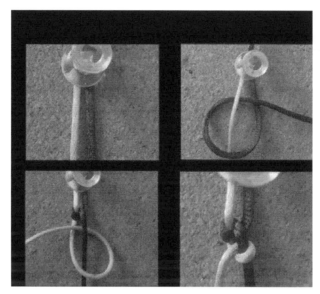

This is a vintage knot that can be used to create wide flat knotted pieces that would be suitable for bracelets, belts, bag straps, and similar. The width of the finished piece is based on the number of central cords used.

CHAPTER 2:

Macramé Patterns

Alternating Square Knots

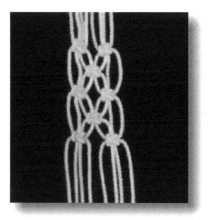

This is the right knot to use for basket hangings, decorations, or any projects that are going to require you to put weight on the project. Use a heavier weight cord for this, which you can find at craft stores or online.

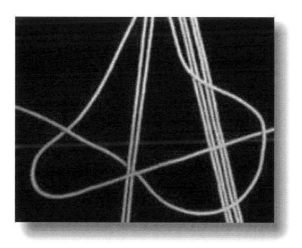

Don't rush, and make sure you have even tension throughout. Practice makes perfect, but with the illustrations to help you, you'll find it's not hard at all to create.

Start at the top of the project and work your way toward the bottom. Keep it even as you work your way throughout the piece. Tie the knots at 4-inch intervals, working your way down the entire thing.

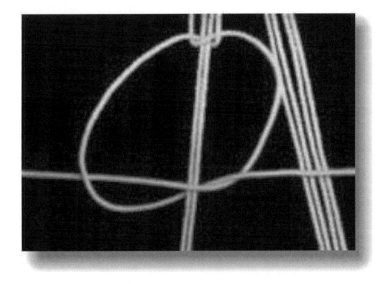

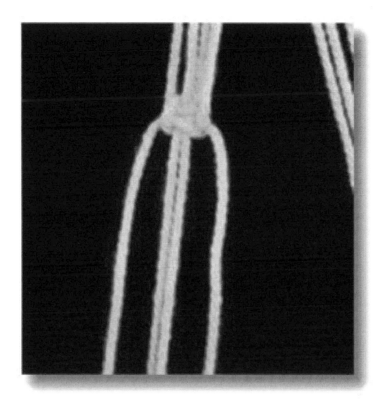

Tie each new knot securely. Remember that the more even you get the better it is.

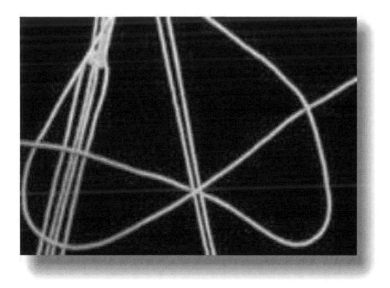

Work on one side of the piece first, then tie the knot on the other side. you are going to continue to alternate sides, with a knot joining them in the middle, as you can see in the photo

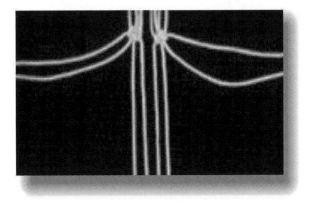

Again, keep this even as you work throughout.

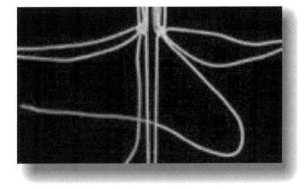

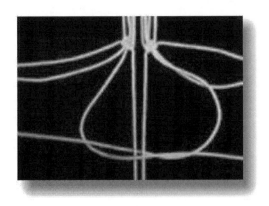

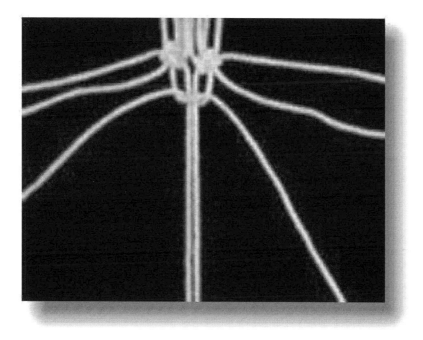

Bring the knot in toward the center and make sure you have even lengths on both sides of the piece.

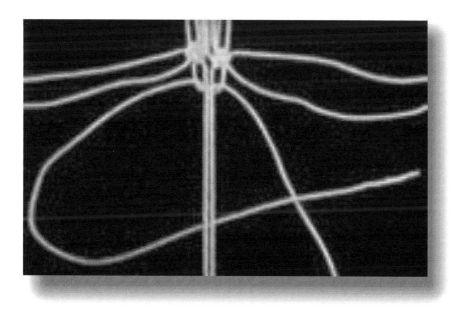

Pull this securely up to the center of the cord, then move on to the part on the cord.

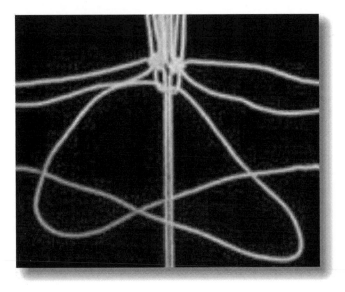

 You are going to gather the cord on one side for the set of knots, and then you are going to go back to the other side of the piece to work another set of knots on the other side.

Work this evenly, then you are going to come back to the center.

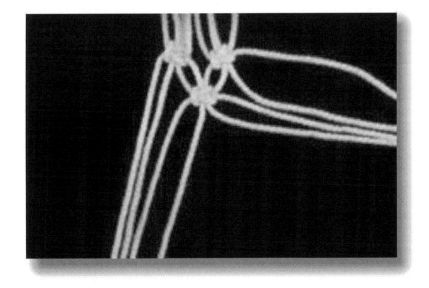

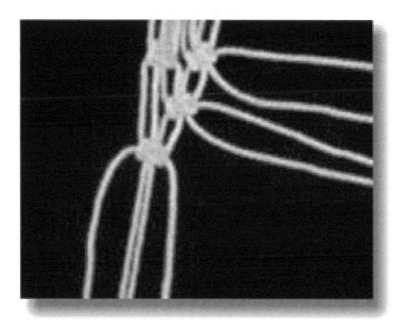

It's a matter of sequence. Work on the one side, then go back to the beginning, then go back to the other side once more.

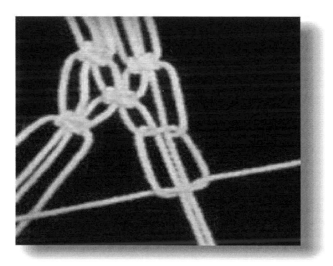

Make sure that you have all your knots secure and firm throughout, and do your best to make sure it is all even.

It is going to take practice before you can get it perfectly each time, but remember that practice does make perfect, and with time, you are going to get it without too much trouble.

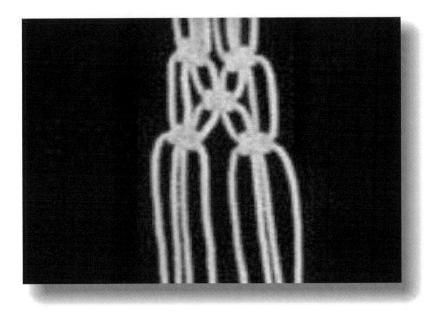

Snip off all the loose ends, and you are ready to go!

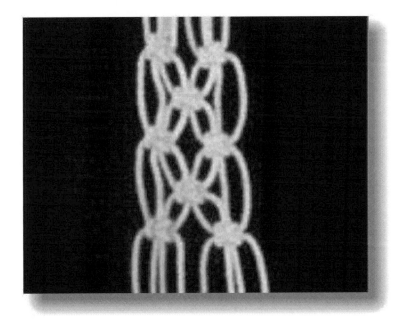

Capuchin Knot

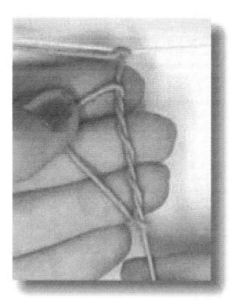

This is a new beginning knot for any project and can be used as the foundation for the base of the project. Use lightweight cord for this – it can be purchased at craft stores or online, wherever you get your macramé Materials:

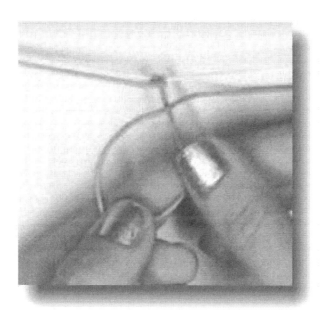

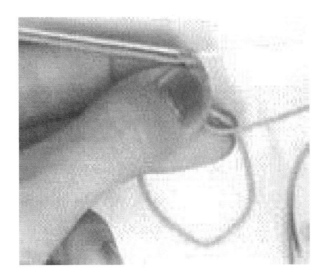

Start with the base cord, tying the knot onto this, and working your way along the project.

Twist the cord around itself 2 times, pulling the string through the center to form the knot.

Do your best to make sure it is all even. It is going to take practice before you can get it perfectly each time, but remember that practice does make perfect, and with time, you are going to get it without too much trouble.

Crown Knot

It can be used as the foundation for the base of the project. Use lightweight cord for this – it can be purchased at craft stores or online, wherever you get your macramé Materials:

Use a pin to help keep everything in place as you are working.

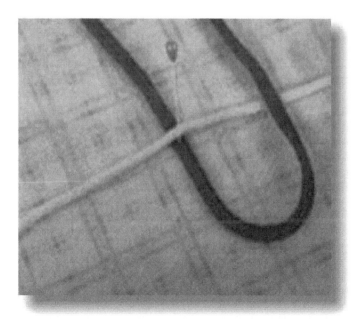

Weave the strings in and out of each other as you can see in the photos. It helps to practice with different colors to help you see what is going on.

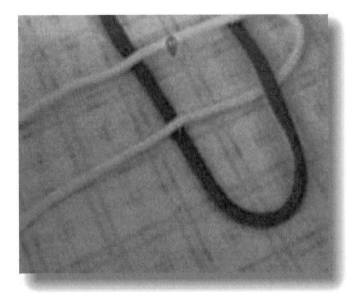

Pull the knot tight, and then repeat for the row on the outside.

Depending on the project. You can also create more than one length on the same cord.

Diagonal Double Half Knot

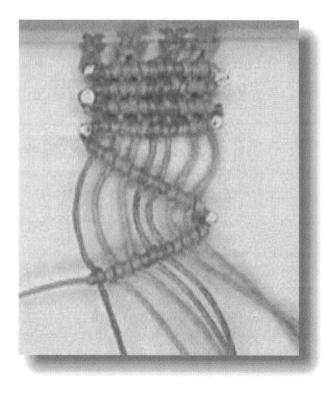

, decorations, or any projects that are going to require you to put weight on the project. Use a heavier weight cord for this, which you can find at craft stores or online.

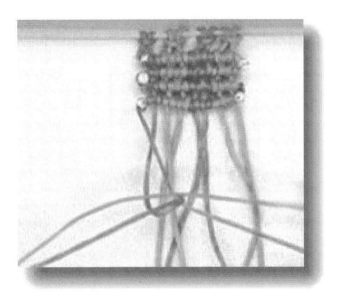

Look at the photo very carefully and look very closely.

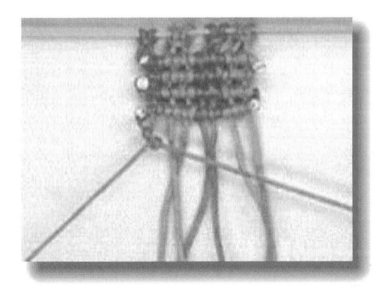

Keep it even as you work your way throughout the piece. Tie the knots at 4-inch intervals, working your way down the entire thing.

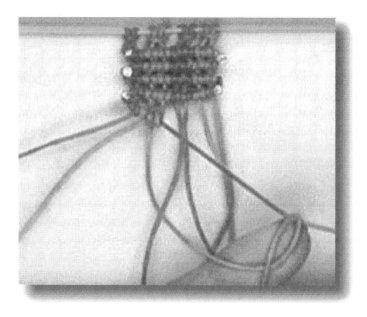

Weave in and out throughout, watching the photo as you can see for the right placement of the knots. Again, it helps to practice with different colors, so you can see what you need to do throughout the piece.

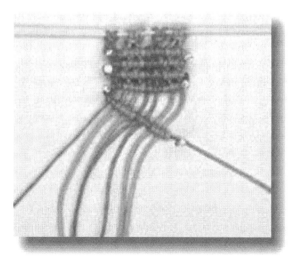

For the finished project, make sure that you have all your knots secure and firm throughout, and do your best to make sure it is all even. It is going to take practice before you can get it perfectly each time, but remember that practice does make perfect, and with time, you are going to get it without too much trouble.

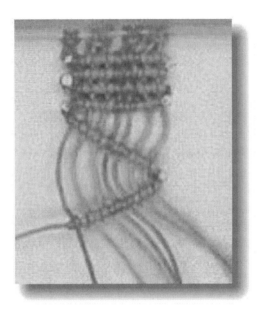

Frivolite Knot

Use lightweight cord for this – it can be purchased at craft stores or online, wherever you get your macramé Materials:.

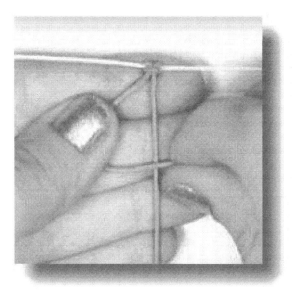

Make sure to follow what is shown in the image.

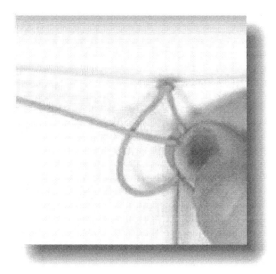

Use the base string as the guide to hold it in place, and then tie the knot onto this. This is a very straightforward knot; watch the photo and follow the directions you see.

Pull the end of the cord up and through the center.

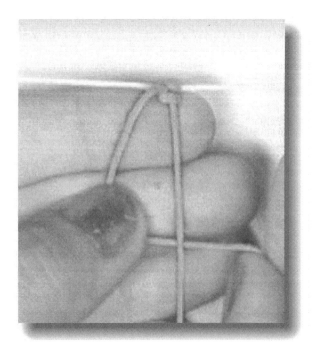

Horizontal Double Half Knot

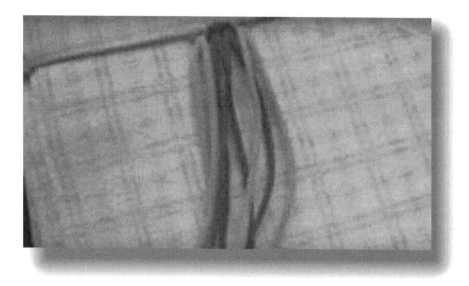

Can be used as the foundation for the base of the project. Use lightweight cord for this – it can be purchased at craft stores or online, wherever you get your macramé Materials:.

Tie the knots

Put 4-inch intervals, working your way down the entire thing.

For the finished project, make sure that you have all your knots secure and firm throughout, it is all even. It is going to take practice before you can get it perfectly each time, but remember that practice does make perfect, and with time, you are going to get it without too much trouble.

Make sure all is even and secure and tie off. Snip off all the loose ends, and you are ready to go!

Josephine Knot

Decorations or any projects that are going to require you to put weight on the project. Use a heavier weight cord for this, which you can find at craft stores or online.

Watch the photos very carefully as you move along with this project and take your time string at the right point of the project.

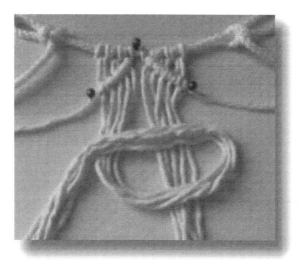

Use the pins along with the knots that you are tying, and work with larger areas all at the same time. This is going to help you keep the project in place as you continue to work throughout the piece.

Pull the ends of the knots through the loops and form the ring in the center of the strings.

That's all.

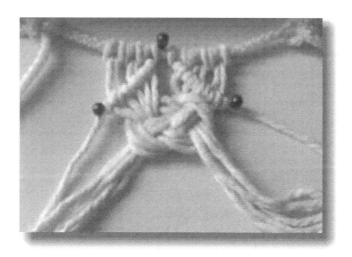

CHAPTER 3:

Essentials and Useful Tools

A side from Kumihimo, knotting and braiding techniques require little in the way of specialized equipment; in fact, most beavers or artisans will probably already have any tools needed in their workbox, so you should be able to go straight away. For details about what you need to get going with Kumihimo, refer to Kumihimo: Tools and materials.

Jewelry Tools

A simple collection of three tools to transform braids or knotting into jewelry is needed. Buying good-quality, fine tools is always worthwhile because these will help you finish tasks quickly and efficiently, but avoid mini-tools because these will make your hands sore when used for long periods.

Wire Cutters

Choose side cutters, or ideally flush-cutters, which cut the wire or headpins to a straight end. Mind to cut into the job or to face away from the tail with the flat side of the cutters.

Round-nose pliers

These pliers are used to make wire or head-pins loops. The jaws are cone-shaped, so you can adjust the loop size by working with tiny loops near the top of the jaws and for larger loops near the bottom. Often work the same distance downwards to make loops of the same size.

They are used to control wire and headpins or to open and close jump rings. Often look for relatively smooth surfaces on the inside of the jaws – pinholes from the local hardware store are unsuitable as apart from being too wide, they are likely to have deep grip serrations that will damage the metal. Blunt-end pliers are the tool for workhorses, but snipe-nose pliers (chain-nose) with tapered jaws allow you to get closer.

Specialist tools although not essential, this kit will help you professionally finish jewelry, so consider investing if you can.

Bent-nose pinions

These are essentially snipe-nose pinions with a right-angle bend in the jaws, allowing you to get into awkward positions and hold wire or headpins as required at a more comfortable angle.

Nylon-jaw pliers

These pliers have a softer material that covers the metal jaws to prevent damage to softer wires and results. They come as round-nose or flat-nose pliers.

Crimp pliers

Available in three sizes-micro, medium, and macro-these pliers are used primarily for closing crimps neatly around bead string thread. The pliers match the wire thickness and the size of the crimp.

Split-ring pinions

With a specially crafted tip for split-ring opening, these will certainly help to prevent broken nails!

Awl

An awl is useful for moving cords and braids through metal finds and easing them.

Warp posts

 Clamp over the edge of the surface of work and set a certain distance apart for winding long cord lengths.

Certain Essentials

These things can place or be found in your toolbox; they will be useful when knotting and braiding.

Scissors

Hold two or three different types of scissors strictly for thread and cord-cutting and do not use them for paper cutting because this would break the blades very easily. Big scissors are suitable for length cutting of threads and cords and small scissors with sharp spots are good for smooth cutting of ends.

Needles

All types of needles can make finishing braids and knotting or thread beads easier.

- Sewing needles, A set of sewing needles of various sizes helps you to sew through braids or secure ends after wrapping. Sharps have a tiny hand, but they are very sturdy and can be used to thread small seed beads into tougher strings. Embroidery needles have longer eyes to ease the threading.

- Tapestry needles These have a fairly blunt tip and a large eye and are useful to string larger beads onto a cord or to manipulate knots in place.

- Fine beading needles are used to attach seed beads and other small beads to the braids or to cover joins. Ideal for size 11 seed beads and size 12 or 13 for size 15 seed beads, a size 10 needle. Keep a good stock, as the finer needles will bend and break in particular.

- Twisted wire needles By looping the fine wire over the jaws of round-nose pliers and pulling the tails together, you can make your own needs. Alternatively, they can be bought in a variety of sizes to loop beads onto a cord or thread, or to pull loops or cords to work or neaten ends into braids.

- Big eye needles. These two-pointed long needles are useful for stringing beads on multi-strands of fine threads, but avoid pulling cords through a tight space as the two fine rods that separate the needle at the soldered end.

Pins Dressmaker's pins Useful for braid marking at a specific length, spacing beads or embellishments, or positioning wrapped threads.

Map pins

These short pins with ball ends are ideal when working macramé to protect the cords and threads. Plug it into a corkboard or foam core frame.

Adhesives

To bind cords and threads and render jewelry and other accessories. Choose the best adhesive to match the materials that you stick to, and remember to leave for 24 hours. Glues like G-S Hypo Cement and E6000 are made particularly for jewelry. The glue forms but stays pliable, so it is less likely to crack and break off over time. The G-S Hypo Cement has a fine nozzle that is suitable for applying a small amount for a smooth finish, then using a cocktail stick to apply the glue.

Superglue

These instant glues can be useful because the material is not to be left in place before the glue sets. More likely to run the gel version, so it's easier to be consistent, so add a small volume. Take care, as these glues of cyanoacrylate bind skin.

Epoxy resin

A two-part adhesive very well suited for sticking cords onto metal finds. Wipe off surfaces with a nail polish remover before applying the adhesive to remove greasy fingerprints. A 5-minute epoxy resin shortens drying time, and when used, one that dries clear is less likely to become visible.

CHAPTER 4:

Types of Cord

Macramé stylists make use of different types of materials. The materials can be classified in two major ways; the natural materials and the synthetic materials.

Natural Materials

The qualities of natural materials differ from the synthetic material and knowing these qualities would help you to make better use of them. Natural cord materials existing today include Jute, Hemp, Leather, Cotton, Silk and Flax. There are also yarns made from natural fibers. Natural material fibers are made from plants and animals.

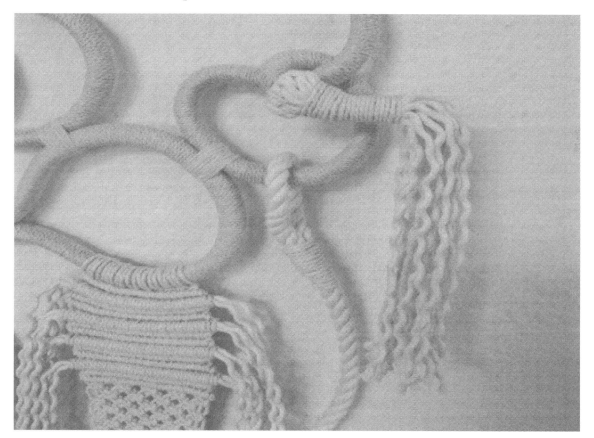

Synthetic Materials

Like natural materials, synthetic materials are also used in macramé projects. The fibers of synthetic materials are made through chemical processes. The major ones are nylon beading cord, olefin, satin cord and parachute cord.

Cord Measurement

Before you can embark on a macramé project, it is essential that you determine the amount of chord you will need. This includes knowing the length of the required cord and the total number of materials you have to purchase.

Equipment: to measure, you will need a paper for writing, pencil, tape rule and calculator. You would also need some basic knowledge of unit conversion as shared below:

1 inch = 25.4millimeters = 2.54 centimeters

1 foot =12 inches

1 yard = 3 feet = 36 inches

1 yard = 0.9 meters

Note: The circumference of a ring = 3.14 * diameter measured across the ring

Measuring Width

The first thing to do is determine the finished width of the widest area of your project. Once you have this width, pencil it down.

Determine the actual size of the materials, by measuring its width from edge to edge.

You can then proceed to determine the type of knot pattern you wish to use with the knowledge of the knot pattern. You must know the width and spacing (if required) of each knot. You should also determine if you want to add more cords to widen an area of if you would be needing extra cords for damps.

With the formula given above, calculate and determine the circumference of the ring of your designs.

Determine the mounting technique to be used. The cord can be mounted to a dowel, ring or other cord. Folded cords affect both the length and width of the cord measurement.

Cord Preparation

Though usually rarely emphasized, preparation of the cords and getting them ready for use in Macramé projects is one of the core pillars of the art of Macramé. At times, specialized processes such as conditioning and stiffening of cords need to be carried out before Macramé projects can be begun. In general, however, cord preparation in Macramé is mainly concerned with dealing with cut ends and preventing these ends from unraveling during the course of the project. During the course of a project, constant handing of materials can cause distortion in the ends which can end up having disastrous consequences on your project. Before starting your project, if you do not appropriately prepare special kinds of cords, like ones that were made by the twisting of individual strands, that cord is likely to come apart, effectively destroying your project completely.

Therefore, cord preparation is extremely and incomparably important to the success of any Macramé project, the preparation of each cord is meant to be done during the first step of making any knot, which is the step where you cut out your desired length of cord from the larger piece.

For cord conditioning, experts recommend rubbing beeswax along the length of the cord. To condition your cord, simply get a bit of beeswax, let it warm up a bit in your hands, and rub it along the cord's length.

This will help prevent unwanted tight curls on your cord. Note that beeswax may be applied to both natural and synthetic materials. For synthetic materials however, only Satin and fine Nylon beading cords actually compulsorily require conditioning. After conditioning, inspect your cords for any imperfections and discard useless pieces to ensure the perfection of your project. After conditioning, then comes the actual process of cord preparation. Cords can be prepared (i.e. the ends can be prevented from fraying) through the use of a flame, a knot, tape and glue.

To prevent unraveling of your cord using a flame, firstly test a small piece of the material with the flame from a small lighter. The material needs to melt, not burn. If it burns, then such a cord is not suitable for flame preparation.

To prepare using a flame, simply hold the cord to the tip of the flame for 2 to 5 seconds, make sure the cord does not ignite, but melts.

Flame preparation is suitable for cords made from olefin, polyester and nylon, and the process is compulsory for the preparation of parachute cords.

The overhand knot is an all-time favorite, but knots such as the figure 8 knot which is best suited to flexible cords can be used if you think the knot might have to be undone at some point of your project. The Stevedore knot can be used to prevent fraying when using slippery materials. Glue is another priceless alternative that can be used to prevent fraying at the ends of cords efficiently. However, not all kinds of glue may be used in cord preparation.

Only certain brands, such as the Aleen's Stop Fray may be used in cord preparation. Household glue might also be used, but only when diluted with water. TO prepare your cord, simply rub the glue on the ends of the material and leave it to dry. If you intend to pass beads over the glued end, roll the cord's end between your fingers to make it narrower as it dries. Nail polish may also be used as an alternative to glue.

A special class of Macramé cords, known as a parachute cord, requires a special form of preparation. Parachute cords are composed of multiple core yarns surrounded by a braided sleeve. To prepare a parachute cord (also called a Paracord), pull out the core yarns from the sleeve, and expose the yarns by about half an inch.

Now cut the core yarns back, so that they become even with the outer sleeve, and then push the sleeve forward till the yarns become invisible.

To complete the preparation, apply flame to the outer sleeve till it melts, and then press the handle of your lighter onto the sleeve while it's still warm to flatten the area and keep it closed up. The melted area will look darker and more plastic than the rest of the material.

Finishing Techniques

Finishing techniques refer to the methods by which the ends of cords, after knots have been created may be taken care of to give a neat and tidy project. Finishing is often referred to as tying off. Several finishing knots are available and are extremely effective methods for executing finishing processes. Reliable finishing knots include the overhand knot and the barrel knot.

Folding techniques are also dependable finishing techniques. For flexible materials like cotton, all you need to do is fold the ends flat against the back surface and add glue to the ends to hold them in place. For less flexible materials, fold the cords to the back, then pass them under a loop from one or more knots, and then apply glue, allow it to dry, and cut off excess material.

Finally, you can do your finishing with the aid of fringes. You may choose between a brushed fringe and a beaded fringe.

Adding Cords

During Macramé projects, you would constantly be faced by the need to add a cord to an existing cord or any other surface such as a ring or a dowel. The process of adding cords to surfaces is usually called mounting. To add extra cords to a ring or dowel, the most common technique to use is the Reverse Larks Head Knot. When adding cords to already existing cords in use, however, it is important that the new cords blend into the overall design. To prevent lopsidedness of the pattern, it is also important to add an equal number of cords to both sides in some projects. It is also important to avoid gaps when adding new cords. You can add new cords to an already existing cord using the square knot, the linked overhand knot and of course the regular overhand knot. Other techniques used for adding cords include the diamond stitch and the triangle knot.

CHAPTER 5:

Macramé Indoors: Feathers, Wall Hangings, Pillows, Mason Jars

Macramé Feathers

Materials:

Macramé Cording.

Sharp Scissors.

Stiffening Spray.

Wire Brush.

Tape Measure

Steps:

Cut the following cord lengths: Big Feather – 1 – 24" piece inches, 10 – 12" pieces inches, 10 – 10" pieces, 10 – 8" pieces (31 total cords) Small Feathers – 1 – 12" piece inches, 6 – 6" pieces inches, 4 – 4" pieces, 4 – 3" pieces (15 total cords)

1 First, take your longest cord and fold it in half. This is the 24" piece, for the large feather. This is the 12" one, for the small feathers. That long piece is our feather's "spine." Then, take and fold

one of your longest cords in half. Place it perpendicular to the right under the spine of your feather.

2 Take another long cord and fold it in half. Pull the part of the loop through the first cord you've laid down (not the backbone). Pull it through your feather over the back.

3 Take the first cord ends and pull them through the second cord loop.

4 Drag cords close now.

5 Now we will repeat steps 1-4, but we'll switch sides. Take one of the longest strings, and split in half. Place your loop (instead of the right) on the left side.

6 Now take another thread, fold in half and loop it to the left through the loop. Pull the ends up, and this loop around.

7 Pull each cord close, holding the sides alternating – right, left, right, left, etc. When all of your longest cords are used, turn to your medium cords, using the same method. Switch to your tiniest cords then.

8 Using all your strings, brush them out with your wire brush to create the strands. Keep the spine at the same time, so that no ties are pulled off.

Tip: If you find your spine still stretched for quite a long time, you can only trim it even further.

Flip over your feather and clean both sides to ensure that the cords are all brushed out.

Brush out the cord for the fringe Step

9 Take your scissors and trim your feather after you brush it all out.

10 Sprinkle the feather with stiffening spray to stiffen the feather so that it can lie flat while it hangs.

Follow this procedure to make the feathers smaller, or whatever size you want!

Macramé Wall Hanging

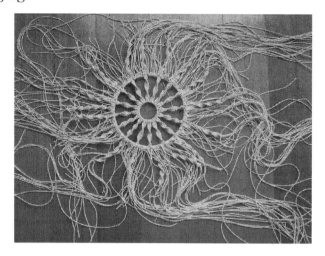

Materials:

Macramé Rope – 4 mm rope – cords (twelve) 12 – 16" (as in feet) will be needed. Note this is a long hanging wall, which is why we need longer cords. Also, you need 1 shorter piece of cord to act as your hanger. Only tie it with a simple knot on either end there.

A dowel or string

Steps:

Tie some cord around the end of your dowel. This will be the hanger for our project. Having a Macramé wall hanging while it's standing is much better than sitting flat.

Start by folding the 16' cords in half. Verify that the ends are even.

Place the cord loop under your dowel and thread through the loop the ends of the rope. Tight drive. That's the head-knot of your first Reverse Lark. (For assistance see simple Macramé knots).

Repeat step # 3 with 11 cords left over.

Allow the first 2 rows of Square Knots. (For assistance see simple Macramé knots).

Render now 2 rows Alternating Square Knots.

Now make another 2 rows of knots in Square.

Follow this pattern (2 rows of square knots, 2 rows of alternating square knots) until you have 10 rows in all.

Working from left to right-make double half hitch knots around your piece in a diagonal pattern.

Working from right to left now-make double half-hitch knots around your piece in a diagonal pattern.

Create 2 more square-knots lines. We will finish the hanging wall with a set of spiral knots-which is essentially just a sequence of half-square knots (or left side square knots). (Do not complete the right side of the square knot, only consistently make the left side square knots, and it will spiral to you.)

Macramé Pillow
Materials:

Macramé Cord Scissors Sewing Machine / Thread (optional)

Pillow cover and attach Dowel or Stick Tape Measure To this pillow, you can either start with a pillow cover that you already have or make a simple pillow cover. But don't just make it yet-see first Stage 5.

Steps:

1 Cut the cords in! To make this pattern, you'll need 16-12-foot cords.

2 Use reverse-lark head knots to tie all 16 of your cords to your dowel.

3 The pattern for this cover is just 1 alternating square knot in the line. Leave a little gap between each knot-around half an inch as a reference point. What's more, having a bit of space makes the project go much faster.

Create two horizontal rows of (left-to-right, then right-to-left) or double half-hitch knots until you touch down.

4 Now that we're done with the pattern cut off the excess from the bottom but keep a little fringe

Now you're either going to remove your dowel or simply cut it off at Step 5: How can you add this to your pillow cover?

Here's how to attach your Macramé pattern to your pillow. Before you sew it up, if you're making a cover yourself – you're essentially going to line up the pattern to the front of your cover, leaving the cut ends a little over the top hang.

Lay down the pattern over the front and put the back piece on top!

Place the back piece over your cover and Macramé template-right sides facing each other-essentially you make a sandwich here, and the Macramé is called the "meat."

Now just patch your pillow cover's top seam-go over the ropes too! It takes some degree of finesse, but you can.

Shove the Macramé pattern within your pillow to stitch the rest of your cover, and stitch the remaining seams as usual.

Flip it straight out. Now you should have your Macramé pattern added to the top of your pillow (coming out from inside between the seams).

Take and loop a cord through your pattern ....

Take the other hand through your pillow on the bottom ... do this many times (crisscross) and knot it!

And it is! It's left your fringe dangling from the edges.

Even if the pillow cover is ready-made?

Mirror Wall Hanging
Materials:

Macramé Cording: 4 mm

Mirrored octagon

2 inches Wood ring

Wood beads: 25 mm w/10 mm hole size

Strong scissors.

Steps:

Cut 4 pieces of cording macramé into sections of 108 inches (or 3yds). Cut the strips in half and tie all four of them with a Lark's Head knot on the wood loop. Tightly and closely pull the knots. Separate two head knots from the Lark and begin to tie them into a square knot. Start tying into the second two Lark's Head knots two square knots. As you start the second knot of the square, loop it through one of the sides of the other two knots into a wide knot of the square. Fasten 7 square knots on both sides. Break the ends after the knots have been tied. Two strings per side and four in the center. To secure the frayed ends, apply tape to the ends of the thread. This will make inserting the beads simpler. Congratulations. That's been the toughest part! The others are easy ties to tie and even get the sides.

In each of the 2 side cording lines, apply one bead. Tie a knot on both sides under the bead to keep them even. Connect the four cords in the middle to a simple or (overhand knot) about 1/14 inch below the beads. Take a cord from the center and add it to the sides of the two cords. Tie the three on both sides in a knot. Apply the mirror to the end of the knot. Add one of the three sides to the mirror's back to hold it steady. Place clear knots in all 3 side cables at the bottom left and right side of the mirror. Trim the cords again on all three sides. Return one to the back of the mirror on either side and add 2 to the front of it on each side.

Flip the mirror over and tie together all the cords. Flip over the mirror and loosen the knot at the front. Inside the knot, slip the back cords and straighten the knot. Cutting the cord ends up to around 14 inches. Take the ends or loose the cord and let them break. Combine the ends of the cording to fluff ends with a comb. Hang up and have fun!

Macramé Mason Jars

Materials:

Macramé Cord

Mason Jars Scissors

Macramé Wood Rings

Steps:

On both jars, cut the cords at the same lengths — at the end, you'll have to cut off the excess on the regular-sized jar. Still, having too much cord is still better than getting too little!

Creating a Macramé mason jar the larger mason jar has a pattern of one alternating square knot all the way around. For each jar, you'll be cording is 6 feet long.

For the larger jar, you'll need 6 cords, and the smaller jar will require 8 cords.

Standard Mason Jar (known in this tutorial as Standard): The Pattern is 2 square knots followed by 2 alternating square knots all the way around.

To begin each jar: Take two of your 6 ft ropes and fold them over the container's lip — secure them with a solitary square knot. Bigger: Take one of your 6 ft lines and fold them over the container's lip — with a standard knot tight.

Start with the head knots of the lark. Proceed with the head knots of the lark

2. Join remaining lines: Regular: take the remainder of your 6 ropes and bind them to your container utilizing the head knots of the reverse lark. Bigger: take the rest of your 5 strings and

affix them to your container utilizing the head knots of the reverse lark. The knots space consistently around the container's edge.

Making scattered square knots produce square knots 3 scattered. Tie Square Knots: Regular: make 2 knots in the square right around. Bigger: Make a 1-column exchanging square knot around the container as far as possible. Continue the pattern down the jar: Make a row of 2 alternating square knots now normal. Continue on these alternating rows of square knots until you reach the bottom of the pot. Larger: Start along the way with another series of alternating square knots. Repeat so until it hits the jar's rim.

Alternating Mason jar square knots Hint: Have you got a handle on your pot? Getting the knots around or around the handle just fits around it.

Creating fringe Macramé 5 on the bottom of the Mason jar. Finish the bottle: Regular / Larger: Cut off any excess rope before you get to the bottom of the jar, but leave it a little there and comb it out for a fringe look.

However – if you really wanted to cover the whole pot, you might use smaller sized rope and make alternating square knots very tightly weaved.

CHAPTER 6:

Macramé Indoors: Curtains, Baskets, Dragonflies

Macramé Shower Curtain

Materials:

Laundry rope (or any kind of rope/cord you want)

Curtain rod

Pins

Lighter

Tape

Steps:

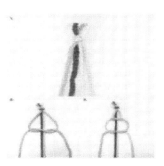

Tie four strands together and secure the top knots with pins so they could hold the structure down.

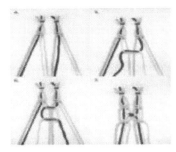

Take the strand on the outer right part and let it cross over to the left side by means of passing it through the middle. Tightly pull the strings together and reverse.

Repeat crossing the thread over four more times for the thread you now have in front of you. Take the strand on the outer left and let it pass through the middle, and then take the right and let it cross over the left side. Repeat as needed, then divide the group of strands to the left, and also to the right.

Repeat until you reach the number of rows you want.

Gather the number or ropes you want—10 to 14 is okay, or whatever fits the rod, with reasonable spacing. Start knotting at the top of the curtain until you reach your desired length. You can burn or tape the ends to prevent them from unraveling.

Braid the ropes together to give them that dreamy, beachside effect, just like what you see below.

Tie four strands together on the same foam core board and place pins in the top knot to keep those in place beneath the two center strands. Take the right outer strand (pink) and pass it over the other two center fibers to the left side. Take the left (yellow) outer strand and pass it under the pink strand that is behind the middle fibers, and on the other side over the pink strand. Push tightly the two strands. Then, in the first step, you just reverse what you did! Take the leftmost strand (now the pink) and lay it over two strands in the middle. Take the last right strand (which is now the yellow) and transfer it under the pink, behind the two middle strands, and on the other side over the pink. Pull the two strands tightly until they create a knot from the woven strands. That's the most difficult part! These basic motions are repeated by the rest of the steps. Put in two right strands of the first knot for a new group with two leftmost strands of the second knot.

Repeat with the new group your basic knot by taking the outer right (purple) strand and passing it over the middle two strands to the left side. Take the outside (green) left and pass it through the purple strand, after the medium strands, and across the purple strand on the other side. Push closely the two fibers. Now turn the first step back! Take the leftmost strand (which is the purple now) and lay it over two strands in the middle. Take the extreme right strand (the green) and pass it under the purple, behind the two middle strands and across the violet on the other side. Pull closely these two threads. By moving the two leftmost threads and the two rightmost strands, divide the middle group of strands. Repeat the fundamental knot with both classes and continue until so long as you like.

Build 14 rope classes, each with four lines, all 100 inches long. It make a clean knot to cut two cords twice as long (thus 200 inches) on top of the curtain and then hung strands across the rod at the middle point and tied up a knot to create a group of four strands. Since doing this method with big ropes is much larger than the thread.

You can see that making the simple knots with the yarn is really the same idea, but only on a much larger scale. Render the base knot near the top of all 14 bands and then made a new knots line below and above them (as in the yarn Steps:). Then go down a new row, take knots under the original knots and keep the knots rowing until you finish all the rows you need. Make sure you stay back while you make your knots to make sure you tie your knots in even rows. Drop the rest of the strands to complete the curtain until 5 rows of knots were completed.

Contrast Basket

Materials:

4mm Macramé cord

Metal ring (just one)

Fabric Glue

Pins and Boards for projects

Steps:

The Contrast Basket has varying measurements for different sizes; the choice of size determines the cord length and quantity. The chart below gives the measurement for the various basket sizes. The basket's height is usually half the width. However, to add to the height, the length of the cords should be increased. If the ring made of bulky plastic or wood, the cords' length may need to be adjusted.

Dragonfly

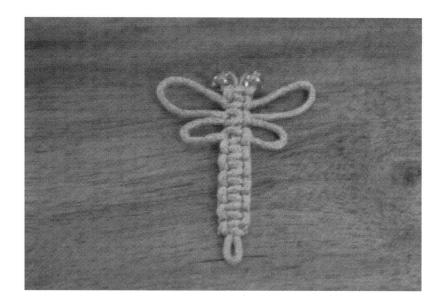

Materials:

Cord material of between 2 and 4 millimeter in length

Half a dozen roller beads or more

Pins and boards for the project

Dry clear glue for fabric.

Steps:

Cut a cord of 72 inches or two yards in length. Use glue to prepare the ends and let it completely dry. The dragonfly's head is created with a single bead. With the cords held your two hands, create a loop and cross the end on the left over that of the right. From below bring the left end through the loop. Tighten and push the tips into the beads, one after the other

Keep the Satin Dragonfly's (SD) head secure by moving the pin through the gap the OK created. Using the cord's left half, create a counter clockwise loop.

Finish OK by shifting the left end through the loop below and then over (from below). Do not make the knot tight.

Through the knot you just made, push the cord's right half through, and rotate in the clockwise direction as it passes over and then under the loop. Draw to the right, and then push it over the cord that was been worked on that is, the half that is on the right.

Finish the OK on the right by pushing the tip into the loop, first under and then over (from below). Position the 2 knots so that both the inner portions and the outer portions can be seen clearly. Put them near bead, and apart with plenty space. It is important to note that the crook, or the rounded area is the inner portion both knots. The Left knot's inner part should be held and moved rightward. Move it through the right knot's outer crossed portion. It should also be passed beneath the segment that leads to the SD's top, and on top of the segment that leads to the end. Bring the right knot's inner portion to the left knot's crossed area. Move it the same way that is below the top segment, and above part that leads to the end. Make the wings of the SD tight, and move ii as close to the bead as you can. Possibly, reposition the knot and eliminate the slack that is on top of the knot. With the ends steady, draw on the loops first. Then with the center tightened, shorten the loops by pulling on the tips. They should have an approximate length on an inch. Repeat the 2nd to 7th step more than once to create extra sets of wings and try to put them closely. Behind the hanger knot, add glue and leave it to dry. Join a bead to the two cords as was done to the first at the top of the SD. Make an OK with both ends working together. Repeat the 8th step multiple times, till you get the desired tail size. Glue the final knot tied both on the outside and on the inside.

A Doorway or Big Window Macramé Curtain

Materials:

Loop

Single hollow/rod curtain

Masking tape

Scissors

Steps:

Place 4 strands on a core board of foams and put the pins in the top and the bottom of the mid strands in order to stabilize the strands.

Take the outside right strand (rose) and go to the left over the other two middle strands. Take the outer (yellow) strand on the left and go to the other side of the pink strand behind the middle strands.

Pull those 2 strands tightly. Reverse what you did in Pull those 2 strands far left (now the rose) strand and put it on the middle two strands. Taking the far-right beach (now yellow) and pass the beach on the other side of the rose on the two center beams.

Pull those 2 strands tightly until they make a knot for the woven strands of the previous step. It is the toughest step! Such fundamental motions are repeated in the other steps.

Repeat 1-3 steps to make another knot next to your first knot with four more threads. Bring the first two right-hand strands to form a new group with two more left-hand strands from the second knot.

Take the outer right lilac strand and cross the middle two strands to the left. Take the left outer strand (green), and cross the strand located at the other side (purple), behind the center strands, and over the purple strand.

Pull those 2 strands tightly. Return now the first step!

Take the far-left strand (now violet) and cross the two middle strands. Take the far right (now green) line, and go under the violet, two middle line, and the violet on the other side. Tighten the two divisions.

Divide the middle group of strands by transferring two strands to the left and two strands to the right. Do the fundamental knot with both classes and proceed with this process until as many rows as you want have been completed.

You can see that the basic knots are generated in steps with the yarn, but on a much larger scale only. Make the basic knot close to the top of all 14 groups, and then produced another line of knots

Then move down another row, make knots and alternate the rows of knots only, until you've finish as many rows as possible. Make sure you step back and make your knots to ensure that your ties are equally connected.

Hang the ropes in your ideal place until you are done braiding. At last cover the masking tape on the right side of the tape (or white tape, where the edging touches the ground (my curtain is 6 1/2 feet high).

Break the tape and leave the string intact from 2/3 to half the band. This helps to prevent the spillage of overtime.

CHAPTER 7:

Macramé Indoors: Rope Lights, Table Runners, Wall Art, Tassels, Fish Bowls

Giant Macramé Rope Light

Materials:

Rope

Cord Light Lamp

Backpack Package

Large boat (to be poured into)

Colt

Steps:

Start by securing your lamp's cord.

Put   the middle of your cord and place it on the lamp string.

Take left and put the lamp's front thread.

And you are forming a small loop on the right side of your lamp string.

Then place the right cord behind the lamp wire.

Pull the entire length of the lamp through the narrow loop to the left of the lamp cord.

Repeat your little hands. The pattern starts to spiral as you add more knots. If you take the top of the lamp wire from the left, the spiral is in the same direction. You'll have to undo the knots if you go on.

How to take a Macramé Knot:

Start by boiling a hole in the cup's bottom and attach the punching nipple to the base socket (make sure you straighten up the small screw on your hand so it does not twist off when you turn the light bulb!)

Place the washing machine on the lamp plate, then the cup, and the base socket. Place the socket according to the Steps: given. Instead the washing machine turned on the threaded tip.

Glide up your rope (the only way to change your socket before beginning knots) and around the end of the threaded nipple. Stick in place.

Macramé Table Runner

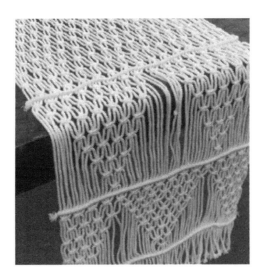

Materials:

-12" wood dowel

– 22 16' 3 mm cotton cloth strands

– The hooks

-2' of twine cotton dowel hanger

-scissors

Steps:

Step 1: At every end, keep your cotton twine and hang it from your door hooks. Fold half of the first 16" rope strand and build a dowel knot.

Step 2: Keep adding a 16" rope beam with a lark headnote to a total of 22. You should then operate with 44 strands.

Step 3: Pull the right outer rope through other ropes (left) and drape the end of the handle of the lock. Use the second seam from the right hand to tie a single knot around the bottom, under the dowel around 6".

Step 4: To attach the base strand with a second knot, utilize a similar strand. This is known as a half-hitch knot.

Stage 5: Make sure they are even and predictable.

Step 6: Repeat the second, third and fourth ropes from the outside, tie up another half-hit knot to make it cool, etc. You'll start to see the pattern. This is a horizontal half-hitch.

Step 7: Keep wrapping consecutive cords in a knot. You don't want it to take the width at the edges nearly enough.

Step 8: Using the external four strands from the right again and make a square knot around 1.5" underneath the horizontal knots. For more details on a square knot, see the Macramé storage article.

Take the next four strands (five to eight) and make another square knot with 9 to 12 strands. Keep skipping four and tie four before you get done.

Step 9: Right again, use all four strands and tie the knot of around 3" under the dowel.

Step 10: Hold four square knots sets skipped until this row is done.

Step 11: Transfer to the right the two outer strands. Then use three to six strands in step 7 below the horizontal knot lines to create another 11" knot. Use the next four strands to make a new knot of the square about 1.5.

Step 12: Start as shown. Don't do anything with the last two threads.

Step 13: Starting from right again, create another line of horizontal halves, repeating steps 3 to 7

Step 14: Use the same rope base strand from left and create a hilly row of knots horizontally about 2.5" below last row. You will focus on it from left to right.

Step 15: Start from the left side, build a series of square knots with 1" below the horizontal knots, without any strands. Then you build a second set of quadratic knots by skip the first two strands to the left. It is known as a knot that alternates. You do not want much space between these groups, so that if you add each knot you can pull them together tightly.

Step 16: Continue to rotate until you have about 13 rows of square knots. This part is the heart of your table runner and everything else is what you have woven above.

Step 17: Add a horizontal half-hitch knots row from the outside to the right.

Step Eighteen: Drop down about 2.5" to create a new horizontal half hitch row with the same base rope from right to left.

Step 19: Turn right on this section two strands of rope, then tie a square knot of three to six strands. Skip strands seven to 10 and create another knot by using strands 11 to 14. Repeat so that you miss all four strands. You're going to have six lines on the left.

Skip the 1 and 2 lines on the left and attach 3 to 6 strands in a 1.5" square knot below the last row. Then miss the next four strands and complete with the pattern the second-row square knots. It will leave you with six more strands on the right.

Step 20: Measure 11" rights from the end of the horizontal knots and tie the outer four strands to the right of the knots. Keep the next four in a 1.5" knot over the last knot.

Step 21: Repeat all over.

Step 22: Then tie the last horizontal knot half-hitch row to around 1.5" below the square knots row. Taking care as long as you like the ends on the opposite side. Remove the twine of the cotton from the dowel and gently slip all the lark knots. Cut the middle of the lark's knot and add the ends.

Macramé Wall Art

Materials:

Large wooden beads

Acrylic paint

Painter's tape

Paintbrush

Wooden dowel

70 yards rope

Steps:

Attach the dowel to a wall. It's best just to use removable hooks so you won't have to drill anymore.

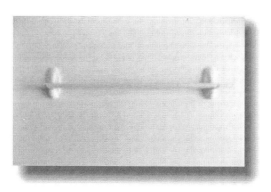

Cut the rope into 14 x 4 pieces, as well as 2 x 5 pieces. Use 5-yard pieces to bookend the dowel with.

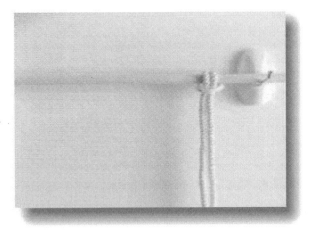

Then, start making double half-hitch knots and continue all the way through, like what's shown below.

Tie the knots diagonally so that they wouldn't fall down or unravel in any way. You can also add the wooden beads any way you want, so you'd get the kind of décor that you need. Make sure to tie the knots after doing so.

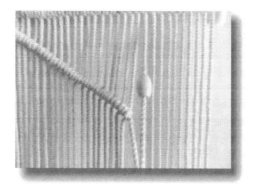

Use four ropes to make switch knots and keep the décor all the more secure. Tie around 8 of these.

Add a double half hitch and then tie them diagonally once again.

Add more beads and then trim the ends of the rope.

Once you have trimmed the rope, go ahead and add some paint to it. Summery or neon colors would be good.

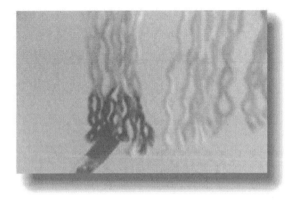

That's it! You now have your own Macramé Wall Art!

Ornament Tassels

Materials:

Small wood rings-if you have that lying around, you can also bend some wire into a circle.

Macramé cord. Use a thinner cord if you want something smoother and tinier.

Scissors

Wire brush for fringe

Macramé tassel hanging from cabinet knob

Steps:

The measures are broken down here. Cut two pieces of cords in length each 48

Using Lark's Head Knots to fasten your cords to the wood frame.

You are going to have four cords in there. Make your spiral knots and go down all the way until you've got a little cord left. That's what's forming our fringe.

Even with your scissors, the cords at the bottom up. Unravel the cords and brush them to form a fringe. Use your scissors to put the fringe on even.

Take a piece of twine from bakers and thread a loop around a ring of wood.

Fish Bowl:
Material:

50 feet nylon string (found at the home improvement shop and comes in all sorts of fun hues!)

Glass or plastic fish bowl

Scissors

Roof noose

Steps:

Stage 1: Cut eight bits of string that are 5 feet in length. Assemble all eight bits of line and tie a big knot toward one side, leaving $1 - 2$ free at the top.

Stage 2: Separate the string into four areas, with two bits of line in each segment.

Stage 3: Take one area and tie the two bits of rope into a twofold knot, leaving a 2nd hole between the principal huge knot you tied.

Stage 4: Rehash with the staying three areas of rope. Hang a fish bowl from the roof with this wonderful macramé hanger! Give your fish a polished home and get spare table space!

Stage 5: Take one bit of rope from an area and consolidate it with a bit of rope from a neighboring segment by tying a twofold knot 2 inches away from the past knots you tied.

Stage 6: Rehash this procedure for the rest of the areas, using one bit of line from two distinct segments.

Stage 7: Presently rehash stages 5 and 6. Take one bit of rope from an area and join it with a bit of string from a neighboring segment by tying a twofold knot 2and away from the past knots you tied.

Stage 8: Spot your fish bowl on the knotted ropes, fixated on the first huge knot you tied. Pull the last details of string up around the fish bowl. The bowl ought to securely rest in the knotted region.

Stage 9: Tie a knot brushing all eight pieces again about 10and – 12and over the highest point of the fish bowl.

Stage 10: Include a roof noose where you need the fish bowl to hang. Slide the noose underneath the top knot, in the middle of the eight bits of rope. Ensure four bits of rope are on either side of the noose to hold the hanger set up.

Stage 11: Include your fish and appreciate! Hang a fish bowl from the roof with this great macramé hanger! Give your fish an in-vogue home and spare table space!

CHAPTER 8:

Macramé Outdoors: Pet Leashes, Jars, Simple Hangers

Pet Leash

Materials:

Swivel Hook

Glue

4mm or 6mm cord material

Project board and pins

Steps:

Put the two cords vertically on our board after getting their corresponding midpoints and tightly place them close to one another. The longer WC should be on the left because that is what will be used to tie the LHK on the HC

A half of the vertical LHK should be made to move using the Wc over or under (as the case may be) the Hc so as to have a counter-clockwise loop. Gradually pulling it left, you should make it go over the WC so as to get the crossing point. Once the crossing point is gotten, tie the other half of the Vertical LHK by passing the Wc under or over the Hc, while pulling it left, pass it under the WC to also make the crossing point.

More Vertical LHK should be tied and should be done from the center in the direction of one end. When the first half of the handle is 6 inches, you should stop.

The whole sennit or cords should be rotated and back to the center, leaving the WC on the right. Loos should be made in clockwise directions as tying of Knots is resumed, and once the handle attains a length of 12 inches, you should stop

The four segments should be brought together, thereby folding the sennit. Locate the WC in the process. Tie a SK using the 2 Wc, and it should be tight. The fillers are going to be the short cords

Folding the 2 WC means we should have 4 cords to work with. A suitable decorative knot by the user should be used alongside this wonderful design, some of the best knots to use alongside it are; the Square Knot, the Vertical larks head and the Half hitches with holding cords. A minimum of six inches material should be attached to the hook at the end of the pet leach.

To attach the hook, two cords should be passed through the loop that is on the hook, and a tight finishing should be tied with the four cords. The usage of glue comes in here as the four cords are being tightened, the glue should be used. When it gets dry, all additional materials should be removed or cut to make the work very neat and beautiful. You may also consider another finishing style which entails that you move the ends in the direction of the strap and put it under the back of the knots so that it can be very firm.

Macramé Plant Hanger Advanced

Materials:

Cord: 4 strands of cord of 13 feet and 1.5 inches (4 meter), 4 strands of 16 feet and 4.8 inches (5 meter), 2 strands of 3 feet and 3.4 inches (1 meter)

Ring: 1 round ring (wood) of 1.5 inches (4 cm) diameter

Beads: wooden beads

Cristal Bowl/Container: 7 inches (18 cm) diameter

Steps:

50. Fold the 8 long strands of cord (4 strands of 13 feet and 1.5 inches and 4 strands of 16 feet and 4.8 inches) in half through the wooden ring.

50. Tie all (now 16) strands together with 1 shorter strand with a gathering knot. Hide the cut cord ends after tying the gathering knot.

50. Divide the strands into 4 sets of 4 strands each. Each set has 2 long strands and 2 shorter strands. Tie 5 Chinese crown knots in each set. Pull each strand tight and smooth.

4. Tie 8 square knots on each set of four strands. In each set the 2 shorter strands are in the middle and you are tying with the 2 outer, longer strands.

5. Tie 15 half square knots with each set.

6. Drop down 5.5 inches (14 cm), no knots, and tie an alternating square knot to connect the left two cords in each set to it.

7. Drop down 3.15 inches (8 cm) and tie again an alternating square knot with 4 strands.

8. Drop down 1.5 inches (4 cm). Place your chosen container/bowl into the hanger to make sure it will fit, gather all strands together and then tie a gathering knot with the leftover shorter strand. Add a bead to each strand end (optional). Tie an overhand knot in each strand and trim all strands just below the overhand knots.

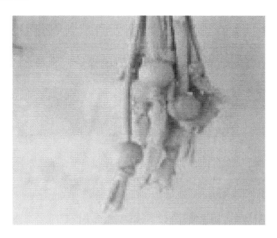

Jar

Materials:

Scissors

Jars

Macramé Cording

Fairy shines when you're finished to things in the jars.

Steps:

Measure the cording you have. Now that you've cut your first piece of cording, you want to cut the exact same length of three more pieces. For a total of four cords of equal size.

Fold half of the cords. Attach a knot to the top of the fold. This is going to be the cute little part of the hanger. Tug the knot to make it smooth and nice by tugging on the cords. Hang it up on something – a door knife, a cabinet knife, etc. It is much easier to tie the nodes as it hanged. Take two cords and tie down a little bit of a knot. Repeat this for everyone until you've got something like that. Make the knots the whole way around. Now, please. Take two of the knots you've just made and take a cord from each of those knots and tie the cords with another knot. Go around all the way until you have four knots. Make sure they're all the same. It will be your second lines of ties and you'll see the forming of the hanger. This is the time of your light bulb! Repeat and make another knot, third row.

Put in the container and make sure it fits. When it doesn't, just change your knots as much as you can or stretch them out. If it suits in there – then just tie into a big knot all the loose ends at the bottom. This big knot is going to be your jar hanger's bottom. The excess hanging from the knot can be trimmed or kept for a long time. Stuff every jar with the lights of the fairy. Hang them up now and enjoy them.

Mini Pumpkin Macramé Hanger

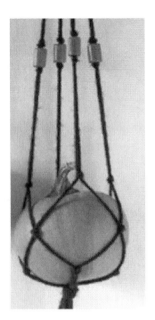

Materials:

Black thread or line.

Metal loop.

Hollow pearls

Scissors

Steps:

Cut 4 yarn strands about 3 times the completed hanger length. Fold the threads in the middle of the metal hoop.

The yarn strands are then divided into two groups.

Connect a knot to each group.

Cord a wooden bead on each thread, then tie another knot just below the bead.

Join a pair of knots a couple of inches apart.

Then tie two neighboring strings together and repeat each string. Then tie with the first line the last line.

Continue this process and bring another string together.

Finally, tie all the strings in a large knot.

Macramé Plant Hanger Beginner

Materials:

Cord: 10 strands of cord of 18 feet and 0.5 inches (5,5 meter), 2 strands of 3 feet and 3.3 inches (1 meter)

Ring: 1 round ring (wood) of 1.6 inches (4 cm) diameter

Container: 7 inches (18 cm) diameter

Steps:

1. Fold the 10 long strands of cord in half through the wooden ring.

2. Tie all (now 20) strands together with 1 shorter strand with a gathering knot. Hide the cut cord ends after tying the gathering knot.

3. Make a square knot using all cords: use from each side 4 strands to make the square knot; the other 12 strands stay in the middle.

4. Divide the strands in 2 sets of 10 strands each. Tie a square knot in each set using 3 strands on each side (4 strands stay in the middle of each group).

5. Divide the strands in 3 sets of 6 strands for the outer groups and 8 strands for the group in the middle. Tie a square knot in each set using 2 strands on each side.

6. Divide the strands into 5 sets of 4 strands each and make a square knot with each set.

7. Continue with the 5 sets. In the 2 outer sets you tie 4 square knots and in the 3 inner sets, you tie 9 half knots.

8. Using all sets tie 7 alternating square knots by connecting two strands in each set with the right two strands of the set to it. In the first, third, fifth and seventh row you are not using the 2 outer strands on each side.

9. Repeat step 7 and 8. In repeating step 8 you tie 5 alternating square knots instead of 7 alternating square knots.

10. To help you with the steps, number the strands from left to right, numbering them no.1 to no. 20.

11. With the 4 middle strands (no. 9 tot 12) you make 14 square knots.

12. Make a square knot with the set of 4 strands no. 3 to 6 and the set of 4 strands no. 15 to 18.

13. Divide the strands into 4 sets of 4 strands (ignore the set with the 14 square knots in the middle) and tie 12 square knots in each set.

14. Drop down 2 inches (5 cm).

15. Make 5 sets in the following way and tie in each set a square knot:

Set 1 consists out of strands no. 5, 6, 1 and 2

Set 2 consists out of strands no. 3, 4, 9 and 10

Set 3 consists out of strands no. 7, 7, 13 and 14

Set 4 consists out of strands no. 11, 12, 17 and 18

Set 5 consists out of strands no. 19, 20, 16 and 15

16. Drop down another 2 inches (5 cm), no knots. This is the moment to place your chosen container/bowl into the hanger to make sure it will fit. If you need to leave more space without knots in order to fit your container, you can do so.

17. Gather all strands together and then tie a gathering knot with the leftover shorter strand. Trim all strands at different lengths to finish your project.

CHAPTER 9:

Macramé Outdoors: Christmas Ornaments, Intermediate Hangers, Feathers

Mini Macramé Christmas Ornaments

Materials:

Macramé Cord

Hardness

Blueberry or peanut

Masking tape

Scissors

Get the Twig Cords

Steps:

Cut a little twig in the beginning and use the lark's knot to tie 6 cords to the end.

How do you build a lark knot in 4 steps?

To tie a knot of a lark, first fold it halfway and lie down over the top of the twig in the center.

Bend the loop over the back of the twig and pull both ends up. Pull close. Pull strong All 6 cords repeat.

White Christmas decoration of the mini Macramé with twinkle lights.

Mini Macramé Square Ornament Knot for Christmas

First Knot Square

The first chain, which is three square knots, must be started once the strings are on the twig. These knots are connected to four cords so that the first four cords begin to be divided on the left.

How to tie a square knot in four measurements to Macramé:

To make the square knot, pull out the left cord to look like a "4" number.

Then tuck under the fourth string at the end of the first string.

So pick up the end of the 4th cord and pick the gap between the first and second cord that looks like the four.

Tighten the 1st and 4th thread ends and move the nudge to the tip.

How to tie a square knot in a macramé college

So do the same thing for the second half of the square knot, but in the other direction. You form the 4 cords with the first and fourth cords but with the 4 cords on the right side.

Take the fourth first string.

Then feed into the 2nd and third strings the 1st string tail and into the 4th shape through the opening.

Tighten the first and fourth thread ends, and you've got the first square knot.

1-3 degrees

Steps to tie a knot in macramé

Make four pieces of cord working. Keep another square knot and another square knot in the top row.

For the second section, you can only make 2 square knots. The first is divided into cords to do this. The second knot in row 2 will be followed by the next four cords. At the other hand, the other two cords are still left.

Use the four-string center of a row just to form a square knot for the third row.

You can change the stress, try to keep your knots twisted and evenly spaced. Four or five rows

Small knot Macramé, taped to a table

Repeat row 2 for row 4 with 2 square knots, leaving both cords at the ends.

Repeat row 1 for row 5 with 3 knots square.

Line 6 -Half Hook Knot

Take the first string and move the part horizontally to the half knot. It will be your lead thread.

Take the second cord from behind the lead and through the hole you made. Now make the same knot again with the same 2nd thread. This is half a jump. It is a half jump.

Continue through the rest of the strings so that the lead cord is pulled through the other cords horizontally and directly.

To save the knots, push the lead thread.

Finishing of the decoration

Four steps to build a mini-Macramé

Cut the ends directly into a "V" down or up on the base to complete.

Then wear a hairbrush or a comb to brush the cord and build the fringe edge. Once you smooth it off, you can have to change the shape a little.

Cut the twig ends, then add a piece of string to hang the ornament up.

7-point Snowflake

Materials:

A 1.5-inch ring

Any household clear drying glue or fabric

2mm or 14 yards white cord material

Project board and pins

Steps:

All the cords should be mounted to the 1.5-inch ring with LHK. It can be done by folding the cord and placing it under the ring, then bring ends over the front of the ring and down. The ends should be passed over the folded area. A reverse half hitch should also be tied, passing the ends under and over the ring and under the cord. All the other cords should go through this step, and at the end of this step; the cords should be organized into a group of 7 having four cords. All the knots should be well tightened so that it won't loosen later on. Two SK should be tied with each group of four cords. The fillers should also be pulled so as to tighten them firmly; this ensures that the first rests against the knots that are on the ring. The four cords from the two SK should be numbered. The cords should be alternated by using cords 3 to 4 from an SK and using cords 1 to 2 from the other SK. At this juncture, one must be careful in selecting the four cords that come from the two adjacent knots while tying the ASK in a circle or ring.

The other cords should also follow after step 3 in order to complete the second row

The cords should be alternated again so that the same group is used as is done in step 2. The third row of the ASK should be tied all the way around the 7-point snowflake. Ensure that the knots in this row are a half-inch beneath the knots from the second row.

A picot has been made beneath every of the knots of step 5 using the four cords we just did. Now, let's get back to business. A SK should be tied below one of the knots that was tied in row three.

We need to make sure the knot rests against the one tied in step 5 above, so we move the knot up allowing it to form two picot loops

Still, with those same four cords, we will tie another SK that is close to the one that was recently tied. Before tightening the knots, glue should be applied to the fillers. Once the glue gets dried, the ends should be trimmed to 1 inch, and a fringe should be formed by separating the fibers at the ends of the 7-point snowflake

Steps 6 to 8 should be repeated with other set of cords

There is a higher percentage that the knots may loosen as time goes on if a cotton cable cord is being used and although this is an optional step but it is also advised. The snowflake can be turned over, and fabric glue should be applied behind each knots. Another thing to take note of about the fabric glue to be used is that it must be such that it dries clear.

Macramé Plant Hanger Intermediate

Materials:

Cord: 8 strands of cords of each 26 feet and 3 inches (8 meter), 1 short strand of cord

Wooden Ring: 1 round ring (wood) of 1,6 inches (4 cm) diameter

Container/Flowerpot: 7 inches (18 cm) diameter

Steps:

1. Fold 8 strands of cord, the long ones, in half over and through the ring. Now you have 16 strands of cord in total. Group them in sets of four strands.

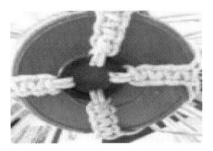

2. Tie 4 square knots on each set of four strands.

3. Drop down 3.15 inches (8 cm).

4. Tie 4 strands in each set with the right two of the set to it. Repeat on each of the 4 sets.

5. Drop down 4.3 inches (11 cm).

6. Repeat step 4, starting with the 2 right strands this time.

7. Take 2 strands of 1 set and make 10 alternating half hitch knots. Repeat for the 2 left strands of that set. Repeat for all sets.

8. Drop down 3.9 inches (10 cm) and tie a row of 48 half knots on each set of four strands.

9. Take the 2 middle strands of each set and make 8 alternating half hitch knots. You leave the 2 strands on the side of the set as they are (without knots).

10. Tie a row of 30 half knots on each set of four strands.

11. Use a new short strand of cord to make a gathering knot around all strands.

12. Cut off and fray the ends as desired.

Macramé Feathers
Materials:

5mm single wind cotton string

Texture stiffener

Sharp texture shears

Feline brush

Ruler

For a medium measured plume, cut:

1 32" strand for the spine

10-12 14" strands for the top

8-10 12" strands for the center

6-8 10" strands for the base

Steps:

Overlap the 32" strand into equal parts. Take one of the 14" strands, overlap it down the middle and fold it under the spine.

Take another 14" strand, crease it down the middle and supplement it into the circle of the top-level strand. Presently pull the base strands all the path through the top circle. This is your knot!

Pull the two sides firmly. On the following line, you'll interchange the beginning side. So, if you laid the even strand from left to right the first time, you'll lay the level strand from option right to left straightaway. Lay the first collapsed strand under the spine, string another collapsed strand into its circle. Pull the lower strands through the top circle. Also, fix.

Continue onward and work gradually down in size.

At that point, give it a rough trim. This helps direct the shape as well as assists with brushing the strands out. The shorter the strands, the simpler, to be completely honest. It likewise helps to have a sharp pair of texture shears!

After a rough trim, place the quill on a strong surface as you'll be using a feline brush to brush out the cording. Next, you'll need to harden the quill. The cording is delicate to such an extent that it'll simply fall if you get it and attempt to hang it. Give it splash, or two, and allow to pursue at least a few hours. When your plume has hardened up a bit, you would now be able to return and give it a last trim. It's smarter to trim just a little more! What's more, you may need to modify your trim contingent upon how regularly you're moving the piece. When you're ended cutting, you can even give it another wanderer of texture stiffener for good measure. And afterward, you'll be ready to hang your piece!

CHAPTER 10:

Macramé Lifestyle

Double Beaded Macramé Bracelet

Materials:

2m 1mm black waxed cord

40cm 2mm black waxed cord

60 4-6mm beads (hole must be at least 1mm wide)

1 10-12 flat beads or button (hole must be central and at least 2mm wide)

PVA glue

Clear nail varnish

Tools List

Macramé board and Pins (optional)

Craft knife or sharp pointed scissors

Steps:

Step 1 - Dip the ends of the 1mm cord into the clear nail varnish. If using super glue add a drop to each end. Allow to dry. This stops the ends of the cord fraying and makes it easier to thread the beads on in the further steps.

Tie and loop in the end of the cord big enough so the flat bead will fit through with some pressure. If the fit is too loose the bracelet may come unfastened. Pin the loop to your macramé board, if using.

Step 2 - Fold the remaining waxed cord in half. This will be used to tie the knots. Place this cord under the length attached to the board and tie one square knot over the cord length and the short end left from creating the loop.

Pull the knot tight.

Step 3 - Thread one bead on to each end of the knotting cord. Push these up the cord until they are resting against the central cord.

Step 4 - Now tie one square knot under the beads. While tying the knot adjust the thread tension and beads as needed so that the beads are touching the central cord.

Step 5 - Repeat steps 4 and 5 until you have added 30 pairs of beads.

Step 6 - Cut off the remaining knotting cords and cover the ends and a small area around them in PVA glue. Do not worry about the glue showing as it will dry clear. Allow the glue to dry until it is at least touch dry.

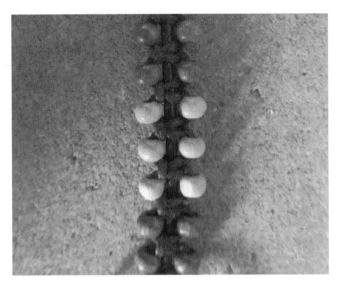

Step 7 - Thread the button or flat bead on to the central cord and leaving a few millimetres for movement tie a knot to hold it on the cord. Trim off the remaining central cord leaving a short end. This end can be dipped into clear nail varnish to prevent it from fraying or left as it is.

Endless Falls Macramé Bracelet

Materials:

• 60cm length of 2mm black waxed cotton cord

• 40 inch length of red waxed cotton cord

• 1 8-10mm flat bead

Tools List

• Macramé board and Pins (optional)

• Scissors

• Ruler

• PVA glue

Steps:

Step 1 - Fold the black cord in half and lay it in from of you or pin to your macramé board.

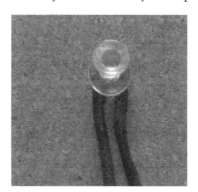

Step 2 - Fold the red cord I half and place the half-way point underneath the black cords.

Step 3 - Cross the red cords over the front of the black. It does not matter which cord is on top but ensure that it is the same in each knot or the pattern will not form correctly.

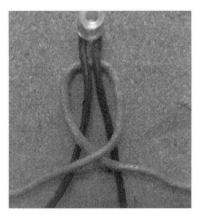

Step 4 - Pick up the black cords and thread them through the loop formed by the red cords and between the two black cords.

Step 5 - Tighten the knot by pulling the black cords downwards. Position the knot approximately 1cm below the black cord ends, creating a loop. This loop forms part of the bracelets fastener so needs to be tight fit for the bead to pass through.

Step 6 - Cross the red cords over the front of the black cords.

Step 7 - Pick up the black cords and thread them through the loop formed by the red cords and between the two black cords.

Step 8 - Pull the black cords downwards to tighten the knot until it rests beneath the first knot.

Step 9 - Repeat steps 6-8 until the bracelet measures 7.5 inches long. Holding all four cords at the cross over point with one hand while threading the black cords with the other is a good technique for tying this type of knot.

Step 10 - Now tie one square knot using the red cords and pull the knot tight

Step 11 - Cut off the excess red cords and one of the lengths of black cord.

Step 12 - Cover the cut cord ends and surrounding area in PVA glue and leave until dry.

Step 13 - Thread the flat bead onto the remaining black cord. Leaving a 3mm gap, tie an overhand knot to secure the bead.

Step 14 - Cut off the remaining cord leaving a short end. The cord end can be dipped in PVA if desired to stop it from fraying.

Zig Zag Bracelet

Materials:

• 60cm length of 2mm black waxed cotton cord

• 150cm length of 2mm black waxed cotton cord

• 16 8mm oval beads (must have a 2mm hole minimum)

• 1 15mm disk bead or button with central hole (minimum hole diameter of 4mm) Tools List

• Macramé board and Pins (optional)

• Scissors

• Clear nail varnish (optional)

• PVA glue

Steps:

Step 1 - Fold the shorter length of cord in half and place it round a pin on your macramé board, if using. If not just lay the cord on a flat surface.

Step 2 - Fold the longer length of cord in half and tie one square knot around the shorter cords.

This knot needs to be placed so that the loop created in the end of the shorter cords is a tight fit for the disk bead to fit through.

Step 3 - Tie a further four square knots.

Step 4 - Thread eight beads on to each of the central cords.

Step 5 - Pick up the longer cord on the right and take it across the central cord, under the first bead and then under the central cords so it come out back on the right side under the first bead on the right side central cord.

Step 6 - Repeat step 5 until you have wrapped the right cord around all the beads, moving the beads into place as you go.

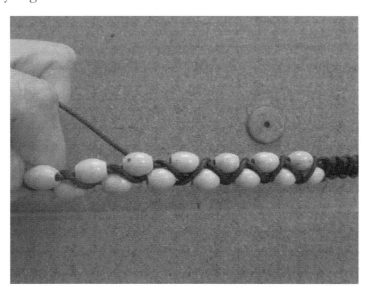

Step 7 - Holding the right cord in place at the bottom of the beads, repeat steps 5 and 6 using the left side longer cord.

Step 8 - Now tie one square knot to secure the wrapped cords.

Step 9 - Tie another four square knots to match the ones at the start of the bracelet.

Step 10 - Cut off the excess long outer cord lengths and cover the ends and surrounding area with PVA glue. The glue will secure the ends and dries clear so will not show. Allow the glue to dry.

Thread the disk bead onto the two centrals cord and leaving a gap of a few millimetres, tie an overhand knot to secure. After cutting off the excess cord in step 11, the ends can be dipped into clear nail varnish if desired. Once dry this will stop the cord from fraying.

Starlight Earrings

Materials:

2 ft Blue Lagoon C-Lon cords, x8 (4 per earring)

2 gold earwires

2 eye pins

2 blue beads, 4mm

2 gold beads, size 6

26 size 11 blue seed beads

52 size 11 gold seed beads

Steps:

Take an eye pin place on it a size 11 blue seed bead, a 4mm blue bead and another size 11 seed bead. Curve the end into a loop and trim.

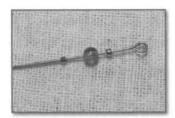

Place a gold earwire onto the top loop. Cut a cord in half and attach it to the lower eye hook via a Lark's Head Knot (LHK). Repeat with the other 3 cords. Separate cords 4-4.

Left 4 cords:

Tighten left 2 LHK's.

Row 1: Place the inner cord to the left and down slightly as the holding cord (HC). Tie double half-hitch (DHH) knots onto it with the other 3 cords; inside to outside.

Row 2: Find the inner cord and place it out to the left as the HC. Tie 1 DHH knot onto it, then place a size 11 gold seed bead onto the HC. Tie 1 DHH knot. Place a gold seed bead onto the HC. Tie 1 DHH knot.

Row 3: Repeat row 2.

Right 4 cords:

Tighten LHK's.

Row 1: Place the inner cord to the right and down slightly as the holding cord (HC). Tie DHH knots onto it with the other 3 cords; inside to outside.

Row 2: Find the inner cord and place it out to the right as the HC. Tie 1 DHH knot onto it, then place a size 11 gold seed bead onto the HC. Tie 1 DHH knot. Place a gold seed bead onto the HC. Tie 1 DHH knot.

Row 3: Repeat row 2.

Find the center 2 cords and thread a size 11 blue seed bead onto each one. Place inner right cord over inner left then tie a DHH knot with the left cord. For this "Blue Seed Bead Section" we will use all size 11 blue seed beads

Place another bead onto the 3rd cord in from the right. Find the cord that you tied the last DHH knot with and place a bead on it (4th cord in on the right). Tie a DHH knot with the 4th cord in onto the 3rd cord in.

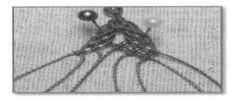

Bead the 2nd cord from the right. Find the 3rd cord from the right and bead it then tie a DHH knot with the left onto the right. Ignore outer right cord for now.

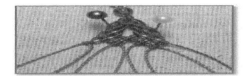

Bead the 3rd cord in on the left. Bead the 4th cord in from left. DHH knot the 3rd cord onto the 4th cord.

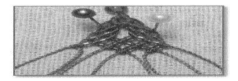

Bead the 4th cord in from each side. Tie left beaded cord onto the right beaded cord.

Bead the 3rd & 4th cords in from the right. Tie left onto right

Bead 2nd & 3rd cords in from the left. Tie left onto right.

Bead 3rd & 4th cords in from the left. Tie left onto right.

Bead the 4th cord in from each side. Tie left onto right. (End of Blue Seed Bead Section).

Using size 11 gold seed beads, bead as follows: outer cord on each side; 1 bead. Inner 2 cords; 3 beads each. Remaining 4 cords; 2 beads each.

Take the outer left cord and thread on 1 blue seed bead then place it to the right as the HC. Tie 1 DHH knot with the outer cord. Place a blue bead on the HC then tie a DHH knot with the next cord in. Repeat once more.

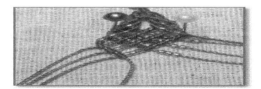

Take the outer right cord and thread on 1 blue seed bead then place it to the left as the HC. Tie 1 DHH knot with the outer cord. Place a blue bead on the HC then tie a DHH knot with the next cord in. Repeat once more.

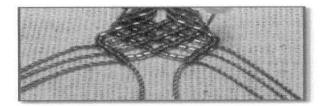

Place a gold seed bead onto each HC. Place one HC through a size 6 gold bead, then thread the other HC through the same bead from the other direction.

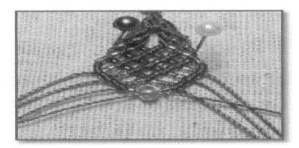

Take the left HC and place up and to the left. Tie a DHH knot onto it with the inner left cord. Tighten up against previous row. Place this cord with the HC. Tie a DHH knot with the inner left cord around both HC's, then and add this cord to the HC's. Repeat once more.

Repeat on the right side.

Glue, trim, glue again.

Macramé Bag

Steps:

To Make the Handle:

We'll start by hitching the tie of the bag. You'll need to tie every half of the tie independently, so the length of each bit complete length of the tie.

Complete four knots. Beginning with the knot on the right, take the inward string and circle it around the external string. Fix the knot and this is what it ought to resemble. Rehash the past knot, just using the following string this time. Knot the opposite side of the ties using the equivalent hitching strategy, just turning around the course this time. This is the two sides done. Rehash this for the two sides multiple times. Once more, using the equivalent tying technique, interface the two strands by broadening the knots. This is what the expanding line resembles.

Rehash these all-inclusive lines multiple times. At that point alter the course and knot from left to directly for the following 3 lines. At that point rehash the side knots. When you've done this, you have completed a large portion of the tie! Rehash this for the other lash and band, we'll associate them later on. To polish off the knotwork, rehash a similar knot.

Clip off one of the strands in the knot, at that point proceed with the tying another knot using the following strand. This is what the completed end will resemble. To join the lashes together, line up the closures and sew together with needle and string. To make the body of the rope pack, cut 10 bits of string that are multiple times the ideal length of your bag.

As a reference, the pack we made is 15" (38cm). Knot it onto the gold band using the collapsed end like previously. The body of the rope pack will be ended with box ties. Taking two strings as an afterthought, circle it around the two center strands. Rehash the knot, and pull the knot tight. Rehash the knots on the remainder of the strands, make sure to keep the separations between the knots and the bands the equivalent. We did our own 3" down from the circle.

Keep doing box knots for the subsequent column, just using the strings one strand over this time. Knot 3 columns of box knots on the two sides, before tying the sides of the bag by using two strands from either side. Keep doing box knots until the pack is the size you are after. Cut off the parts of the bargains in the event that you don't need any tuft ends, and put a touch of paste into the knots to make sure about them. Flip the pack out.

Hoop Earrings

Materials:

Contact glue,

Synthetic yarn,

Scissors.

Jewelry caps

Earring hooks.

Steps:

First of all, wrap 3 meters of thread over your fingers, hold it and tie it with more ribbon, cut the threads on the opposite end, use another piece of string and wrap it around the related part, tie it from behind and use glue to fix the knot. Finally, use scissors to cut the excess piece.

At this point, we should already have our two fringes ready to turn them into beautiful earrings. From here, we have several options; the option that we recommend is to use jewelry caps for ornaments and contact glue.

The last step is to use two earring hooks on each cap. You can use jewelry pliers if you need to open and fix the rings or any other material you use. You can get all the materials used in specialized jewelry stores or by recycling old earrings that you no longer apply.

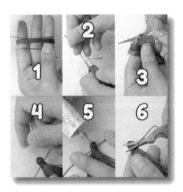

Folded Braid Keychain

Steps:

1) Cut three bits of rope somewhat more than twice the length you need for the completed custom keychain.

2) Stack them, even the strands, and wrap one end with a small elastic band a couple of inches from the ends.

3) Do a straightforward mesh. Stop when you are the same distance from the closures as the elastic band is.

4) Circle one end through the keychain. If you'd like, put the elastic band around the two closures to hold them erect.

5) Tie knots in the sections of the bargains to wrap it up.

Choker Necklace

Materials:

3 strands of black C-Lon cord; two 7ft cords, one 4ft cord

18 - green beads (4mm)

7 - round silver beads (10 mm)

Fasteners: Ribbon Clasps, silver

Glue - Beacon 527 multi-use

Note: Bead size can vary slightly. Just be sure all beads you choose will slide onto 2 cords.

Steps:

Optional – Find the center of your cord and attach it to the top of the ribbon clasp with a lark's head knot. If this is problematic, you could cut all the cords to 7ft and not worry about placement. (If you really trust your glue, you can skip this step by gluing the cords into the clasp and going from there).

Lay all cords into the ribbon clasp. Add a generous dap of glue and use pliers to close the clasp.

You now have 6 cords to work with. Find the 4 ft. cords and place them in the center. They will be the holding (or filler) cords throughout.

Begin your Alternating Lark's Head (ALH) chain, using the outmost right cord then the outermost left cord. Follow with the other right cord then the last left cord. For this first set, the pattern will be hard to see. You may need to tug gently on the cords to get a little slack in them.

Now slide a silver bead onto the center 2 cords.

The outer cords are now staggered on your holding cords. Continue with the ALH chain by knotting with the upper right cord then tie a knot with the upper left cord.

Finish your set of 4 knots, then add a green bead

Tie four ALH knots followed by a green bead until you have 3 green beads in the pattern. Then tie one more set of 4 ALH knots.

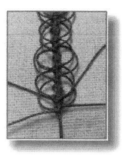

Slide on a silver bead and continue creating sequences of 3 green, 1 silver (always with 4 ALH knots between each). End with the 7th silver bead and 1 more set of 4 ALH knots, for a 12" necklace. (Use this to shorten or lengthen as you choose).

Lay all cords in the ribbon clasp and glue well.

Crimp shut and let dry completely. Trim excess cords.

Lantern Bracelet

Materials:

3 strands of C-Lon cord (2 light brown and 1 medium brown) 63-inch lengths

Fasteners (1 jump ring, 1 spring ring or lobster clasp)

Glue - Beacon 527 multi-use

8 small beads (about 4mm) amber to gold colors

30 gold seed beads

3 beads (about 6 mm) amber color (mine are rectangular, but round or oval will work wonderfully also)

Note: Bead size can vary slightly. Just be sure all beads you choose will slide onto 2 cords (except seed beads).

Steps:

Find the center of your cord and attach it to the jump ring with a lark's head knot. Repeat with the 2 remaining strands. If you want the 2-tone effect, be sure your second color is NOT placed in the center, or it will only be a filler cord and you will end up with a 1 tone bracelet.

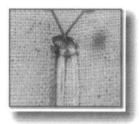

You now have 6 cords to work with. Think of them as numbered 1 thorough 6, from left to right. Move cords 1 and 6 apart from the rest. You will use these to work the spiral knot. All others are filler cords. Take cord number 1 tie a spiral knot. Always begin with the left cord. Tie 7 more spirals.

Place a 4mm bead on the center 2 cords. Leave cords 1 and 6 alone for now and work 1 flat knot using cords 2 and 5.

Now put cords 2 and 5 together with the center strands. Use 1 and 6 to tie a picot flat knot. Loosen it up and try again. Gently tug the cords into place then lock in tightly with the spiral knot.

Notice here how I am holding the picot knot with my thumbs while pulling the cords tight with my fingers.

Tie 8 spiral knots (using left cord throughout pattern).

Place a 4mm bead on the center 2 cords. Leave cords 1 and 6 alone for now and work 1 flat knot using cords 2 and 5. Now put cords 2 and 5 together with the center strands. Use strands 1 and 6 to tie a picot flat knot.

Place 5 seed beads on cords 1 and 6. Put cords 3 and 4 together and string on a 6 mm bead. Tie one flat knot with the outermost cords.

Repeat this step two more times.

5 sets of spirals from the center point. Thread on your clasp. Tie an overhand knot with each cord and glue well. Let dry completely. As this is the weakest point in the design, trim the excess cords and glue again. Let dry.

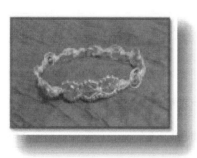 

Macramé Spiral Earrings

Materials:

Lighter

Earring hooks

Jump rings

4mm light cyan glass pearl

1 mm nylon thread

Steps:

Cut three pieces of nylon thread at 100 cm. One of these would be the nylon thread and the rest would both be the working threads. A crown knot should then be tied around the holding thread.

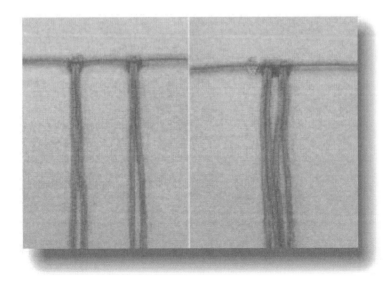

Check the left holding thread and make sure to add a jump ring there.

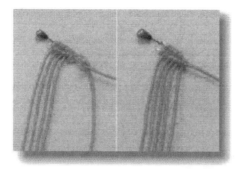

Over the four working threads, go ahead and place the left holding thread there. Use the four working threads to hold the thread and the make a half hitch knot on the remaining thread.

Tie 4 half hitch knots on the leftmost thread and then slide a pearl onto the nylon thread. Secure with a half hitch knot.

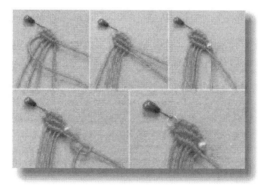

Repeat for 25 times to create a perfect spiral.

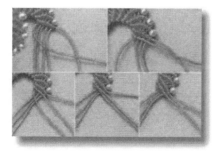

To fasten, get your holding thread again (the leftmost thread, in this case), and let it overlap the thread you are currently holding. Cut one holding thread after tying a half hitch knot.

Tie two more half hitch knots and slide a pearl onto the rightmost thread. Make sure to use the thread in a half hitch again.

To finish, just cut some extra threads off and burn the ends with a lighter. Make sure to attach earring hooks, as well.

Summery Chevron Earrings

Materials:

Ear wires

Small chain

Nylon/yarn (or any cord you want)

Wire

Pliers

Scissors

Hot glue gun

Steps:

Fold the cord into four, and then tie a base/square knot as you hold the four lengths. Once you do this, you'll notice that you have eight pieces of cotton lengths with you. What you should do is separate them into twos, and tie a knot in each of those pairs before you start knotting with the square knot. It's like you're making a friendship bracelet!

Use the wire to make two loops out of the thread and make sure the center and sides have the same width.

At the back of the bracelet, make use of hot glue to prevent knots from spooling.

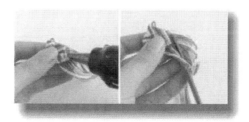

Fold the bracelet around the wire shortly after putting some glue and letting it cool.

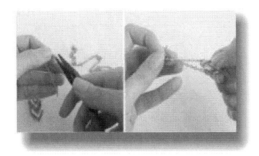

Use hot glue so knots wouldn't come down again. Make sure to cut the excess thread.

Cut the chain to your desired length—or how you want the earrings to look like. Secure the ear wire as you find the middle of the chain.

Enjoy your new earrings!

Hearty Paperclip Earrings

Materials:

Paper clips

Embroidery thread

Earring hooks

Glue

Water

Paint brush

Steps:

Bend some paper clips until they resemble hearts. Take note that you may have to try a lot of times because it's expected that you may not get the effect right away. Once you have made some hearts, glue the ends to keep them secure.

Wrap embroidery thread just to coat the clips, and then leave some inches of thread hanging so you could make half-hitch knots out of them.

Tie knots until you reach the end and paint with a mix of water and glue to keep secure.

Let dry and then add the earring hooks.

Fringe Fun Earrings

Materials:

56" of 4-ply Irish waxed linen cord

2 brass headpins

2 brass ear wires

2 hammered brass 33mm metal rings

22 glass 6mm rounds

Round nose forceps

Chain nose forceps

Scissors

Steps:

Make eye pins out of the headpins by twisting the tip and making a loophole, much the same as what's demonstrated as follows.

String a glass round to form a single loop and then set aside before cutting in half.

At the end of one cord, make a 3" fold and then go and knot around the brass ring.

Make two half-hitch knots just around the ring.

String a glass bead so that you could form an overhead knot. Trim until you reach 1/8" and the make an overhand knot again. Trim once more to 1/8".

Macramé Bracelet

Materials:

Scissors or razor blade

A crayon or T-pin or foam frame

A hemp cord or a string of choice

Steps:

Step 1

The width of the wrist is first calculated. Then cut two bits of hemp cord with the aid of the scissors. The cut pieces will be at least three times the length of the wrist or even the diameter initially measured. For example, if the measurement is 5 inches, two strands of 15 inches should be cut.

Step 2

One strand is partially folded. When the handle is kept in a horizontal position, the folding strand is protected with a loop over the pencil which ensures that loose ends are placed behind it. Those loose ends should be tightly pulled and crossed by the loop.

This cycle should also be replicated in the second strand. You'll finally have to hang this pencil down with four lines. Mentally, you can mark 4 strands as 1, 2 3 4 from right to left. Any labeling technique you find simple can be used.

Step 3

Therefore, beach 1 will be moved to the west over beach 2 and beach 3 (which are the two main beaches) and then below beach 4.

Step 4

Take strand 4 at this step behind both strands 2 and 3 through the loop created by strand 1. Pull strand 1 and strand 4 tightly to ensure a half-square knot is achieved.

Step 5

You can now conduct a crossing process. Continue this crossing until the bracelet eventually reaches your desired duration. Spirals will be formed as the half-square knots start to operate.

Step 6

The loops have gone out of the crayon here. Pull strand 2 and strand 3 to develop the loop size marginally. Instead, the four threads are tied together and the job is secured by two knots. Those are main knots. Those strings that you assume are unwanted should be cut off and reached as close to those knots as possible.

Step 7

Now you put your watch on your wrist. To hold the bracelet on your handle, move the knot through the loop.

Celtic Choker

Materials:

3 strands of black C-Lon cord; two 7ft cords, one 4ft cord

18 - Green beads (4mm)

7 - Round silver beads (10 mm)

Fasteners: Ribbon Clasps, silver

Glue - Beacon 527 multiuse

Note: Bead size can vary slightly. Just be sure all beads you choose will slide onto 2 cords.

Steps:

1. Optional – Find the center of your cord and attach it to the top of the ribbon clasp with a lark's head knot. It is easier to thread the loose ends through and pull them down until the loop is near the opening, then push the cords through the loop. Repeat with the 2 remaining strands, putting the four-foot cord in the center. If this is problematic, you could cut all the cords to 7ft and not worry about placement. (If you really trust your glue, you can skip this step by gluing the cords into the clasp and going from there).

2. Lay all cords into the ribbon clasp. Add a generous dap of glue and use pliers to close the clasp.

3. You now have 6 cords to work with. Find the 4 ft cords and place them in the center. They will be the holding (or filler) cords throughout.

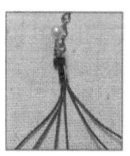

4. Begin your Alternating Lark's Head (ALH) chain, using the outmost right cord then the outermost left cord. Follow with the other right cord then the last left cord. For this first set, the pattern will be hard to see. You may need to tug gently on the cords to get a little slack in them.

5. Now slide a silver bead onto the center 2 cords.

6. The outer cords are now staggered on your holding cords. Continue with the ALH chain by knotting with the upper right cord...

Then tie a knot with the upper left cord.

7. Finish your set of 4 knots, then add a green bead

8. Tie four ALH knots followed by a green bead until you have 3 green beads in the pattern. Then tie one more set of 4 ALH knots.

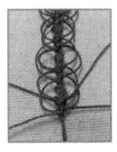

9. Slide on a silver bead and continue creating sequences of 3 green, 1 silver (always with 4 ALH knots between each). End with the 7th silver bead and 1 more set of 4 ALH knots, for a 12" necklace. (Use this segment to shorten or lengthen as you choose).

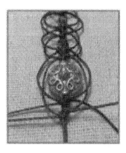

10. Lay all cords in the ribbon clasp and glue well.

11. Crimp shut and let dry completely. Trim excess cords.

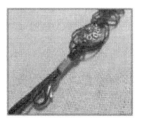

Pet Leash

Materials

Swivel Hook

Glue

4mm or 6mm cord material

Project board and pins

Overhand Knot

Buttonhole Clasp

Leash

The length of the material (Leash) after the work is done should be determined by you and after you and after it has been selected, you should try out this calculation

Length of leash (in inches) = WC /3 (in yards)

The length of the Holding cord also increases by 0.5 yards for every 10 inches the length of the leash is beginning from 20 inches which is 2 yards long (i.e., 20 inches = 2 yards, 30 inches = 2.5 yards, 40 inches = 3 yards….) till you get to your desired leach's length. The total amount of materials needed is, therefore dependent on this calculation.

Steps

Put the two cords vertically on our board after getting their corresponding midpoints and tightly place them close to one another. The longer WC should be on the left because that is what will be used to tie the LHK on the HC. A half of the vertical LHK should be made to move using the WC over or under (as the case may be) the HC to have a counter-clockwise loop. Gradually pulling it left, you should make it go over the WC to get the crossing point. Once the crossing point is gotten, tie the other half of the Vertical LHK by passing the WC under or over the HC, while pulling it left, pass it under the WC to also make the crossing point. More Vertical LHK should be tied and should be done from the center in the direction of one end. When the first half of the handle is 6 inches, you should stop. Folding the 2 WC means we should have 4 cords to work with. A suitable decorative knot by the user should be used alongside this wonderful design, some of the best knots to use alongside it are; the Square Knot, the Vertical larks head, and the Half hitches with holding cords. A minimum of six inches of material should be attached to the hook at the end of the pet leach. To attach the hook, two cords should be passed through the loop that is on the hook, and a tight finishing should be tied with the four cords. The usage of glue comes in here as the four cords are being tightened, the glue should be used. When it gets dry, all additional materials should be removed or cut to make the work very neat and beautiful. You may also consider another finishing style which entails that you move the ends in the direction of the strap and put it under the back of the knots so that it can be very firm.

Fish Bone Macramé Bracelet

Steps:

Step 1 - Fold the shorter blue cord in half and lay it in front of you.

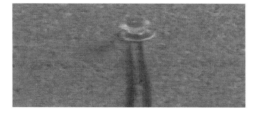

Step 2 - Fold the long blue cord in half and tie one square knot around the shorter cord.

This knot should be positioned so that the loop created is a tight fit for the bead/button to fit through.

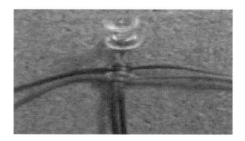

Step 3 - Use the red cord to tie a square knot underneath the bead.

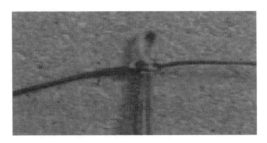

Step 4 - Thread on the first bead.

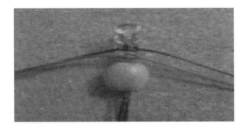

Step 5 - Carry the blue cords over the red and tie a square knot underneath the bead.

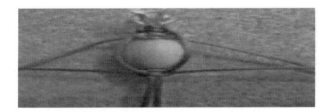

Step 6 - Carry the red cords over and tie a square knot underneath the blue knot.

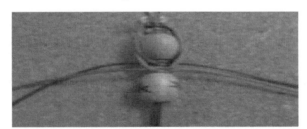

Step 7 - Thread on a second bead.

Step 8 - Repeat steps 5 and 6.

Step 9 - Continue in this way until all the beads have been added.

Step 10 - Leaving a 3mm tail cut off the remaining knotting cord on one side. Use the lighter to melt the ends and stick them to the back of the knots.

Take care with the melting cord as it gets very hot and can stick to your skin and burn. Use a needle or point of the scissors to press down the cord.

Step 11 - Repeat step 10 with the remaining cords.

Step 12 - Thread on the disk bead/button. Leave a 3mm gap between the final knot and the bead and tie an overhand knot.

Black and Red Macramé Bracelet

Steps:

Step 1 - Fold the shorter red cord in half and lay it flat in front of you. These are the designs central cords.

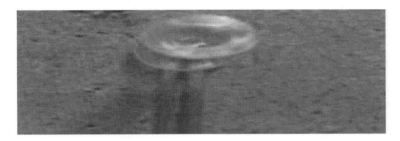

Step 2 - Fold the black cord in half and tie one square knot around the red central cords.

This knot needs to be positioned so that it creates a loop that the bead/flat button can pass through tightly. This forms the bracelets fastener.

Step 3 - Fold the longer red rattail cord in half and tie one half knot around the red central cords underneath the black square knot.

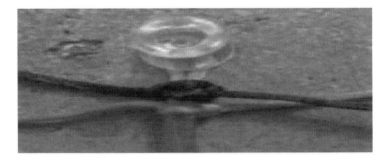

Step 4 - Tie a further four half knots always starting with the same side cord so that the knots begin to form a spiral.

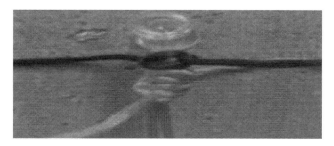

Step 5 - Carry the black cords over the red and tie one square knot underneath the half knots.

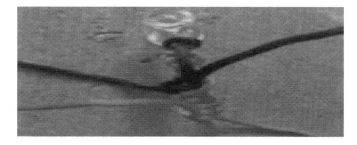

Step 6 - Pass the red cords under the black and tie five half knots.

Step 7 - Continue in this way until you have tied 18cm of knots.

If you have the bracelet pinned to a board or solid surface the bracelet will twist as the spirals forms so you may find it easier to unpin and re-pin it as you work. The black cords should be flat, only the red knotting cords form the spiral.

Step 8 - Turn the bracelet over and trim away all the excess knotting cords leaving 3mm ends.

Step 9 - Gently melt the cord end with the lighter and press them against the knots.

Heated rattail cord becomes very hot and can stick to your skin and burn so this step is safest carries out using a needle or scissors point to press on the melting cord.

Step 10 - Thread the flat bead/button onto the central cords. Push it up to the knots and leaving a 3mm gap tie an overhand knot to secure the bead. Cut off any excess cord and gently melt the ends to prevent fraying.

Macramé Camera Strap

Materials:

Macramé Loop

Four fasteners

Clothing spinner

Industrial adhesive resistance

Scissors

Steps:

Step 1: Cut 2 lengths of the Macramé thread, each 4 yards.

Step 2: Fold each cord length to make one yard on one side and 3 yards on the other. Attach the intermediate points by the flap of a swivel clasp that holds the long ends of the strands external.

Step 3: Tie each cord by its own loop and safe it around the clasp.

Step 4: Start tying a square knot. Take the left (longest) cord, cross it over the middle and the bottom of two cords (longest one). Bring up and down the right cord beneath the center of the two and the left cord. Pull this tight. It is half of the square knot.

Step 5: Complete the reverse move 4 square knot. Cross in the middle of two the right chord, then the left chord in the middle of two, then the right one. Pull close and finish the square with a knot.

Step 6: Continue to tie square knots to the appropriate camera strap length.

Step 7: Trim all four ends of the thread. Join all four cords through another pivoting bond. At the bottom of each thread, fold the cords over the clasp and hold clothespins until the adhesive dries.

Remove the clips and pop the strap when the glue is hot on your frame.

Day Glow Earrings

Materials:

36" Irish-waxed linen cord

3" 2.5mm crystal chain

2 3" headpins

2 large kidney ear wires

2 12mm beads

Scissors

Cutters

Round nose pliers

Chain nose pliers

Steps:

Tie an overhand knot by using 18" waxed linen, and make sure to leave 3". Make sure it reaches 1 headpin.

String ceramic on both ends of the cord, then wrap the headpin with a long cord.

Using a square knot, and make sure to wrap the loop.

On top of 1 kidney wire, hold a 1 ½" of crystal chain. Place the rest of the waxed linen under the crystal and let it go criss-cross around the ear wire.

End the loop with a square knot and clean the ends by trimming them.

Put the beaded dangle onto the wire.

As for the second earring, you should String ceramic on both ends of the cord, then wrap the headpin with a long cord. Using a square knot, and make sure to wrap the loop. On top of 1 kidney wire, hold a 1 ½" of crystal chain. Place the rest of the waxed linen under the crystal and let it go criss-cross around the ear wire.

End the loop with a square knot and clean the ends by trimming them, as well.

Filigree Lace let Bracelet

Materials:

66" length white C-Lon cord, 4 strands

6 clear beads, 5mm

56 clear beads, 3mm

5 clear beads, 4mm

1 bead for button closure, about 7mm

164 clear seed beads

Glue - Beacon 527 multiuse

Note: You can vary the bead sizes slightly. Just be sure the beads you choose will slide onto 2, and sometimes 3 cords. (The seed beads only need to fit onto one cord).

Steps:

Find the center of the cords and lightly tie an overhand knot. Pin this onto your project board. Tie about 9 flat knots (for 7mm button closure bead). Now undo the overhand knot and fold the flat knots into a horseshoe shape. Using the outer cord from each side, tie 1 flat knot.

2. Take the rightmost cord and place it over all others down to the left to work Diagonal Double Half Hitch (DDHH) knots from right to left. Put 1 clear seed bead on each cord, then tie another set of DDHH knots from right to left.

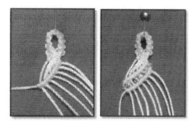

3. Separate cords into 4-4. Working with left 4 cords bead as follows: on the left most, cord put 4 clear 3mm beads with a seed bead between each one. The following cord in gets 5 clear seed beads. The following cord in needs a 5mm clear bead. And the last cord of this segment gets 5 clear seed beads. Use the outer 2 cords to tie a flat knot around the inner cords.

4. Working with right 4 cords: Place a 3mm clear bead on the center 2 cords. Place a seed bead on the right most cord. Now use this right most cord to tie an Alternating Lark's Head (ALH) knot around the other 3 cords. Repeat 4 times.

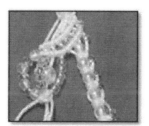

5. Using the left most cord as a holding cord, work DDHH knots from left to right. Place a seed bead on each cord then work another set of DDHH knots (from left to right again) using the left most cord as your holding cord.

6. Separate cords into 4-4. Working with left 4 cords: Place a 3mm clear bead on the center 2 cords. Place a seed bead on the left most cord. Now use this left most cord to tie an ALH knot around the other 3 cords. Repeat 4 times.

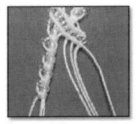

7. Working with right 4 cords: the right most cord gets 4 clear 3mm beads with a seed bead between each one. The following cord in from the right needs 5 seed beads. The following cord in gets a 5mm clear bead. And the last cord of this segment gets 5 seed beads. Use the outer 2 cords to tie a flat knot around the inner cords.

8. Repeat steps 2-7 for pattern until you have about 6 1/2 inches in length.

9. Separate cords into 3-2-3. On the left set of cords, place a 4mm bead. With the center 2 cords thread on a 3mm bead, a 4mm bead and another 3mm bead. On the right 3 cords place three 4mm beads. Find the outermost cord on each side and tie a flat knot around the rest.

10. Thread your button bead onto the center 4, or 6 cords if possible. Use the outer cords to tie a flat knot. Glue flat knot and let dry. Trim excess cords.

Macramé Bracelet with Rattail Cord and Glass Beads
Materials:

30cm length of 1mm rattail cord

140cm length of 1mm rattail cord

1 10-12mm disk bead or button with central hole (hole must be 1mm minimum)

8 6mm black glass spacer beads

4 6mm white glass spacer beads

3 6mm patterned glass spacer beads

Tools List:

Macramé board and pins (optional)

Ruler

Lighter

Steps:

Step 1 - Fold over the first 5cm of the shorter length of cord and lay in front of you. These are the central cords.

Step 2 - Fold the longer cord in half and place the center point underneath both cords.

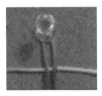

Step 3 - Starting with the left side cord tie one half knot.

Step 4 - Tighten the knot fully and position it to create a 10mm loop in the end of the shorter length of cord. This loop will form part of the bracelets fastener and needs to be a tight fit for the disk bead to fit through. Adjust as needed to suit your bead.

Step 5 - Always start with the left side knotting cord, continue tying half knots until you have a Sennett 3.5cm long. The Spiral pattern can be seen forming within a few knots. Pull the first few knots tied a little tighter than normal to hold the loop created in step 1 securely. The completed section of bracelet, including the loop should measure approximately 4.5cm.

Step 6 - Thread one black bead, a patterned bead and a second black bead onto the central cord and move these up to the bottom of the knots. Tie one half knot underneath the beads to hold them in place. This knot should not to too tight. The beads should be sitting freely with the cords around them not squashed together.

Step 7 - Tie a further four half knots.

Step 8 - Repeat step 6, this time adding one white, one black and then a second black bead. Tie four more half knots.

Step 9 - Repeat steps 6-8 until all the beads have been added to the bracelet.

Step 10 - Continue tying half knots until you have a 3.5 cm Sennett to match the one at the beginning of the bracelet.

Step 11 - Cut off the excess knotting cords leaving a 3mm tail. Gently melt this tail using the lighter and fuse them to the final knot.

The melted rattail cord can get very hot and stick to skin so it is best to use the point of the scissors, a needle or similar item to carry out this step.

Step 12 - Thread the disk bead on to the central cord. Leave a gap of 3mm between the last knot and the bead and tie an overhand knot to secure the bead. Trim of the excess central cord and gently melt the end to prevent fraying.

Macramé Shopping Bag
Materials:

Jute Rope

Bag Handles

Steps:

1. Split 2.3-meter long rope into 10 lengths. Fold them in half and thread through the gap on the bag handle to the folded middle. Take the ends of the rope and move through the loop you made in this earlier stage. Tight drive. Repeat this until 5 pieces of rope are attached to the handle of each bag.

2. Starting at one end, separate two pieces of rope from each other and push the rest sideways. With those two pieces, we will make the first knot. This is the knot that we will use in the tutorial, so keep moving to the next few steps if you get confused.

Make a right strand bend, so it crosses the right angle over the left rope.

Take the rope on the left (which is still straight) and thread that you made with the two ropes through the gap. Push both ends of the rope away before the knot is shaped and is in the right position. You want the handle to be about 5 cm forward.

Take the left-hand rope to complete the knot, and this time bring it over the right.

This time the right-hand rope is threaded through the gap. Push the tight knot over again. This is a double half hitch knot now complete.

3. Use the remaining ropes on the handle to make four more of those knots in a line. Then continue again but skip the first rope this time, and the second and third knot. Move on down the line. This time, you'll make four knots, and there's no knotting of the first and last rope.

4. Make the third row the same as the first one (thus five knots, without losing any ropes) once you have completed the second row.

5. Repeat steps 2-4 on the second handle once the third row is done. If that's finished, but the two handle facing each other together with the backsides.

6. Keep knotting in this pattern until you are left with around 10 cm of rope on the ends.

7. Cut rope length 4 meters long. Handles to tie this into the last side knot.

8. Take one front and one back string and wrap the rope around them. Then take another two knots (one from the front and one from the back) and do the same again. Act before you make it to the top.

9. Draw the rope which hangs down. Connect these strands together to stay in place in knots. To strengthen these, you should apply some glue. Combine it to form a fringe.

Side by Side Macramé Bracelet
Steps:

Step 1 - Gently heat the ends of each cord to make it easier to thread on the beads and prevent fraying.

Fold one cord in half and secure to your Macramé board (if using).

Step 2 - Fold a second cord in half and use it to tie one square knot around the cords on the Macramé board.

Position this knot to create a small loop in the end of the first cord. This loop should be sized so that the flat bead/button fits through with a little pressure.

Step 3 - Fold the final length of cord in half and use it to tie one square knot underneath the knot tied in step 2.

You should now have six cords, grouped in three sets of two.

Step 4 - Regroup the cords into two sets of three.

Step 5 - Working with one set of three cords, thread one bead purple and one silver bead on to the outer cords.

Step 6 - Using these two outer cords, tie one square knot around the central cord below the beads.

Step 7 - Thread two more beads on to the outer cords and place them below the two already added to the bracelet.

Tie one square knot around the central cord below the beads.

Step 8 - Repeat step 7 until all the purple and silver beads have been added to the bracelet.

Step 9 - Return to the beginning of the bracelet. Thread the cord nearest to the row of silver beads through the first silver bead.

Step 10 - Thread one lilac bead onto the first cord in the set of three. This is the cord furthest from the beads.

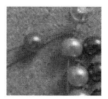

Step 11 - Position this bead in line with the beads already added to the bracelet and tie one square knot beneath it.

Step 12 -. Add one lilac bead to the first cord and tie one square knot underneath it.

Step 13 - Repeat step 12 to add the lilac beads to the bracelet.

Step 14 - Separate the cords into three sets of two again.

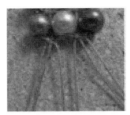

Step 15 - Use the four outer cords to tie two square knots around the two central cords.

Step 16 - Turn the bracelet over and trim of the two sets of outer cords, leaving a 3mm tail.

Step 17 - Gently melt the cord ends and fuse them to the back of the knot.

Take care with this step as the melting cord is hot and can stick to your skin.

The point of the scissors can be used to press it into play.

Step 18 - Thread the disk bead/button onto the remaining two cords. Leaving a gap of 2mm between the last square knot and the bead, tie an overhand knot to secure. Trim of any excess cord and gently heat the end to prevent it fraying.

Macramé Sunscreen Holder

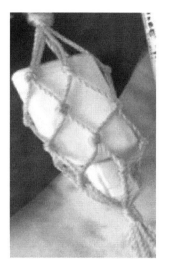

Materials:

Line

Carabiner Cer

Sun screen

Large empty bottle

Manager

Scissors

Candle

Steps:

1. Cut 5 pieces of string about 20cm long.

2. Fold one big knit in half and tie in the middle. Type the knot down to keep it.

Group the string into 5 pairs and each pair into 1" knot. Take another 1" down and tie the next set line.

4. Use this for about four rows of knots or span the length of your bottle. Glide into your bottle to test the fitness and number of knots required. Put the bottle down in the cap side for easy use.

5. Once the fit is correct, tie a big knot to hold the bottle with the strands.

6. Place each chord over the heat to melt the ends of the candle to prevent sprays.

7. Add a carabiner to your knot and add it to your curtain.

Rhinestone Bracelets
Materials:

11 cm (4 1/4 in) of 4 mm (stretched) rhinestone cup chain

2.5 m (2 3/4 yd) of 1 mm nylon knotting cord

E6000 jewelry glue

Pinboard and map pins (optional)

Steps:

Cut a length of 50 cm (20 in) from the knotting cord and fold both pieces in half.

1 Pin or tape the short duration with the loop overhead to the work surface. Bind the longer piece of cord to an overhand knot around the short end.

2 Operate 3 cm (1 1/8) "of square knots for a 17.5 cm (7 in) long bracelet (see Macramé Basics: Macramé Knots). Attach a pin or tape to secure the knots in place at the bottom.

3 Lie the length of the cup chain above the threads of two cords. Work a square knot over the cup chain between each rhinestone (see Adding Beads to Macramé: Adding Rhinestones). Look at the top of the previous square knot to see where the bar is: if it is on the right, then start the next square knot with the right cord; if it is on the left, start with the left cord. Continue to work a square knot between each rhinestone, changing the side you start the knot to keep the knots in place.

4 Finish the macramé with a square knots segment of 3 cm (1 1/8 in) or work along the length to suit the other end. Check the bracelet length and change if needed. Function a two-strand knot

over two strings, and thread the strings in pairs (see Chinese Knots: Knot button). Gradually strengthen the button knot, dragging the cords through, so that it sits from the square knots around 3–5 mm (1/8–1/4 in).

5 Add a small glue to the inside of the button knot where the cords appear in the middle and trim the cords until the glue has dried. Test that the loop at the opposite end of the bracelet runs snugly over the knot ring. You can move a little by pulling down or up the center core cords of the macramé knots. To secure the loop to the appropriate size, apply a little glue on the reverse side.

Beaded macramé bracelet Start the bracelet exactly like the rhinestone bracelet, and instead of adding the cup chain in the center section, pick up a seed bead size 6 (3.5 mm) on each outer cord and tie the next square knot (see Adding Beads to Macramé: Adding Beads to Working Cord). A 17.5 cm (7 in) bracelet will need 20 seed beads.

Double Coin Knot Cuff
Materials:

9 m (10 yds) 2 mm leather cord

3 x 9 mm internal dimension end caps magnetic fastening

Steps:

1 Cut the leather cord into three equal pieces, 3 m (31/3 yd) long. Referring to Chinese Knots: Double Coin Knot, tie a double coin knot using all three strands starting in your left hand with a clockwise loop and pulling down the working end (right-hand tail) over the thread. Complete the

166

knot and make it tight, so that the top loop is relatively wide and all three strands are smooth and neatly aligned.

2 Make a second double coin knot, this time starting with a loop in your right hand, bringing the working end (left-hand tail) down through the loop, around the other tail, and doubling back to create the second knot.

3 Firm the second knot, adjust the position so that the previous knot is fairly close but does not overlap. Make sure none of the cords are twisted and that they all lie flat inside the knot.

4 Continue to tie double coin knots one by one, and swap the starting position from side to side each time.

5 Analyze the length of the cuff until you've made six knots. If required, adjust the distance between each knot to allow for the fastening.

Overlap the cords after the final knot to create a circle. Either tie the cords together or stitch them across to hold the cord flat, depending on the style of your end cap (see Finishing Techniques). Trim the ends and use epoxy resin glue to hold into the end caps.

Prosperity Knot Belt

Materials:

8.5 m (9 yds) 2 mm wax cotton cord

12 mm (1/2 in) long buckle

Small piece of leather

E6000 jewelry glue

Steps:

1. Fold the cord in half to locate the center and tie a double coin knot in the middle, beginning with a loop on the left side. Referring to Chinese Knots: Prosperity Knot, a somewhat loose knot of prosperity tends to tie in. Firm by raising all of the overlapping cords up, one at a time, to the top of the knot, until two loops are left at the bottom.

2 Pull through the top left cord to pull one side of the bottom loop up. Repeat on the other side. Then pull the tails one by one to get the knot tight.

3 Repeat the firming up the process if necessary, to create a 12 mm (1⁄2 in) wide, closely woven prosperity knot. Hold the knot tightly in two hands between fingers and thumbs, and agitate gently to align the cords in a pattern that is even more woven.

4 Tie a double coin knot to the tails, this time starting with a loop on the right side. If the knot is tied, change the location, so it is similar to the knot of success but does not overlap it. Carefully set up because you won't be able to change it later.

5 Continue to tie alternative stability and double knots of coinage.

Remember to alternate the side on which the start loop is an on-left loop for the knot of prosperity and the right loop for the knot of the double coin.

6 Stop after tying a prosperity knot once the belt has the appropriate length allowing for overlap. Loop the ends twice on either side around the belt buckle to fill the void, and stitch tightly backward.

7 Cut a 1 x 3 cm (1⁄8 x 11⁄8 in) leather strap to create the belt loop.

Apply glue to one end of the leather strip and hold below the buckle over the stitched cord ends. Loop the strap around the belt, so it overlaps on the opposite side, leaving a loop wide enough to pass through the other end of the belt. Apply glue to the overlapping strip and stay until the adhesive seals. Leave before use, for 24 hours.

Snake Knot Tie Backs
Materials:

5 m (51⁄2 yd) 3 mm teal elastic cord

Swarovski Elements: XILION beads 5328, 4 mm pacific opal and chrysolite opal, 54 each

Seed beads 11 (2.2 mm) blue marbled aqua and silver-lined crystal

Nylon beading thread

Size 10 beading needle

Tapestry needle

Two end caps with 3 x 9 mm internal dimension

Epoxy resin adhesive

168

Steps:

1 Cut a 45 cm (18 in) length of Referring to Knotted Braids: Snake Knot, work the braid on your snake knot.

2 Tie a knot to a beading thread at the end of a nylon length (or equivalent color), and thread 10 beading needle. Bend the braid from the end about 5 cm (2 in), so you can see the pattern of the cord between the loops on one side. Place the needle of a tapestry between the two straight braid lengths you can see.

3 Move the needle of the tapestry through the braid to escape between the loops on the other side. Leave the needle in place for the tapestry; this is the direction the finer threaded needle takes through the braid.

4 Hold the nylon thread between two lateral loops above the needle. Pick an aqua seed bead, a pacific opal XILION, an aqua seed bead, a silver seed bead, a chrysolite opal XILION, a silver seed bead, an aqua seed bead, a pacific opal XILION, and an aqua seed bead.

5 Place the beads through the braid at an angle, then take the beading needle back alongside the tapestry needle. Remove all needles simultaneously.

6 Pull the thread taut over the braid to protect the beads. Between the next loops thread the tapestry needle again through the braid, in order to attach another line of beads. This time the XILIONS order is inverted, adding two opal chrysolite and one opal pacific.

7 Repeat to add bead lines, stopping from the end of the braid about 5 cm (2 in) apart. Sew firmly in ends of thread.

8 Cut the cord to the same length, leaving the tails approximately 2 cm (3⁄4 in) long. Mix a bit of epoxy resin adhesive and put a cocktail stick within one end cap. Place two of the cord ends in the end cap and force the remaining cord in place using a cocktail stick (or awl). At the other end, repeat to add an end cap, and leave to dry.

Macramé Brooch

Materials:

1.5 m (1¾ yd) of each SuperlonTM cord in violet, lilac, coral, light gray and dusky pink

20 cm (8 in) of 1 mm (19swg) half-hard sterling silver wire

Seed beads: size 6 (3.5 mm) matt silver, size 10 (2 mm) colored peach, size 11 (2.2 mm) silver-lined crystal and smart raspberry gold luster

10 cm (4 in) square

Brooch back

Jewelry tools

Chasinine tools

Steps:

1 Set the SuperlonTM cords ready for use: red, lilac, coral, light blue, and dusky pink.

2 Take on a purple cord a silver-lined crystal seed bead and drop to the middle. Fold the cord in half, and put it on one side of the 'V' over the cable. Take the tails over the wire and through the loop back to form the head knot of a reverse lark (Knotting Basics: Simple Knots).

3 Work on either side of a half-hitch (see Macramé Basics: Macramé Knots). With the other colored cords repeat measures 2 and 3, adding a bead each time.

4 Lay the outline of the wire on the baseboard of the foam, and place the tape in position.

* Bring the lilac end cord in parallel to the cable. Act with each cord in effect a double half-hitch

5 Place a map pin at the end of the rope, then take the purple cord back in a slight angle around the vertical cord. Secure with tape or clip on a spring. Work with the dusky pink cords and the first grey cord in double half-hitches. On the next grey thread, pick up a color-lined peach seed bead and again work double half-hitches.

6 Work double half-hitches with first coral cord, then pick up on the next coral cord two silver-lined crystal seed beads; secure with double half-hitches. On the first lilac thread, add three emerald raspberry gold luster seed beads, securing again with double half-hitches.

7 Work double half-hitches on the next lilac cord before finishing with silver crystal, 6 matt silver, and silver crystal on the remaining lilac cord. Run the last half-hitch of the pair.

8 Repeat from * in step 4 six or seven times, depending on the stress, before the half-circle of macramé curves around to touch again the thread. Again, take the purple cord back to the outer edge and work straight half-hitch rope. Function double half-hitches over the wire for every cord in place.

9 Tuck all of the silver wire cord tails behind it. Take on the first dusky pink cord two silver-lined crystals, a size 6 matt silver seed bead, and two silver-lined crystals. Function on the other side of the wire 'V' shape a double half-hitch. The next dusky pink cord is attached without beads.

10 Repeat on the two grey cords and then work the wire down, inserting beads on the first of each color, reducing the number of silver-lined beads as the distance between the wires narrows.

11 Work a semicircle in macramé to suit the first line, finishing with a half-hitch rib straight. Function the first cord with a double half-hitch, and add a silver-lined crystal. To secure the bead, work another double half-hitch with the same thread. Repeat with each cord in seconds.

12-Fold the cord over the back of the macramé, and thread with tiny stitches invisibly. Trim sparingly. Cut UltrasuedeTM into place invisibly around the edge to match every semicircle and stitch.

13 Knit a brooch on the reverse side of the brooch, stitching straight through to the right side, then going back to the reverse side so that the small stitch between the macramé knots is covered. Sew the ends tightly into.

Macramé Bracelet

Materials:

Scissors or a razor blade

A pencil or foam board or a T-pin

A Hemp rope or a string of one's chosen Steps:

Steps:

1 The circumference of the wrist is measured first. Next, with the help of scissors, cut two sections of the hemp thread. The parts cut should be at least three times the wrist length, or rather, the initially measured diameter. For example, if the measurement obtained was 5 inches, then two strands should be cut, each measuring 15 inches.

2 One strand is folded halfway round. Holding the pencil in a flat position, the collapsed string is extended onto the barrel of the pencil to hang a circle simply over its front, and furthermore to guarantee that remaining ends hang behind it. Those loose ends should be passed through the loop, then held tightly. Repeat this cycle again with the second strand. You will eventually have four strands hanging down the pencil. In mental terms, you can mark these four strands as 1, 2 3 4, from right to left. Whatever labeling technique you consider simple, you can use it.

3 Strand 1 will then be taken to the left side, above both Strand 2 and Strand 3 (which in turn are the two middle strands), and below Strand 4 afterward.

4 Take strand 4 behind both strands 2 and 3 at this point through the loop, which shaped strand 1. Pull both strand 1 and strand 4 tightly to ensure a half square knot is realized.

5 You will know a method of crossing a strand by now. Continue this cycle of crossing the strand until the bracelet eventually reaches the length you might like. Spirals are created from half-square knots as you continue to work.

6 The loops are slipped off the crayon here. Then, pull strand 2 and strand 3 to be able to that just a bit the size of the loops created. Afterward, all four threads are placed together, and two ties tied together as a way of securing the work. These are essential knots. All strings you find unwanted should be cut off, and that should be done as similar as possible to these knots.

7 You've got your wrist bracelet on now. Then the knot will be passed around the loop to help secure your wrist bracelet.

Macramé Tote Bag

Steps:

1. Cut 10 ropes 2.3 meters wide. Fold half and fill the middle of the folded handle with the void. Take the ends of the rope and cross the last step of the loop you made. Pull close. Pull strong.

Continue to attach 5 pieces of cord to each bag handle.

2. Separate two rope bits at one end and move the remaining rope to the other. We'll make the first knot with these two parts.

Turn the left corner in the right corner and make a curve.

Take the left (still straight) rope and fill the room with the two ropes you made. Remove the two corners until the knot is rising and in the right place. You want the handle to be approximately 5 cm.

Take the left hand rope and this time put it right to complete the knot.

This time, thread through the gap the right side rope. Bring the knot tight again.

3. Create four more knots in a row on the handle with the rest of the ropes. Then continue again, but the first rope is missing this time and the second and third ones tie. Continue along the route. You make four knots this time and you don't knot the first or the last rope.

4. When the second row is done, make the third row the same as the first (five knots without missing ropes).

5. Upon completing the third section, repeat steps 2-4 in the second handle. After that, bring the two handles face to face together.

6. Take both end ropes from the front of the bag and back to begin the next row. Fasten the ties on the front and back on the other end. You are then faced with the last lines on the front and back. Tie these together. Tie them together. Tie them together. Tie them together.

7. Knead until the strands are approximately 10 cm left of the rope.

8. Cut the length of the rope 4 meters. Use the same technique to tie it to the last knot of the handle.

9. Take the front and back strand and wrap the cord around. Place a double hitch knot and take two additional knots, one on the front and the other on the back. Act before you. Work before you do.

10. Taking off the hanging rope. Link these strands instead of knots. You should apply some glue to cover them. Put it together to make a sheet.

Striped Clove Hitch Keychain

Steps:

1) Start with two 20 or so bits of string (you can generally cut them shorter, so it's smarter to begin long). Circle each through the keyring with a larkspur hitch, making the outside strands somewhat longer than the ones within.

2) Include vertical clove hitch knots with a couple of different shades of yarn. This video has simple guidelines to kick you off, including how to gauge your yarn. We completed two columns each in the initial two colors, and one line in the third color.

3) Make a full square knot in the center.

4) Include another arrangement of vertical clove hitch, turning around what you did on the top.

5) A fast trim of the closures polishes it off.

6) Interlaced and macramé keychains

Macramé Guitar Strap

Materials:

Macramé List

Active Clasps

Nice areas.

Industrial resistance to adhesive

Scissors

Steps:

Step 1: Cut 2 macramé cord lengths, every 4 yards.

Step2: Fold the length of each string so that one yard is on one side, and three yards on the other side. Insert the centers on the thread outside, which leave the long ends, in the flat part of the swivel handle.

Step 3: Push each cord into its own circuit and close its knot.

Step 4: begin making a knot of a square. Take the longest left string and cross the middle of each string and underneath the left string. Take the right cord under the center two and the left cord up and down. Pull this taut. That's half your knot square.

Step 5: Complete square knot with reverse step 4. Intersect the right cord over the center two and the bottom left; then, under the center two, across the center and over the left cord. A quick pull and a square knot was completed.

Step 6: Keep adding your square knots for your camera strap to the right length.

Step 7: Trim all four ends of the thread. In a pivoting knot, join all four cords. At the end of each string, put a dollop of adhesive, fold the strings and hold clothespins in put until the adhesive is soft.

Replace the clips until the glue is dry and pop your strap!

Macramé Top

Materials:

Plain white cotton T-shirt (long is better than short)

Dylon Pink Flamingo Dye

Salt

Bucket

Spoons/stick for stirring

Small container for mixing dye

Rubber gloves

Hanger

Steps:

Step one

Mix the dye as per the manufacturer's Steps: and thoroughly wet the T-shirt. We used half a packet of dye, as we were only dyeing a couple of T-shirts. Choose a 100% cotton garment or one with as high a cotton percentage mix as possible, as human-made fibres such as polyester or viscose won't absorb the dye.

Step two

Put your T-shirt on a hanger (it's the easiest way to control the dyeing process) and dip it into the dye bath, approximately two thirds of the way up the shirt, for 30 seconds. This first dip needs to be really quick.

Step three

For the second dip, put the T-shirt back into the dye bath two thirds up the dyed section. This time leave for a minute or two. Keep an eye on the color – once you're happy with the ombré effect that's starting to appear, take the T-shirt out of the bath and rinse the dyed section with warm water. Be careful not to get any pink dye on the white section.

Step four

Add another tablespoon of dye to the bath and mix thoroughly. Put only the lower third of your T-shirt back in for three or four minutes. Check the ombré effect – if you think the base needs to be darker, leave in the bath for a few more minutes. Once happy, rinse the dyed part until the water runs clear and leave to dry.

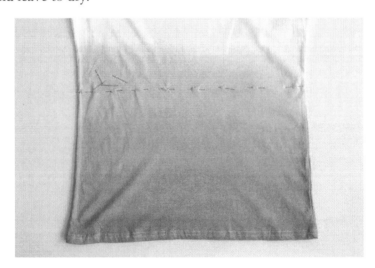

Step five

Give the T-shirt a good press as you need it to be flat for the next steps. Run a line of pins where you want the top of the macramé section to start – ours began 26cm (10¼") up from the hem.

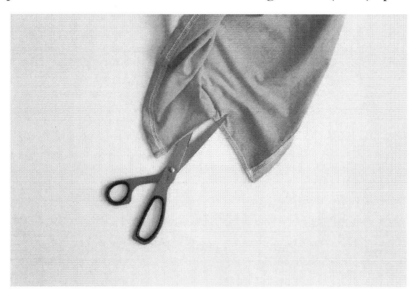

Step six

Remove the seams up to where you've pinned by cutting very closely to the edge of the stitching. This gives a neat finish.

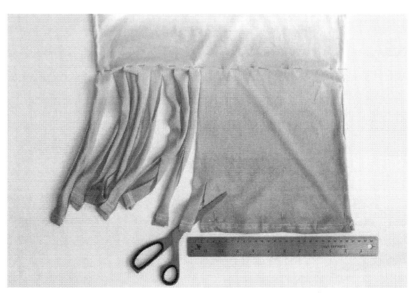

Step seven

Measure the T-shirt's width and divide by two – this will give you the number of strips you need to cut. If the number is odd, then round down to the nearest even number (you need an equal number of strips and it's better if they're thicker rather than thinner). Cut the strips up to the pinned line.

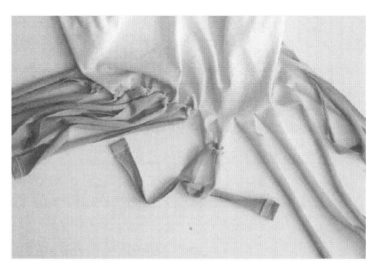

Step eight

Take the first two strips on the outside edge (we worked left to right) and tie together in a double knot. You want the tension to be firm but not over-pulled. Continue knotting in pairs along the whole of the T-shirt front and back.

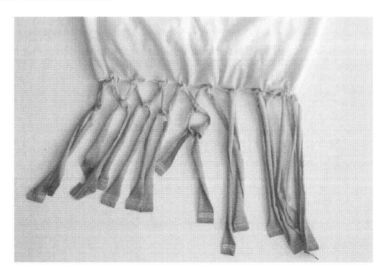

Step nine

For the next row, take two strips from the next-door knots and knot together 2.5cm (1") below the first row. Continue front and back. You should start to see a triangular shape forming.

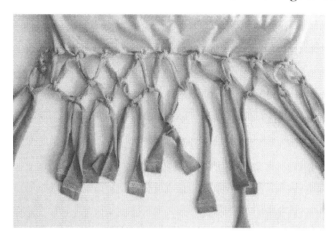

Step ten

Repeat the above step to create another row of knots. This time a diamond shape will have formed. If you're working with a really long T-shirt then you could add a few more rows of knots – we liked the cropped effect we created, so have kept to just three.

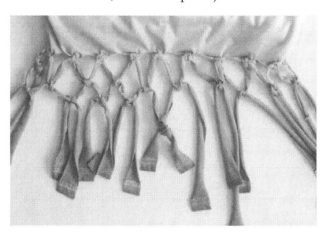

Step 11

To finish, cut off the over locked hem from the bottom of each strip so they curl up neatly. Now all you need is a sunny day to show it off.

Climbing Vine Keychain

Materials:

Measure out 3 cords of Peridot C-Lon, 30" each

1 key ring

2 (5mm) beads

8 (plus extra for ends) pink seed beads

4 (plus extra for ends) gold seed beads

12 (plus extra for ends) green seed beads

8 (plus extra for ends) 3mm pearl beads (seed pearl beads will work also)

Note: You can vary slightly the bead size. Just be sure that 2 cords will fit through the 2 main beads (the 5mm size beads)

Steps:

1. Fold each cord in half and use to attach it to the key ring. Secure onto your work surface with straight pins. You now have 6 cords to work with.

2. Separate cords into 3 and 3. Using the left 3 cords, tie 2 flat knots. Repeat with the right 3 cords.

Tassel and Macramé Key Chains

Materials:

1 keyring

3/16 natural cotton piping cord

Beads

Weaving floss or yarn

Small rubber band (keychain only)

Scissors

Steps:

For both, you'll start with two 50 or so bits of line. Circle each through the keyring with a larkspur hitch, making the outside strands go around 2/3 the length of the string. (See the free download for step by step photographs.)

For the keychain, make around five square knots, include the globule, make a half square knot underneath it, and tie the rest of in a decoration.

For the keychain, make around 16 half square knots and end it off with a decoration.

To give your decoration the ideal extravagant shaft, use your preferred colors of yarn.

Separate the rope at the closures, trim it up, and you're done!

Pizzaz Anklet

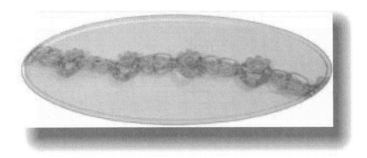

Materials:

C-Lon cord, 5 ft 6 in., Rose (x1), Mint (x1), Apricot (x1)

5mm button bead (x1)

Light green size 11 seed beads (x108)

Pink size 11 seed beads (x64)

Light pink size 6 seed beads (x40)

Beacon 527 glue

Steps:

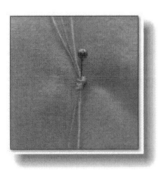

Place all 3 cords together and find the center. Tie a loose overhand knot at the center point and place the cords on your project board as shown with the green on the left and the pink on the right:

185

Using the outer most cord on each side, tie about 10 flat knots around the inner cords. Untie the overhand knot and place the flat knots in a horseshoe shape. Pin the ends in place and check to see if your button bead will fit (snugly) through the opening. Adjust flat knots as necessary.

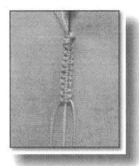 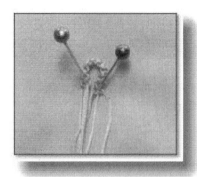

Rearrange the cords so that both green cords are on the left, the apricot cords are in the center and both pink cords are on the right. Using the outer cord on each side (green and a pink) tie a flat knot.

Separate the cords 2-2-2. Find the second cord in from each side and thread on 3 size 11 light green seed beads.

Take the left apricot cord and tie a VLH knot onto the beaded cord to the left of it. Tug gently on the apricot cord to form an arc. Now take the right apricot cord and thread it through the arc, then tie a VLH knot onto the beaded cord to the right. Tug gently on the apricot cord to form an arc.

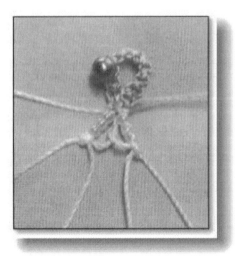

Find the left cord (green) and attach it to the beaded green cord with a VLH knot. Tug gently to create an arc to the outside. Repeat with the right cord (pink onto pink).

187

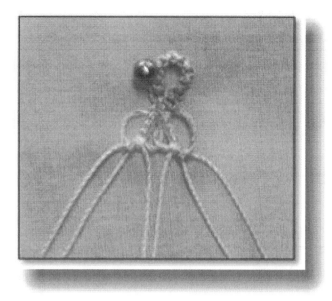

Repeat steps 4-6, then tie a flat knot with the outer cord on each side. Note: As you go on, if the left green cord is getting too short, swap it with the longer green cord next to it either before or after this flat knot.

 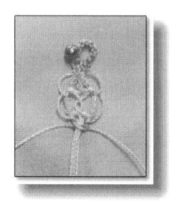

Take the left cord and thread on four size 11 pink seed beads, one size 6 pale pink seed bead and another four size 11 pink seed beads, then set it aside. Find the right cord (pink) and place it to the left, over the other 4 cords, as the holding cord (HC). Tie diagonal double half hitch (DDHH) knots onto it from right to left.

Find the right cord and thread onto it three pale pink size 6 beads. Skip the next cord in and place on the next cord a size 6 pale pink bead.

Take the HC from the left and place it to the right. Tie DDHH knots onto it from left to right. Retrieve the set aside cord and use it along with the far right cord to tie a flat knot around the other cords.Repeat steps 4 through 10 until you have reached 9 1/2 inches. With the center 2 cords, thread 2 or 4 cords through the button bead. Use the remaining cords to tie a flat knot around it. Glue the back of the flat knot and let dry. Then trim the cords and glue once more.

For this one you can use Teal, Blue Lagoon and Amethyst cord:

Cheap Macramé Sanitizer Holder

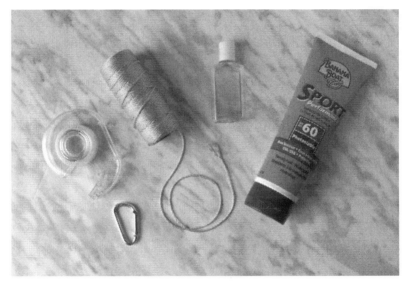

Materials:

String
Carabiner
Sanitizer
Small empty bottle

Tape
Scissors
Candle

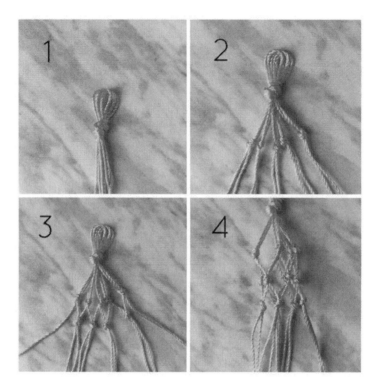

Steps:

Cut 5 pieces of string about 20" long.

Fold in half and tie one big knit in the center. Tape the knot down to keep it set up.

Gathering the string into 5 sets and knot each pair about 1" down. Presently another 1" down, take one string and knot it with the string from the pair close to it.

When the fit is correct, attach a major bunch with all the strands to hold the bottle set up.

Key Chains with Beads and Tassels:

Steps:

1) For both, you'll start by tying a 10-16 piece of yarn to your key ring with a larkspur hitch.

2) Include the beads.

3) Cut yarn for a tuft—we used around 20 bits of yarn. (You pick the length and softness. Make it twice the length you need your tuft.) Center it under the dot and tie it on with a straightforward knot. Take care of your dabs and decoration and double the knot.

4) Overlap the tuft into equal parts and wrap the neck with yarn or dental floss.

5) Trim the closures.

Barefoot Macramé Sandals

Materials:

Pure cotton yarn or macramé cord

Scissors

Large hole beads, for instance: the silver spacer beads.

The Bulldog clips.

Steps:

Make 3 pieces of yarn or cords about 3m long then locate the middle point of the strips and make a knot. It's important the yarn is long; it will be needed for the ankle straps.

On one of the sides of the knot, braid strands of 2-3 inches together.

Loose the knot which was earlier made, and tie it again once you've made a spiral loop along with the strand that is braided. This creates what is called a toe loop of your sandal!

The major sandal part, which goes down from the ankle, to cross the foot's front and then towards the toe, generally, is made using square knots. There are half a dozen strands to use now, so, divide them into 3 strands, with each having two strands.

From the right side, put that strand on top of the one in the middle, making D-shaped looking loop. The strand located on the left should be threaded underneath the one in the middle and inside the loop with D-shape.

To make or create the leading section of the square knot, pull the right and the left strands. In the opposite direction, do the same thing for the left side. Move the strand on the left side over the one in the center, then thread the strand on the right-hand side under the one in the center and backwards into the D-shaped loop. Draw the strands on the right and on the left from the one in the middle to finish the first square knot.

Make two other square knots, in addition to the first square knots tied. Next, thread the round beads made of silver on the strand in the center. Then around this same bead, begin the initial part of the next SK.

Repeat steps 6 and 7, there should be a total 10 beads, which would be joined to the center strand with macramé SK. A few more beads are needed for bigger sizes).

Complete the section with beads by making 1 or 2 plain SK that have no heads and separate the strands in two with each split have about 3 heads. Braid the strands to form the straps for the ankle, till a length/diameter of about 50 centimeters is reached. This will allow you to wrap them round your ankles a few times. Alternatively, another bead made of silver can be added towards the end between a SK for some decoration. When doing this, it is important to make two knots (double knots) towards the bottom part of the final square knot so as to make it firm. Cut off any remaining unused thread and repeat the steps above to make the sandal's second leg,

Serenity Bracelet

Materials:

White C-Lon cord, 6 ½ ft., x 3

18 - Frosted Purple size 6 beads

36 - Purple seed beads, size 11

1 - 1 cm Purple and white focal bead

26 - Dark Purple size 6 beads

1 - 5 mm Purple button closure bead

(Note: the button bead needs to be able to fit onto all 6 cords)

Steps:

Take all 3 cords and fold them in half. Find the center and place on your work surface as shown:

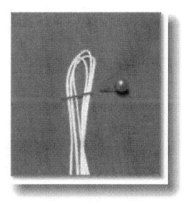

Now hold the cords and tie an overhand knot, loosely, at the center point. It should look like this:

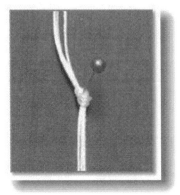

We will now make a buttonhole closure. Just below the knot, take each outer cord and tie a flat knot (aka square knot). Continue tying flat knots until you have about 2 ½ cm.

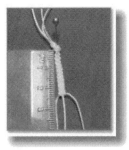

Undo your overhand knot and place the ends together in a horseshoe shape.

We now have all 6 cords together. Think of the cords as numbered 1 through 6 from left to right. Cords 2-5 will stay in the middle as filler cords. Find cord 1 and 6 and use these to tie flat knots around the filler cords. (Note: now you can pass your button bead through the opening to ensure a good fit. Add or subtract flat knots as needed to create a snug fit. This size should be fine for a 5mm bead). Continue to tie flat knots until you have 4 cm worth. (To increase bracelet length, add more flat knots here, and the equal amount in step 10).

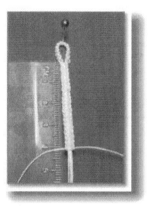

4. Separate cords 1-4-1. Find the center 2 cords. Thread a size 6 frosted purple bead onto them, then tie a flat knot with cords 2 and 5.

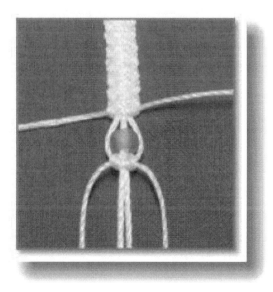

5. We will now work with cords 1 and 6. With cord 1, thread on a seed bead, a dark purple size 6 bead and another seed bead. Repeat with cord 6, then separate the cords into 3-3. Tie a flat knot with the left 3 cords. Tie a flat knot with the right 3 cords.

6. Repeat step 4 and 5 three times.

Find the center 2 cords, hold together and thread on the 1cm focal bead. Take the cords out (2 and 5) and bead as follows: 2 size 6 dark purple beads, a frosted purple bead, and 2 dark purple beads. Find cords 1 and 6 and bead as follows: 2 frosted purple beads, a seed bead, a dark purple bead, a seed bead, 2 frosted purple beads.

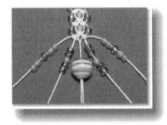

With cords 2 and 5, tie a flat knot around the center 2 cords. Place the center 4 cords together and tie a flat knot around them with outer cords 1 and 6.

Repeat steps 4 and 5 four times.

Repeat step 3.

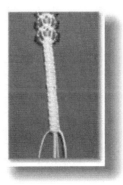

Place your button bead on all 6 cords and tie an overhand knot tight against the bead. Glue well and trim the cords.

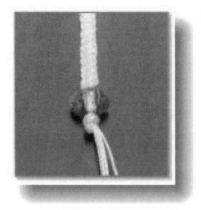

CHAPTER 11:

Modern Projects for Macramé DIY

Bohemian Macramé Mirror Wall Hanging

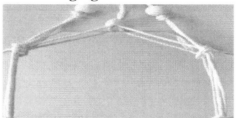

Materials:

Macramé cord: 4 mm

Octagon Mirror

Ring of wood: 2

Wood Beads: Size hole 25 mm w/10 mm

Sharp Scissors

Macramé Mirror Model

Steps:

Cut 4 bits of Macramé into 108 inches (or 3yds). Macramé Larks Mirror Knot

Bend the strips in half and tie all 4 of them on the wooden cord with a head knot of Lark. Tighten the ties and lock them. Divide the two knots of Lark 's Head into a knotted square. Square Knot Macramé Mirror Model. Tie together two knots. Begin to tie two cubic knots into Lark's second two head knots. Mirror Macramé knot square When the second knot is started, bend it to one side of the other two knots to merge it into a big knot. Tie 7 knots square running on each side and all sides. Macramé square knot creator

After the knots are joined, break the ends. Two strings on both hand and four lines in the middle. Place the line on the terms to show the broken terms. This makes it easier to add the beads.

Thanks! It is the most challenging part! The rest connects only basic knots and even gets on the sides. Add Macramé perforations Place one bead on both hands. Place a knot on both sides under the bead to hold it even. Tie 4 strings in the middle or about 1/14 centimeter below the dots. Macramé mirror beaded, Macramé mirror, white Macramé mirror simple knotted. Take a single cord from the middle and attach it to the 2 wires on the ends. Bind the three on both sides in a knot. Connect the mirror even to the knot lengths. Attach one of the three side cords to the mirror back to keep it steady. Secure knots in all three cords at the left and right bottom of the mirror. Separate the three wires again. Put one on both sides of the mirror to place two on the front of the mirror and tie in a knot. Knots on Macramé mirror back, necessary mirror Macramé technology Flip the mirror over and tie all the cords together. Flip the mirror over and loosen the front knot. Glide into the knot, the back cords and straighten the knot. Cut the cord to around 14 inches. Pull the ends or loosen the strings and let the purposes go. Combine a smooth comb with the terms of the thread. Hang, and go!

Boho Christmas Trees

Materials:

A few branches or branches of the garden

Wire of jewelry or other ornamental parts

A brush or a cake

Fishing line hanging

Steps:

Break the yarn in 7-8 inches sections. Take two threads, and fold half of them as a loop. Place a circle under a twig. Take the looped end of the other beam and move the terms of the shaft under the twig into the loop. Connect the thread under the twig at the ends of the rope.

Once enough knotted strands are inserted, separate the threads with a brush or comb. The "almost finished" tree is a little weak, so you have to stabilize it with some starch.

Cut them into a triangle and adorn them with small jewels or beads when the boho trees are high. I just made a little flower star joystick. It takes about 10 minutes for a whole bunch to produce. I think they would make perfect presents or on your Christmas tree, you could hang them.

Macramé Glass Connector Bracelet

Materials:

3 meters of glass connectors

3 meters cords for each bracelet.

2 mm string

Steps:

For the first time, let's make the bracelet. Take a 20 cm piece and slip it over the connector leg. Take the 1 m piece and tie your knot middle. You have two lines now, one to the left and one to the right. Take the right string and slide it into the middle rope and the left strand. Take the left thread; slip it on the center string, then close the knot under the remaining line. Repeat the steps until on the one hand, and you make the bracelet. Finally cut off those ends and then burn them to melt and stick and make the other leg. When you tie the knots, a spiral is formed. It's going to feel like that.

Switch to the second form now. Steps 1, 2, 3 are the same for this method as the first step. The difference is that you don't repeat the same move repeatedly! After tying the first leg, slip the left cord under the cords in the center and over the right wire over the center and left ropes. Tie the knot, which looks like 2 knots. Alternately tie the ties on either hand until the desired length is reached. Repeat the other side of the bracelet.

Change your bracelets with another short cord and the second option instead of a clasp. Combine both ends and tie the knots on both ends.

Dip-Dyed Mobile

Materials:

10 inches sticky fucker

Yellow Pair

Scissors

Big bowl

Fabric sculpture

Hot Water

Handicraft stick

Elastic film

Rubbish bin

Steps

Remove from the stick hoop the external frame. Cut 90 twine pieces (not less than 12 in.) in various lengths. Fold in half a little. Take any folded portion under and over, and then save the ends by the string. Gather twine in 4 beach bunches. Knot together under the ring to protect half an inch. In the hoop repeat. Take 2 twine-pieces from the first battery and tie with 2 second pinch twine-pieces below the first battery of knots. In the hoop, repeat. Using a craft stick to mix 3 table spoon of fabric paint with 3 cups of clean water in a large tub. Hang twine and hold elastic midway. Take the ends of the twine 30 min in a paint-water solution. Place on a 24-hour plastic waste bag to dry. Remove the external elastic and safe sewing loop.

Knotted Chevron Headband

Materials:

Broder floss (6 colors/12 suits my 1/2-inch wide headband)

The satin narrow belt – 1/8 to 1/4 "is perfect.

E6000 or equivalent adhesive plastic

1/2 centimeter long or your favorite headband

Matched thread and needle sewing

Steps:

Start by making your new long friendship bracelet. I've been using 6 strands each 10 feet in length, half by 5 feet, but if your head band is more extensive, maybe your headband would be more significant. Hold a loose knot together and tie the strands and operate the Classic Chevron Friendship Bracelet (or pattern for you) until the strip is 1 to 5 inches longer than the length of the headband. Untie the knot upon completion. Get a dot of glue on the back of your headband and put it around your headband. Make sure you cover the band on the front and back and if you have a single face on the satin belt, the right side is off. Cut off the tails one end of the knitted strip and hold it down. Save it for a few minutes. Put some glue on your back and tie the knotted strip to the rope until it is imperfect. So go on gluing and binding, but then behind the knotted thread. Avoid gluing and wrapping when the knotted strip is as far away from the other end. Cut the tails to the end and add the whole length of the super long bracelet to the end. Likely, you will extend it a little to match and that's perfect. (Keep it to the end only if you want to stitch the kneaded portion on the back). Hold on the end of the strip and tie it smoothly on your back to the end of the headband. When you just hang up, you can thread the knotted piece back and forth on the edges and draw it close. This is a right choice because the line has very straight edges.

DIY Stone Necklace

Materials:

Colorful Embroidery Floss

Rock(s)

4 mm cord – 24-36 centimeters per arm, whatever you want.

6 mm ring break - Clasp Lobster

A big needle - Scissors - Pin (split ring pinches are especially useful)

Steps:

First, cut the four corsets to about 18 inches in length. This was enough to cover a stone measuring 2-3 inches. You won't have to be as large if your stones are smaller, but it's still better to be bigger than you are! Take a one-cord chain and split loop chain. (You can replace a standard jumping ring, but it will not slip out later) Place the ring in the chain center and tie the chord in the middle of the other three chords. It produces a central ring of 8 9-inch strands in the middle. Next, put two cords next to each other. Connect a knot in each and link it from the middle ring of each chain approximately 1/2 "as shown above. Put another knot about 1/2 inch from each pair of wires in the earlier knots. You start to divide and rotate pairs and create knots within a short distance of the previous ones. **Note:** if your stone is fragile, your knots could be closer and closer to the central ring. You build a sort of board with your stone, and the distance between knots defines how full the hole is. You would have to try to find the lengths that work best for you. Try to place your stone in the net while you try to determine if your sleeve suits well. Once you've made a net wide enough to accommodate your stone, stick and tie it around the rock safely. Here's a tightening tip – break the strings into two pieces and bind the pieces once you secure a shoe, so the stone has two knots to make.

Cut the ends to make a tassel and finish your DIY's shirt!

Neon Macramé Jar

Materials

Neon String

Clean Vessels

Aluminum foil tray

Washi tape

Scissors

Accurate knife

Cold glue tool

Tape measurement

Steps

Cut 5 strands of cord approximately 6' each. Fold them in the middle and tie the knot overhand, you should have 10 3' cord strands now. This is more than sufficient for a jar – change these lengths if your container is smaller / larger. Even the smaller jars with fewer strands and bigger jars with more strands can be compared. Use a cord or lighter to avoid additional spray if the cable is sprayed after it is cut. Tie two pieces together with your measuring tape from the original big knot. Repeat with the other branches. Repeat the step but split the joined strands and bind them together, as shown in the figure, just about 2 "apart from the neighboring knots. Checking your Macramé net fit over the pot every time is a good idea. If you want to change how the net looks, you just untie your knots and make another test. Keep the knots tied to make sure your container is correct. Avoid the net approaching the mouth of the pot. Hot glue the two beaches in the jar on the lower part of the container. In the concentric zone, it is best done without touching the floor, so that the box would be flat. Using the accurate knife to cut off the big initial knot. When the original big knot is cut off, the jar will be flat on top of the surface. If the rope is very thick, use hot glue to cover those raw edges. At the bottom of the pot, tie the string to the strings of the bottle. Use the same knife to cut off any excess material. Heat any raw edges to avoid scrubbing as before. Measure the jar's mouth circumference and cut the aluminum strip 1/2 "longer; the jar thread will at least cover its width. There's no problem if still be some texture when you are done, because this adds value to the surface! Using hot glue to protect the aluminum strip mouth of the container.

Macramé Hanging Plant Holder

Materials

Knot row

Lamb

Solar panel

Mini bottle clean

Movie

Scissors

Candle Light

Steps

Cut 5 string pieces about 20 "long. Fold in half and tie the middle of the big sweater. Tap the knot to catch it. Group the string into 5 pairs with about 1 "down each knot pair. Take one additional 1 "down and tie the rope to the next set. Maintain approximately 4 rows of knots, or cover your bottle length. Glide through your bottle to see how solid you are and how many knots. Tie a large knot to safe the bottle after the fit is right. Place each string piece on a candle to melt ends and avoid spraying. On the top of your knot put the carabineer and add it to your belt.

Macramé DIY Guitar Strap

Materials

Macramé List

Active Clasps

Nice areas.

Industrial resistance to adhesive

Scissors

Steps

Cut 2 Macramé cord lengths, every 4 yards. Fold the length of each string so that one yard is on one side, and three yards on the other side. Insert the centers on the thread outside, which leave the long ends, in the flat part of the swivel handle. Push each cord into its own circuit and close its knot. Begin making a knot of a square. Take the longest left string and cross the middle of each series and underneath the remaining strand. Take the right cord under the center two and the left cord up and down. Pull this taut. That's half your knot square. Complete square knot with backward step 4. Intersect the right cord over the center two and the bottom left; then, under the center two, across the center and over the left cord. A quick pull and a square knot were completed. Keep adding your square knots for your camera strap to the right length. Replace the clips until the glue is dry and pop your strap!

Hanging Macramé Fish Bowl

Materials

50-foot nylon string (found in all sorts of fun colors in the hardware shop!)

Fish glass or plastic cup (I used a ½ gallon glass bowl) - Scissors

Steps

Cut eight 5-foot-long pieces each. Collect all eight parts of a rope, tie a large knot on one end and leave 1? – 2? Loose at the top. Loose at the top. Loose at the top. Loose at the top. Divide the cord into four sections, each one with two cord pieces. Create a section and tie the two parts of the cord in a double knot, leaving a 2? The gap between you connected the first significant knot. Repeat the other three parts of the thread. Hang out a fish tank from the wall with this beautiful Macramé hanger! Give your fish a stylish home and save your table room! Take a portion of a cord and connect it with an adjacent cord segment by joining a 2-knot? You tied away from the knots before. Then repeat the steps. Take a portion of a cord and connect it with an adjacent cord segment by joining a 2-knot? You have moved away from past ties. Repeat the rest of the bits. Place the fishbowl on the knotted cords of the original broad knot. Pull the loose cord ends around the water bowl. The container will rest safely in the knotted area. Hang out a fish tank from the wall with this beautiful Macramé hanger! Give your fish a stylish home and save your table room! Are you adding a knot that incorporates all eight pieces around the bottom of the fish tank? Make sure you have ample space to clean the bath. Tie another knot at the very end of the loose strings and pull it as tightly as you are able.

Macramé Speaker Hanger

Materials

Measuring tape

Fabric glue

Brass rings

50 yards Para cord

Steps

Cut 16 cords that are 15 yards long, and then cut two cords that are 2 yards long, and finally, cut 2 cords that are 60 inches long. You must wrap the two rings together using two cords and tying with the crown knot. Make use of half hitch stitches to secure the wrap and then find the center of the cord. Make sure to secure them on the surface and to hold them close together. Eight of the two cords should then line up centrally so that they would be able to hold the speaker.

Now, go and bundle the long cords by wrapping and pulling them tightly together and letting the first end pass under the last coil. Wrap securely so it would not unravel. Make sure to pull more cords from the bundles and then tighten the wraps on the center with your working cords. Let the lower portion come together by using square knots and make sure that you go and tighten the first half of it. Tie the second Half around the board and then turn the board around after letting the rolled coils pass through at one end of the ring.

Use half-hitches to arrange the center and let the rolled bundles dangle on the other end of the ring. Fold the sennit so you could match it with the last couple of knots and wrap the scrap cord around it. Now, put the hanger horizontally on your workspace and secure with square knots. Let the working end pass through the middle of the bundle and then bring the working end around the bundle that you are using. Let it pass over the front and under the cord's back and keep wrapping as firmly as you can until you see something that looks like a loop. Take the pin away from the secured end and pull until you reach the knot inside. Make use of fabric glue to coat this with and trim the ends. Let flame pass through it to secure it, as well. Tie five half knots to keep the hanger secure and start suspending on the wall or ceiling—whichever you prefer. Place some beads before tying the knot again, and then make use of fillers as working cords before firmly tightening the knot. Create 25 more square knots and push the knots up to eliminate spooling. Repeat the process until your desired length.

Finally, make a figure-eight knot and make sure to pull the end tightly before tying several more.

Giant Macramé Rope Light

Materials

Rope

Cord Light Lamp

Backpack Package

Large boat (to be poured into)

Colt

Steps

Start by securing your lamp's cord. Take a left and put the lamp's first thread. And you are forming a small loop on the right side of your lamp string. Repeat your little hands. The pattern starts to spiral as you add more knots. If you take the top of the lamp wire from the left, the spiral is in the same direction. You'll have to undo the knots if you go on. How to take a Macramé

Knot Start by boiling a hole in the cup's bottom and attach the punching nipple to the base socket (make sure you straighten up the small screw on your hand, so it does not twist off when you turn the light bulb!)

Place the washing machine on the lamp plate, then the cup, and the base socket. Place the socket according to the instructions given. Instead, the washing machine turned on the threaded tip. Glide up your rope (the only way to change your socket before beginning knots) and around the end of the threaded nipple. Stick in place.

A Doorway or Big Window Macramé Curtain

Supplies

Loop

Single hollow/rod curtain

Masking tape

Scissors

Steps

Place 4 strands on a core board of foams and put the pins in the top and the bottom of the mid strands in order to stabilize the strands. Take the outside right strand (rose) and go to the leftover the other two middle strands. Take the outer (yellow) strand on the left and go to the other side of the pink strand behind the middle strands. Pull those 2 strands tightly. Pull those 2 strands far left (now the rose) strand and put it on the middle two strands. Taking the far-right beach (now yellow) and pass the beach on the other side of the rose on the two center beams. Pull those 2 strands tightly until they make a knot for the woven strands of the previous step. It is the toughest step! Such fundamental motions are repeated in the other levels. Repeat 1-3 steps to make another knot next to your first knot with four more threads. Bring the first two right-hand strands to form a new group with two more left-hand strands from the second knot.

Take the outer right lilac strand and cross the middle two strands to the left. Take a left outer strand (green), and pass the strand located at the other side (purple), behind the center strands, and over the purple strand. Pull those two strands tightly. Return now the first step! Divide the middle group of strands by transferring two strands to the left and two strands to the right. Do the first knot with both classes and proceed with this process until as many rows as you want have been completed. You can see that the basic knots are generated in steps with the yarn, but on a much larger scale only. I made the basic knot close to the top of all 14 groups and then produced another line of knots then I move down another row, make knots and alternate the rows of knots only until I've finished as many rows as possible. Make sure you step back and make your knots to ensure that your ties are equally connected. I hang the ropes in your ideal place until you are done braiding. At last cover the masking tape on the right side of the tape (or white tape, I used "sleeping tape") where the edging touches the ground (my curtain is 6 1/2 feet high). Break the tape and leave the string intact from 2/3 to half the band. This helps to prevent the spillage of overtime.

CHAPTER 12:

Innovative and Modern Ways to Use Macramé in Home Décor

Modern Macramé Hanging Planter

Plant hangers are lovely because they give your house or garden the feel of an airy, natural space. This one is perfect for condominiums or small apartments—and those with minimalist, modern themes!

Plant Pot

Materials

50 ft. Par cord (Parachute Cord)

16 to 20 mm wooden beads

Steps:

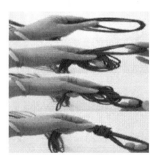

First, fold in half 4 strands of the rope and then loop so you could form a knot.

Now, divide the cords into groups of two and make sure to string 2 wires through one of the wooden beads you have on hand. String some more beads—at least 4 on each set of 2 grouped cords.

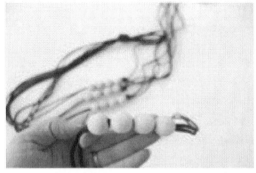

Then, measure every 27.5 inches and tie a knot at that point and repeat this process for every set of cords.

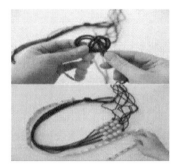

Look at the left set of the cord and tie it to the right string. Repeat on the four games so that you could make at least 3" from the knot you have previously made.

215

Tie another four knots from the previous knot that you have made. Make them at least 4.5" each.

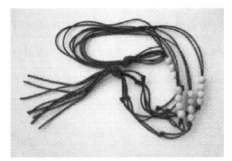

Group all of the cords and tie a knot to finish the planter. You'll get something like the one shown below—and you could just add your very own planter to it!

Mini Macramé Planters

Succulents are all the rage these days because they are just so cute and are decorative! What's more is that you can make a lot of them and place them around the house—that will give your place a unique look!

Materials:

Small container

Garden soil/potting mix

Succulents/miniature plants

¼ inch jump ring

8 yards embroidery thread or thin cord

Steps:

Cut 36-inch of 8 lengths of wire. Make sure that 18 inches are already enough to cover enough half-hitches. If not, you can always add more. Let the thread loop over the ring and then tie a wrap knot that could hold all the cords together.

Create a half-twist knot by tying half of a square knot and repeating it multiple times with the rest of the cord.

Drop a quarter inch of the cord down and repeat step twice.

Arrange your planter and place it on the hanger that you have made.

Nail to the wall, and enjoy seeing your mini-planter!

Amazing Macramé Curtain

Macramé Curtains give your house the feel of that beach house look. You don't even have to add any trinkets or shells—but you can, if you want to. Anyway, here's a high Macramé Curtain that you can make!

Materials:

Laundry rope (or any kind of rope/cord you want)

Curtain rod

Pins

Lighter

Tape

Steps:

Tie four strands together and secure the top knots with pins so they could hold the structure down.

Take the strand on the outer right part and let it cross over to the left side using passing it through the middle. Tightly pull the strings together and reverse what you have done earlier.

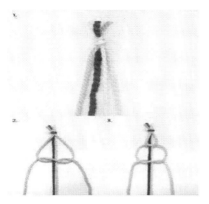

Repeat crossing the thread over four more times for the yarn you now have in front of you. Take the strand on the outer left and let it pass through the middle, and then take the right and let it cross over the left side. Repeat as needed, and then divide the group of strands to the left, and also to the right. Repeat until you reach the number of rows you want.

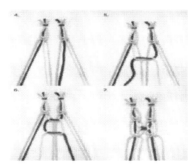

You can now apply this to the ropes. Gather the number or lines you want—10 to 14 is okay, or whatever fits the rod, with proper spacing. Start knotting at the top of the curtain until you reach your desired length. You can burn or tape the ends to prevent them from unraveling.

Braid the ropes together to give them that dreamy, beachside effect, just like what you see below.

That's it, you can now use your new curtain!

Macramé Wall Art

Adding a bit of Macramé to your walls is always fun because it livens up the space without making it cramped—or too overwhelming for your taste. It also looks beautiful without being too complicated to make. You can check it out below!

Materials:

Large wooden beads

Acrylic paint

Painter's tape

Paintbrush

Wooden dowel

70 yards rope

Steps:

Attach the dowel to a wall. It's best just to use removable hooks so you won't have to drill anymore.

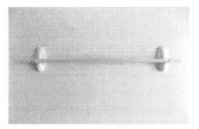

Cut the rope into 14 x 4 pieces, as well as 2 x 5 pieces. Use 5-yard parts to bookend the dowel with. Continue doing this with the rest of the rope.

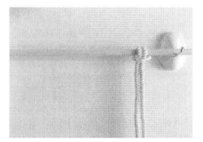

Then, start making double half-hitch knots and continue all the way through, like what's shown below.

If you get to the last part of the dowel, tie the knots diagonally so that they wouldn't fall or unravel in any way. You can also add the wooden beads any way you want, so you'd get the kind of décor that you need. Make sure to tie the knots after doing so.

Use four ropes to make switch knots and keep the décor all the more secure. Tie around 8 of these.

Add a double half hitch and then tie them diagonally once again.

Add more beads and then trim the ends of the rope.

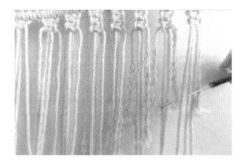

Once you have trimmed the rope, go ahead and add some paint to it. Summery or neon colors would be right.

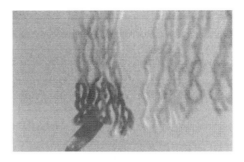

That's it! You now have your own Macramé Wall Art!

Hanging Macramé Vase

To add a delicate, elegant touch to your house, you could create a Macramé Vase. With this one, you'll have to make use of basket stitches/knots—which you'll learn about below. It's also perfect for those who love flowers—and want to add a touch of nature at home!

Materials:

Masking tape

Tape measure or ruler

30 meters thick nylon cord

Small round vase (with around 20 cm diameter)

Steps:

Cut eight ties measuring 3.5 yards or 3.2 meters each and set aside one of them. Cut a cord that measures 31.5 inches and set it aside, as well. Then, cut one cord that measures 55 inches.

Now, group eight lengths of cord together—the ones you didn't set aside, of course, and mark the center with a piece of tape. Wrap the cords by holding them down together and take around 80 cm of it to make a tail—just like what you see below.

Cover the cord around the back of the long section and make sure to keep your thumb on the tail. Then, wrap the cord around the main cord group. Make sure it is firm, but don't make it too tight. If you can make the loop bigger, that would be good, too.

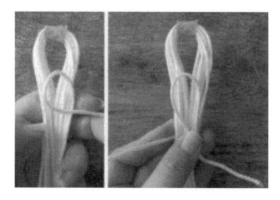

223

Do it 13 more times through the loop and go and pull the tail down so the loop could soften up. Stop letting the cords overlap by pulling them whenever necessary and then cut both ends so they would not be seen anymore.

Divide the cords into groups of four and secure the ends with tape.

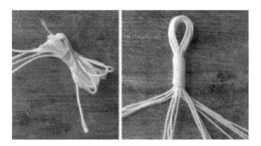

Get the group of cords that you have not used yet and make sure to measure 11.5 inches from the beginning—or on top. Do the overhand knot and get the cord on the left-hand side. Fold it over two of the cords and let it go under the cord on the right-hand side.

Fold the fourth cord and let it pass under the leftmost cord then up the loop of the first cord. Make sure to push it under the large knot so that it would be really firm.

Make more half-hitches until you form more twists. Stop when you see that you have made around 12 of them and then repeat with the rest of the cords.

Now, it's time to make the basket for the vase. What you have to do here is measure 9 centimeters from your group of cords. Tie an overhand knot and make sure to mark with tape.

Let the two cord groups come together by laying them side by side.

Tie the cords down but make sure to keep them flat. Make sure that the knots won't overlap, or else you'd have a messy project—which isn't what you'd want to happen. Use two cords from the left as starting point and then bring the two cords on the right over the top of the loop. Loop them together under the bottom cords and then work them back up once more.

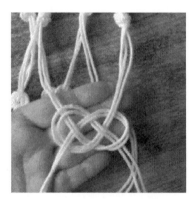

225

Now, find your original loop and thread the same cords behind them. Then, let them pass through the left-hand cords by making use of the loop once more.

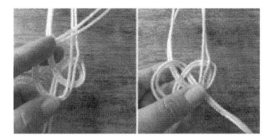

Let the knot move once you already have it in position. It should be around 3 inches or 7.5 cm from the overhand knots. After doing so, make sure that you flatten the cords and let them sit next to each other until you have a firm knot on top. Keep dividing and letting cords come together.

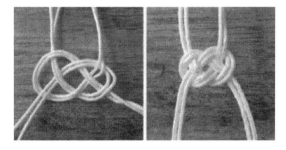

Next, get the cord on the left-hand side and let it go over the 2nd and 3rd cords before folding the fourth one under the first two cords. You'd then see a square knot forming between the 2nd and 3rd cords. You should then repeat the process on the right-hand side. Open the cord on the right side and let it go under the left-hand cord. Repeat this process thrice, then join the four-square knots that you have made by laying them out on a table.

You'll then see that the cords have come together at the base. Now, you have to start wrapping the base by wrapping a 1.4 meter cord and wrap around 18 times.

To finish, just cut the cords the way you want. It's okay if they're not of the same length so that there'd be variety—and they'd look prettier on your wall. Make sure to tie overhand knots at the end of each of them before placing the vase inside.

Enjoy your new hanging vase!

CHAPTER 13:

Decorative Macramé Patterns for your Home and Garden

Macramé Plant Holder

Materials

Metal or wooden ring

Yarn

Potted plant

Steps

Cut four different yarn lengths. Mine were about 2 feet long–you want to make sure that your plant holder is enough to finish! You may need to make the yarn strands even longer, depending on how big your planter is. Fold half the strands of your yarn, and then loop the folded end of your chain. Split the yarn into four yarn groupings of two yarn strands each. Measure several centimeters (I just looked at it) and tie each of the clusters together. Ensure that the knots are about the same length. Document this ad Take the left path of each group and add it to the right way of the next grouping. Keep the knots a little deeper, from the first set of knots only an inch or two. Tie one additional round of knots, repeating the process of knotting each group's left strand to the right strand of the next. Bring the ties pretty close to the last round you made–just half or two inches away this time. Tie all the threads of yarn a little under the last round of knots you made around one inch. Cut off the extra yarn to create a beautiful tassel.

Amazing Macramé Curtain

Macramé Curtains give your house the feel of that beach house look. You don't even have to add any trinkets or shells—but you can, if you want to. Anyway, here's a high Macramé Curtain that you can make!

Materials

Laundry rope (or any kind of rope/cord you want)

Curtain rod

Scissors

Pins

Lighter

Tape

Steps:

Tie four strands together and secure the top knots with pins so they could hold the structure down. Take the strand on the outer right part and let it cross over to the left side employing passing it through the middle. Tightly pull strings together and reverse what you have done earlier. Repeat crossing the thread over four more times for the yarn you now have in front of you. Take the strand on the outer left and let it pass through the middle, and then take a right and let it cross over the left side. Repeat as needed, and then divide the group of strands to the left, and also to the right. Repeat until you reach the number of rows you want. You can now apply this to the ropes. Gather the number of lines you want—10 to 14 is okay, or whatever fits the rod, with proper spacing. Start knotting at the top of the curtain until you reach your desired length. You can burn or tape the ends to prevent them from unraveling. Braid the ropes together to give them that dreamy, beachside effect, just like what you see below. That's it, and you can now use your new curtain!

Macramé Charm and Feather Décor

Charms and feathers always look cool. They just add a lot of that enchanting feeling to your house, and knowing that you could make Macramé décor with charms and feathers take your crafting game to new heights! Check out the instructions below and try it out for yourself!

Materials:

Stick/dowel

Feathers and charms with holes (for you to insert the thread in)

Embroidery/laundry rope (or any other line or thread that you want)

Steps:

Cut as many pieces of string as you wish. Around 10 to 12 bits is good, and then fold each in half. Make sure to create a loop at each end, like the ones you see below: Then, go and loop each piece of thread on the stick. Make use of the square knot and make sure you have four strands for each knot. Let the leftmost strand cross the next two strands and then put it over the strands that you have in the middle. Tuck it under the middle two, as well. Check under the strands and let the rightmost strand be tucked under the loop next to the left-hand strand. Tighten the loop by pulling the outer strands together and start with the left to repeat the process on the next four strands. You will then see that a square knot has formed after tightening the loops together. Connect the strands by doing square knots with the remaining four pieces of rope and then repeat the process from the left side. Tighten the loop by pulling the outer strands together and start with the left to repeat the process on the next four strands. You will then see that a square knot has formed after loops have been tightened together. You can then do a figure-eight knot and then just attach charms and feathers to the end. Glue them in and burn the terms for better effect!

Plant Hanger Bella
Materials

6 strands of the cord of 13 feet and 1,5 inches (4 meters), 4 strands of 16 feet and 4,8 inches (5 meters) and a wooden stick of 11,8 inches (30cm)

Used Knots: A half knot, Lark's Head knot, (Alternating) square knot and Coil knot

Steps:

Fold all strands in half and tie them to the wooden stick with Lark's Head knot. The longest strands are on the outer side (2 strands at the left side and 2 at the right). Make 4 rows of alternating square knots. In the 5th row, you only make 2 alternating square knots on the right and 2 on the left. In the 6th row, you only tie 1 alternating square on each side. Then, with the 4 strands on the side, you tie 25 half (square) knots. Put this for sides, left and right side. Take 4 strands from the middle of the plant hanger, first drop down 2,4 inches (6 cm of no knots) and then tie a square knot with the 4 center strands. Now with the 4 strands next to the middle, Dropdown 3.15 inches (8 cm of no knots), and tie a square knot. Drop down 2,4 inches (6 cm of no knots) and tie 2 (alternated) square knots by taking 2 strands from both sides (right and left group). Then 3 alternating square knots with the other groups. These knots must be about at the same height where the strands with the half knots have ended. Take the 2 outer strands of the left group, which you made 25 half knots, and take the 2 outer strands of the group on the right. First dropping down 2.4 inches (6 cm of no knots), you tie a square knot with these 4 strands. Drop down 2,4 inches (6 cm of no knots) and make another row of alternated square knots using all strands.

Drop down 2.4 inches (6 cm of no knots) and make 5 rows of alternated square knots. Be careful: this time leaves NO space in between the alternated square knots and you make them as tight as possible. Drop down as many inches/cm as you want to make the fringe and tie at all ends a coil knot. Then cutoff all strands, directly under each coil knot.

CHAPTER 14:

Project Ideas for Advanced Macramé

DIY Plant Hanger

Materials

Cord

Scissors

Measuring Tapes

Washi Tape

A Doorknob, Or A Hook, Etc.

Knowledge of Various Knots

Steps

They require cords of 8 x 5.4 m. You have to weigh the first cord duration and then use that to calculate the other seven, and you don't have to use anything to measure it. You need 1 by 1 m and 1 by 2 m for this pattern too. You'll want to put up the plant hanger at someplace until you're finished. Some people use a ring above to make the hanger. In reality, if you build your plant hanger (it is a little tricky, a natural alternative is to use a ring) you don't need one: bring the eight strands together and then fold them in half, and you've got 16 strands with a loop. Tape below the loop, about 7 cm. Now you'll take the 2 m cord and hook it up to the end of the circle with a lark's ear. You may also loop through the center of the loop like a vertical lark's head with the correct rope knotted: take the right cord through the circle, and then beneath the loop, and then thru the line-stretch (not too close, enough to catch it). You then take the same cord, slip through the loop, take it up and then pull through the thread-tighten it. Try to do this before half of your circle is finished, and take the left cord and try to do it again the opposite way around. Now you've got a right, colorful circle, but it doesn't fit neatly together. With the 1m cord, knot the loop together using a "Gathering Knot" utilizing this form (cut all the extra wire that sticks out and force them into your knot). At last, you can start. I think the most complex part is already completed. However, you can use a ring, too. Now split the 16 strands into 4 sections of 4 and begin knotting: a 25 cm segment of spiral stitch in one group knot. That is replicated with the other 3 classes, would make sure anywhere the pattern is the exact duration. So, create no knots for the 15 cm, allow the strings to hang loosely, and then create a standard broad knot. It has been repeated for both classes. Now you tie the square knot to the length of 25 cm. It is replicated with the remaining 3 levels, again make sure the sequence is all the same duration. Now you allow the string free for about 10 cm, and tie two square knots, but using 2 lines of 1 group and 2 strings of the adjacent group. For the remaining 3 classes, this is echoed; make sure that no strands cross any strands and only neighboring strands are knotted together. First, you leave about 10 cm as it is again and take each of the adjacent threads and tie them using two square knots. Now you've come to the finishing and you can easily bind all the strands together in a significant knot. Should not over press the ties or the template bends Seek to hold the knots consistent but it should be simple and don't pull the knots too fast The hanger ends up about 1.4 meters long and suits perfectly with 15 to 25 cm diameter plates Practice the ties or you'll get very irritated Using different cord size/thickness/form can result in a smaller or larger plant hanger.

Rope Lights – Macramé

Materials

Rope or Cording - Lamp Cord - Socket Kit

· Small Vessel (that can be drilled into) - · Glue

Steps

You can get 35 yards for the big string, and it comfortably covers about 15 feet of your lamp cable. You can get 40 yards with the smaller one, however, and it can conveniently cover around 8 feet. Begin by connecting the wire to the light. You might clip it onto a wall for videos, in actual life you 're going to want to secure it to things like a back chair or doorknob to stabilize it. Find your cord core, and position it behind the wire of the lamp. Take the left-hand side and place it over the lamp wire top. Then making a full loop on the left side of the lamp wire under the right side of the thread. So, take the correct thread, and position it behind the fence of the light. Pull the entire length through the tiny loop you built on the left side of the lamp string. Pause. Pause. As you make more and more knots the pattern begins spiraling. As long as you continue from the left side and push it over the top of the wire of the lamp the spiral would travel in the same direction. Whether you pull the right hand over or bring the wrong side under the loop, the instructions will turn and the ties will need to be undone. When all the connections have been made, it is time to rig the plug. You should do so before knotting if you like, it's all up to you. You'll need some form of cup or planter for your socket cover. You can use a thirsted copper cup and a plastic discount cup which you can spray painted white or whatever color you want. But you can use whatever! A wooden tub, a pottery planter, the sky is almost the limit! Start by drilling a hole down into your cup. And fasten the treaded tip to the base of the plug. Also, make sure you fix the tiny screw on the side so that when you twist the light bulb the socket doesn't unscrew! Place the washer onto the lamp string, then the cup, then the base plug. Place the cap on. Then screw the machine over the tip with yarn. Slide the rope up (this is the only change you won't need to create if you wire your socket until you work on your knots) and around the end of the tip cord. Glue on the spot. Ta-da!

DIY Dream catcher

Materials

Twine

420mm Ring

175mm Ring

40mm Ring

Steps:

Using a 40 mm loop, the larks head tie the twine into the circle and then use half tie twist to build the spiral know-how function. Spiral out before the next 175 mm ring is fit for connecting. Further twine is then larks heading all the way around on the 175 mm ring (making it seem like a magnificent sea creature), there are plenty of twines to dispute at this stage! The final ring of 420 mm is connected, so several severe macramé knots will now occur.

Laptop Mat

Materials

Wooden board

4-5 clips

Scissors

Measuring tape

Steps

Knots used: Square Knot, Diagonal double and horizontal double half hitch. Measure 48 bits of 3 m yarn and split. Leaving around 10 cm of thread, the yarns are tied to a wooden board using 4-5 clips to begin knotting. Tie 12 knots in line, from left to right. Cross out the first two lines. Build a square knot with two strands of the first square knot, and Two strands of the first row's second square knot. Continue to tie 10 more knots in square to have Eleven knots in a series. Create rows of square ties, missing the first. Two strands for the fourth, sixth, eighth, and tenth sets. Full one side with double half-hitch horizontal. Skip three threads and the next Five knots in the line. Avoid five threads and the following Four knots in the front. Ignore the future. Three square ties and the seven ribbons. Miss the next two square relationships and the nine threads. Avoid eleven threads and one square knot then.

Move to 12th row: Use the 3rd strand as the keeping rope, attach Ten double half hitch diagonally downwards from left to right. Using the 24th strand as the keeping string, attach Ten double half hitch diagonally downwards from right to left. Skip the 25th strand and tie the next 5 knots in the line. Avoid the 25th-27th strand and tie the next Four ties. Miss the 25th-29th strand and tie the next Three knots. Miss the 25th-31st strand and tie the next Two knots. Remove the 25th-33rd strand and tie the next One knot. Link 10 double half hook from left to right diagonally down using the 25th strand as holding the thread. Using the 46th strand as the keeping string, attach 10 double half hitches diagonally downwards from right to left. Tie the square knots to build a Thirteen to Twenty-one row diamond pattern. Try to tie the design with square knots and a double half hook diagonally until you get the template. Full a double half-hitch horizontal. Line 34 to 43: make rows of square knots, missing the first 2 lines for row 34, 36, 38, 40, and 42. Split the two ends smooth and even to the desired length.

Macramé Chandelier

Materials

Lampshade

Scissors

35m of Cotton Rope

Iron

Steps

You can dismantle a cheap Ikea lampshade to the surface. You want the wrapping covered so that the wire is left behind. Cut the rope to fit first, our parts were 3 meters a piece or 118 inches, then cut it into three strands afterward. You should undo the rope to get the beautiful soft tassel feeling, and then iron it to make it straighter. Fold the two pieces of string in half until you bind them to the base of the lampshade using a head knot of the reverse larks. Start the first row by tying half knots on the chandelier. Measure 1-inch from the top row of knots, and continue to match the first row of square knots. Measure 1-inch down again after finishing the first section, and then continue knotting the second set of square knots using alternating strands from the previous row. The next row should consist of two rows of half knots with no gap in between, forming a dense woven border at the bottom. You'll do those spinning half-knots instead. Everyone will go for 15 half knots. Measure the twisted parts, then change them so the lengths are the same, otherwise, you have to knit a dense border at the bottom of two more rows of half knots. The final step is to calculate the optimal tassel length and snip away the excess cord.

CHAPTER 15:

Bonus Macramé Projects

Hand Warmer

Hands warmers are great when it's colder. Crochet your hand warmer and use them while driving or outdoor when it gets very chilly.

Finish size: one hand warmer

Materials

Ball of yarn

Crochet hook of 4.5 mm

Scissor

Yarn needle

Sewing needle and thread (optional)

Steps

Yarn over and then draw a loop. Begin with a foundation chain, and for this, work the chain 25 and then make a hoop by split stitch in the first chain

Round 1: Work in half double crochet all around, chain 2, and then turn.

Round 2: Work in chain 2.6 half double crochet work in chain 3, chain till the end, and then work the chain 2 and turn.

Round 3: Work in half double crochet all around, chain 2 and then turn.

Round 4: Work in chain 2.6 half double crochet work in chain 3 chain till the end, then work the chain 2 and turn.

Round 5: Work in half double crochet all around, chain 2 (and then turn.

Round 6: Work in chain 2, 6 half double crochet work in chain 3 chain till the end, then work the chain 2 and turn.

Round 7: Work in half double crochet all around, chain 2 and then turn.

Round 8: Work in chain 2 6 half double crochet, work in chain 3 chain till the end, then work the chain 2 and turn.

Friendship Bracelet

Crochet friendship bands are a straightforward group gift that works up quickly and easily. And, the best part, it fits every age. If someone doesn't like to wear a friendship bracelet, it can be used as a bookmark or keychain instead. Make the following pattern of friendship band and then tweak it as you like.

Finish size: adult size bracelet

Materials

1 ball of crochet thread of size 10, 9mm thread

Crochet hook

Scissor

Steps

Take two strands of yarn, hold them together, and chain 52 stitches in the size that you want. Make a two-toned effect and for this, turn the chain and then work in half double crochet across the row in each chain. Work on the last row of crochet, and for this, turn the bracelet and slip stitch in back loop only (BLO) of each half double crochet in step 1.Cut off the thread by using a scissor, leave 3 inches of yarn at the end and then tie off the ribbon and don't weave in ends.

Macramé Watch Strand

Ways to spice up your wristwatch, well, now's your chance! Make use of this Macramé Watch Strand Pattern, and you will get what you want!

Materials:

Jump rings

Closure

2mm Crimp ends (you can choose another size, depending on your preferences)

Embroidery or craft floss

Watch with posts

Steps

Choose your types of floss, as well as their colors. Take at least ten long strands for each side of the watch. Lash floss onto the bar/posts of the watch and thread like you would a regular Macramé bracelet or necklace. Braid the ends tightly if you want to make it more stylish and cut the ends. Burn it with lighter to secure before placing jump rings and closure.

Use it and enjoy it!

Camera Strap
Materials:

Macramé rope

Swivel fastens

Clothespins

Modern quality paste

Scissors

Steps

Cut 2 lengths of macramé rope, 4 yards each. Fold every length of rope so that there's 1 yard on one side and 3 yards on the opposite side. Addition the midpoints through the level piece of one swivel catch, keeping the long parts of the bargains on the exterior. Pull the parts of the bargains through its own individual circle and pull tight around th fasten. Begin tying a square knot. Take the furthest left string (ought to be a long one), traverse the middle two ropes and under the furthest right (the other long) rope. At that point bring the right line under the middle two and up and over the left line. Pull this tight. This is half of your square knot. Complete the square knot by doing the opposite of stage 4. Traverse the middle two and under the left; at that point cross the left rope under the inside two and over the right. Pull tight and you have ended a square knot. Continue tying square knots until your camera strap is the right length for you. Trim the parts of the bargain's lines. Supplement all four ropes through another swivel catch. Spot a dollop of paste on the end of each line, crease the strings over the catch, and hold set up with clothespins while the paste dries. When the paste is dry, evacuate the clasps and pop the strap on your camera! I love the macramé line for a camera strap since it's excessively lightweight and adaptable, and comfortable around your neck

CHAPTER 16:

More Bonus Macramé Projects

Macramé Shower Curtain

Materials

389 feet of 3/16" cotton rope

Covering or painter's tape

Scissors

Steps

Cut 32 bits of rope, each estimating 12 feet. Fold a little bit of tape over the two parts of the bargains of rope, to forestall fraying. Integrate bits of rope (as appeared in photograph beneath), with the bunch around 10 crawls from the rope closes.

Macramé Table linen

Materials

Swivel Hook

Glue

Board and pins

Square Knots (SK)

Overhand Knot

Buttonhole Clasp

Linen

Steps

Put the two cords vertically on our board after getting their corresponding midpoints and tightly place them close to one another. The longer should be on the left because that is what will be used to tie the on the HC. Half of the vertical should make to move using the WC over or under (as the case may be) theto have a counter-clockwise loop. Gradually pulling it left, you should make it go over theto get the crossing point. Once the crossing point is gotten, tie the other Half of the Vertical LHK bypassing the WC under or over the HC, while pulling it left, pass it under the WC also to make the crossing point. More Vertical should be tied and should be done from the center in the direction of one end. When the first half of the handle is 6 inches, you should stop. The whole sennit or cords should be rotated and back to the center, leaving the WC on the right. Loos should made in clockwise directions as tying of Knots is resumed, and once the handle attains a length of 12 inches, you should stop the four segments should be brought together, thereby folding the sennit. Locate the WC in the process. Tie an SK using the 2 WC, and it should be tight. The fillers are going to be the short cords folding the 2 WC means we should have 4 cords to work with. A suitable decorative knot by the user should use alongside this wonderful design; some of the best knots to use alongside it are; the Square Knot, the Vertical larks head, and the Half hitch with holding cords. A minimum of six inches of material should be attached to the hook at the end of the pet leach. To attach the hook, two cords should pass through the loop that is on the hook. Tight finishing should tie with the four cords. The glue usage comes in here as the four cords are being tighten, the glue should use. When it gets dry, all additional materials should be removed or cut to make the work very neat and beautiful. You may also consider another finishing style, which entails that you move the ends in the direction of the strap and put it under the back of the knots to be very firm.

Macramé Towel holders

Materials

Finished length: around 20" supplies: 1 meters 6-7mm strand which can moan and shatter one decorative ring -- 2" one ornamental ring -- 5" one cosmetic ring -- seven "

Cut: 3 cords 2 yards extended 1-bedroom cable to wrap

Steps

Twist both lawn cords in half a lark's head on seven " rings. Screws onto the best straight under the lark's head. Connect an SK with all the 4 center strings. Proceed to the alternating SK routine until you have tied 7 inches, finishing with 2 SK. Place the 5" ring under both center filler wires. All the ring out of you, and tie and SK with all the four center strings. Proceed to the alternating SK routine until you have tied 11 longer rows. Place all wires through the " ring together with finishes coming to the front. Connect with wrapping cable. Reduce ends to 21/2" and fringe.

Conclusion

O nce you've mastered the simple macramé knots, you're ready to move on to micro-macramé and use the silky cords (more like thread) and delicate glass beads to make gorgeous jewelry. You can also use hemp to make a more natural jewelry style. You can also render your crafts using leather, silk, cotton fiber, rattail, and flax. Once you have the simple knots down, there really are endless possibilities!

One of the great advantages of this hobby is that with a limited investment in equipment and materials, you can get started with your craft. Unlike other wire jewelry or knitting and crocheting, macramé jewelry projects can be easily completed on the go. You won't need rolls of wire and assorted equipment to work on your designs, with nothing more than a sturdy clipboard and some very basic Materials: you can comfortably work in your lap.

Macramé is a great art and for good reasons has made a huge comeback: it's easy to know, it's cheap, and it's simple to do. You will be knotting your way to beautiful bits in no time.

Nowadays, macramé hobby and ability mean different things to different people. The skill is useful for many in a variety of ways. Tying the various knots will strengthen arms and hands. It can be very soothing to the mind, body, and spirit to build a macramé project! Macramé projects call for few resources and demand materials without any chemicals or fumes; it's an earth-friendly, natural ability without a doubt.

Macramé designs range from jewelry, hangers for plants, home decorations, hangers for doors, purses, and belts. Macramé colors and texture provide a wide range of options. Materials range from various jute and hemp thicknesses to twine, woven nylon, and polyester fibers. There are not only wooden beads in projects these days, but even glass and ceramic beads are being integrated into projects as well.

Macramé has changed ... yes, it's all part of the creative cycle that endures on several levels. Both experienced macramé artisans and experts consider it relaxing, enjoyable, imaginative, and satisfying. There are more and more options for superior macramé to improve the decor of your house, wardrobe and personal style for those who just want to use and enjoy the finished pieces To decide a period of time it will take to learn how to macramé depends on various factors such as how easily you will learn this technique. If you have been knitting or sewing for a long time, the degree of difficulty will be slightly lower, as there are some parallels with the process.

So, what are you waiting for? From now on, you are on the path to be a Macramé master, and you are going to fall in love with everything macramé. The world of Macramé awaits, just begging you to dive in and get started.

Macramé can also serve as an avenue for you to begin your dream small business. After perfecting your Macramé skills, you can conveniently sell your items and get paid well for your products, especially if you can perfectly make items like bracelets that people buy a lot. You could even train people and start your own little company that makes bespoke Macramé fashion accessories. The opportunities that Macramé presents are truly endless.

So, stay sharp, keep practicing and keep getting better. Welcome to a world of infinite possibilities!

MACRAME FOR BEGINNERS

An Easy Step-By-Step Guide To Macramé. Projects For Beginners And Intermediate Learners With High-Quality Images For A Much Better Experience.

EMILY SENRA

Table Of Contents

Introduction

In old times Knots and knot lore were closely associated with magic, medication, religious views for much of history. Knots also acted as bases for mathematical structures (for example, by the Mayans), before writing skills were introduced; and string games and other alternate uses were and are still numerous, of course. All these things have been carried out in one way or another and by all cultures since ancient times. They are even being taught all over the world nowadays. Additionally, it is safe to say that it will continue to follow until the day comes that humankind no longer exists.

Macramé as a part of enhancing ties pervades almost every culture, except inside those cultures, it can show in various ways. The carefully braided strings, with the assistance of a needle-like tool, became the item for shaping fishnets. Their purpose in the fashion world has been incredible and well-known among the generation today in making sandals, shoes, jewelry, etc. It is now used also with other products to fashion all kinds of beautiful works of art.

Macramé is closely associated with the trendy youth due to its rapid growth, quick adaptability, and extensive uses. Concerning its use for fashion items, macramé practiced in the materials turned into a necessary spotlight on the making of each beautifying garment, especially on the edges of each tent, dress, and towel. In this, macramé became a synonym for hanging planter. In its traditional forms, Macramé (is an Italian name given in Genoa-its home and place of birth) became one of the most common textile techniques.

Knots are used for the passage of time for several practical, mnemonic and superstitious reasons. The Peruvian Incas used a Quip, made from mnemonic knot (Basically, overhand knots) to help them record and convey information. In the early Egyptians and Greek times,' Hercules ' knot (square knot) was used on clothes, jewelry, and pottery, which had a spiritual or religious meaning.

As a product of the artistic intervention of scholarly artisans, this human intellectual accomplishment became necessary to incorporate modern architecture requiring the use of other materials for trendy artifacts. While macramé art has been created and used for onward creation in most cultures aimed at achieving both practical and artistic appeal, their end products vary from one culture to the next. These innovations, however, are, by definition, integral parts of cultural growth and are the results of the macramé artisans ' revolutionary accomplishments over the years. The use of adornment knotting distinguishes early cultures and reflected intelligence creation. It is an art that fits all ages and abilities. Today, macramé is experiencing a Revival of the 20th century.

Both men and women transition to work with their hands and build not just utilitarian pieces but also decorative ones.

Macramé has also proven to be an excellent natural treatment for those undergoing recovery procedures and helps to restore memories once again, making it a unique experience for all.

Macramé has the added benefit of embracing the self-expression cycle by establishing the underlying purpose concealed within.

CHAPTER 1:

Types of Cord

Macramé stylists make use of different types of materials. The materials can be classified in two major ways; the natural materials and the synthetic materials.

Natural Materials

The qualities of natural materials differ from the synthetic material and knowing these qualities would help you to make better use of them. Natural cord materials existing today include Jute, Hemp, Leather, Cotton, Silk and Flax. There are also yarns made from natural fibers. Natural material fibers are made from plants and animals.

Synthetic Materials

Like natural materials, synthetic materials are also used in macramé projects. The fibers of synthetic materials are made through chemical processes. The major ones are nylon beading cord, olefin, satin cord and parachute cord.

Cord Measurement

Before you can embark on a macramé project, it is essential that you determine the amount of chord you will need. This includes knowing the length of the required cord and the total number of materials you have to purchase.

Equipment: to measure, you will need a paper for writing, pencil, tape rule and calculator. You would also need some basic knowledge of unit conversion as shared below:

1 inch = 25.4millimeters = 2.54 centimeters

1 foot =12 inches

1 yard = 3 feet = 36 inches

1 yard = 0.9 meters

Note: The circumference of a ring = 3.14 * diameter measured across the ring

Measuring Width

The first thing to do is determine the finished width of the widest area of your project. Once you have this width, pencil it down.

Determine the actual size of the materials, by measuring its width from edge to edge.

You can then proceed to determine the type of knot pattern you wish to use with the knowledge of the knot pattern. You must know the width and spacing (if required) of each knot. You should also determine if you want to add more cords to widen an area of if you would be needing extra cords for damps.

With the formula given above, calculate and determine the circumference of the ring of your designs.

Determine the mounting technique to be used. The cord can be mounted to a dowel, ring or other cord. Folded cords affect both the length and width of the cord measurement.

Cord Preparation

Though usually rarely emphasized, preparation of the cords and getting them ready for use in Macramé projects is one of the core pillars of the art of Macramé. At times, specialized processes such as conditioning and stiffening of cords need to be carried out before Macramé projects can be begun. In general, however, cord preparation in Macramé is mainly concerned with dealing with cut ends and preventing these ends from unraveling during the project. During a project, constant handing of materials can distort the ends which can end up having disastrous consequences on your project. Before starting your project, if you do not appropriately prepare particular kinds of cords, like ones that were made by the twisting of individual strands, that cord is likely to come apart, effectively wrecking your project.

Therefore, cord preparation is extremely and incomparably important to the success of any Macramé project. The preparation of each cord is meant to be done during the first step of making any knot, which is the step where you cut out your desired length of cord from the larger piece.

For cord conditioning, experts recommend rubbing beeswax along the length of the cord. To condition your cord, simply get a bit of beeswax, let it warm up a bit in your hands, and rub it along the cord's length. This will help prevent unwanted tight curls on your cord. Note that beeswax may be applied to both natural and synthetic materials. For synthetic materials however, only Satin and fine Nylon beading cords compulsorily require conditioning. After conditioning, inspect your cords for any imperfections and discard useless pieces to ensure the perfection of your project. After conditioning, then comes the actual process of cord preparation. Cords can be prepared (i.e. the ends can be prevented from fraying) through the use of a flame, a knot, tape and glue.

To prevent unraveling of your cord using a flame, firstly test a small piece of the material with the flame from a small lighter. The material needs to melt, not burn. If it burns, then such a cord is not suitable for flame preparation. To prepare using a flame, simply hold the cord to the tip of the flame for 2 to 5 seconds, make sure the cord does not ignite, but melts. Flame preparation is suitable for cords made from olefin, polyester and nylon, and the process is compulsory for the preparation of parachute cords.

Tying knots at the end of the cord is another effective method to prevent fraying. The overhand knot is an all-time favorite, but knots such as the figure 8 knot which is best suited to flexible cords can be used if you think the knot might have to be undone at some point of your project. The Stevedore knot can be used to prevent fraying when using slippery materials.

Glue is another priceless alternative that can be used to prevent fraying at the ends of cords efficiently. However, not all kinds of glue may be used in cord preparation. Only certain brands, such as the Aleen's Stop Fray may be used in cord preparation. Household glue might also be used, but only when diluted with water. TO prepare your cord, simply rub the glue on the ends of the material and leave it to dry. If you intend to pass beads over the glued end, roll the cord's end between your fingers to make it narrower as it dries. Nail polish may also be used as an alternative to glue.

A particular class of Macramé cords, known as a parachute cord, requires a specific form of preparation. Parachute cords are composed of multiple core yarns surrounded by a braided sleeve. To prepare a parachute cord (also called a Paracord), pull out the core yarns from the sleeve, and expose the yarns by about half an inch. Now cut the core yarns back, so that they become even with the outer sleeve, and then push the sleeve forward till the yarns become invisible. To complete the preparation, apply flame to the outer sleeve till it melts, and then press the handle of your lighter onto the sleeve while it's still warm to flatten the area and keep it closed up. The melted area will look darker and more plastic than the rest of the material.

Finishing Techniques

Finishing techniques refer to the methods by which the ends of cords, after knots have been created may be taken care of to give a neat and tidy project. Finishing is often referred to as tying off. Several finishing knots are available and are incredibly effective methods for executing finishing processes. Strong finishing knots include the overhand knot and the barrel knot.

Folding techniques are also dependable finishing techniques. For flexible materials like cotton, all you need to do is fold the ends flat against the back surface and add glue to the ends to hold them in place. For less flexible materials, fold the cords to the back, then pass them under a loop from one or more knots, and then apply glue, allow it to dry, and cut off excess material.

Finally, you can do your finishing with the aid of fringes. You may choose between a brushed fringe and a beaded fringe.

Adding Cords

During Macramé projects, you would continuously be faced by the need to add a cord to an existing cord or any other surface such as a ring or a dowel. The process of adding cords to surfaces is usually called mounting. To add extra cords to a ring or dowel, the most common technique to use is the Reverse Larks Head Knot. When adding cords to already existing cords in use, however, the new cords must blend into the overall design. To prevent lopsidedness of the pattern, it is also crucial to add an equal number of cords to both sides in some projects. It is also essential to avoid gaps when adding new cords. You can add new cords to an already existing cord using the square knot, the linked overhand knot and of course the regular overhand knot. Other techniques used for adding cords include the diamond stitch and the triangle knot.

CHAPTER 2:

Essential and Useful Tools

Yarn

While you can use any yarn, as a beginner, you will find it best to use the yarn options we will outline below since they are easier to work with than others are.

Choosing the Best Yarn for Macrame

Fiber type: Choose from for both plant and animal fibers.

Acrylic yarn: Acrylic is generally a popular yarn among crochet enthusiasts. It is usually among the affordable choices for yarn, comes in a variety of colors and is widely available. It is a more-than-acceptable choice for you as a beginner.

Cotton yarn: It's an inelastic fiber, thereby making it a bit more challenging to work with than wool. However, where you want the item to hold its shape, this quality makes cotton an excellent choice for specific projects.

Wool Yarn: Wool is the perfect choice for you to practice your stitches. It is forgiving of mistakes and is a resilient fiber. If you happen to make a mistake while crocheting, most wool yarns are natural to unravel and even re-use (in crochet, its called frogging). Wool yarn is not suitable for those with wool allergies, but for most, it is a right crocheting choice.

Additional Yarn Tips and Considerations

Yarn weight: Yarns come in different thicknesses as well. This thickness is what we refer to as weight. The importance of the yarn is usually found on the label, where it's numbered 1-7 (from the thinnest to the thickest). It is most comfortable to work with a worsted weight yarn as a beginner, which is #4 on the yarn label.

*Note: you should use the correct crochet hook size for the yarn weight you will be using.

Yarn colour: Choose lighter yarn colours rather than dark ones, as it can get challenging to see your stitches if using yarns with dark colours.

Yarn texture: Choose smooth yarn and not the textured ones. As you begin crocheting, avoid eyelash yarns and any other textured novelty yarns, which can get quite frustrating to work with.

Yarn yardage: Each ball of yarn has different yardage amounts, which relates to the price. You can find two balls of yarn at the same rate; check the yardage to ensure the value of yarn in each ball is approximately the same.

Yarn price: The price of yarn varies significantly from brand to brand and fiber to fiber. It is better to work on the affordable ones so that you get the hang of it before investing a lot of money in very expensive yarns. This is why acrylic, wool and cotton are the top fiber choices, as they tend to be the most affordable.

Yarn colour dye lot: to crochet will need more than one ball of yarn; then, you want to ensure that all the colors match (assuming that you are using the same colourway or colour for the entire project). You do this by checking the "dye lot on the yarn label to ensure that the balls noticeable differences between them.

Washing details: This will be important if you are crocheting something to wear. For instance, you can use wool that is safe to put in the washer and dryer, or you can do so for some wool that must be hand washed and dried flat because it will sink in the dryer. The yarn label contains this information to aid in your selections.

Hooks

The average crochet hook works for anyone, and it favours beginners like you. You will find crochet hooks sold at yarn stores or any major craft retailer. You can also get them online. Few things you need to know about:

Material: A basic crochet hook can be made of several common elements such as bamboo, plastic and aluminum. Most people usually choose aluminum crochet hooks for their first project. There are also fancier crochet hooks made of wood, glass, and clay.

Size: Crochet hooks differ in size; many different formats are measured in numbers, letters or millimetres. For instance, a basic crochet hook set may range from E – J. A general-sized crochet hook is normally H-8 5mm. Size E is smaller than size H; size J is more significant. As mentioned, you should match the size of your crochet hook with the weight of your yarn, which is usually on the label of the yarn. For most beginners, it is generally advisable to work with a size G or H crochet hook and worsted weight yarn.

Hook throat: an inline or tapered less or more flatness to the head of the hook. Since neither is better than the other is, if you find it hard to work with one, try the other.

Metal Wire the web

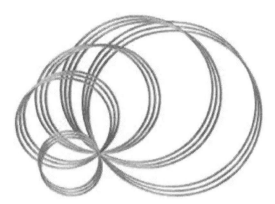

Something else, knitters can exchange skeins each couple of lines to help the color par

There are different business applications for sewing texture made of metal wire by knitting machines. Steel wire of various sizes might be utilized for electric and attractive protection because of its conductivity. Treated steel might be used in an espresso press for its imperviousness to rust. Metal wire can likewise be utilized as gems.

Glass/Wax Sewn glass combines knitting, lost-wax throwing, shape-making, and oven throwing. The procedure includes:

Needles

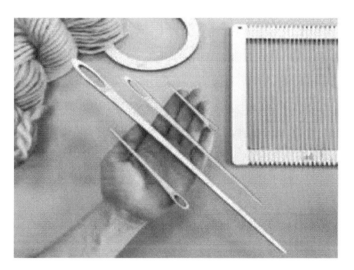

Various materials have various grindings and unexpectedly grasp the yarn; smooth needles, such as metallic needles, help quick knitting, while more unpleasant needles, such as bamboo, offer more erosion are this way less inclined to dropping join. The knitting of new lines happens just at the decreased finishes. Needles with lit tips have been offered to permit knitters to weave in obscurity.

Tape

Use tape on the ends of your cords to keep them from fraying. I suggest masking tape since it will not leave any marks on the cord. When cutting a cord, you can first put tape on the part where you will reduce the cord. Cut in the exact half of the tape to have the end and the beginning of the next cord with tape. Use tape on the terms of your cords to keep them from fraying. I suggest masking tape since it will not leave any marks on the cord. When cutting a cord, you can first put tape on the part where you will reduce the cord. Cut in the exact half of the tape to have the end and the beginning of the next cord with tape.

Clothes rack

To work comfortably, it is recommended to use a clothes rack. Any type of clothes rack will do, although one that is adjustable in height can be helpful. Something similar to a clothes frames can also work: a curtain rail or wooden step ladder might work.

Cord

Cotton is very soft and pleasant to work with, while jute, for instance, could hurt on your hands while working with it. T-shirt yarn is cheap and quite easy to find. But it would help if you considered that most of the T-shirt yarn tends to be a bit elastic, which makes it less suitable for hanging objects that have to carry some weight like plant hangers.

CHAPTER 3:

Charms, Beads and Others

Types of Beading

There are many different ways that beads have been used to create various forms of jewelry and decoration. Beads can be strung, woven, or sewed, and there are several different techniques to achieve a variety of different effects.

Threading: Most typical type of beadwork, this is the act of stringing beads one at a time onto a single strand of thread, wire, or nylon. You can get many different effects using this one simple technique either by varying the beads, varying the length of the thread, or combining multiple threads, twisting the strands, or layering them.

Corralling is a threading type that uses beads to create numerous branches combing off a single row of beads. Think of the way that a piece of coral may branch in different directions. So using corralling, you can be creating a necklace with several small offshoots or a set of earrings that move in various ways.

Stitching is one of the more elaborate and complicated methods of beading. There are several different stitches, including ladder stitches, brick stitches, peyote stitches, and spiral stitches. Most stitching techniques rely on seed beads or other types of tiny beads to weave them together to form things like flowers made entirely out of beads. Loom beading is a method of weaving threads or stitches through a set of beads to create a beads sheet. Bags, tassels, and any kind of jewelry meant to drape on the wearer are using woven using this type of technique. Unlike other types of beading, which don't need special equipment beyond the beads, thread, and possibly a needle, loom beading does require both a set pattern and a beading loom to create the desired effects.

Beaded Jewelry Trends

There are many classic, timeless type of jewelry and beadwork that never go out of style. There are also many different types of beading and jewelry that heats up for a minute, then vanishes into thin air. Remember the super long necklaces that everyone was wearing in the late aughts? You'll be hard-pressed to find anyone still sporting one today.

With jewelry trends that wax and wane so frequently, it can get expensive to try to keep up. You'll need an ever-expanding jewelry case just to contain it all, too. This is part of what's fun about making your jewelry. After all, by creating things yourself, you can:

Bypass trends by creating unique, one of a kind piece of wearable art

Recycle old jewelry pieces by taking them apart and repurposing the beads in new and exciting ways

Whip up the perfect necklace, bracelet, or pair of earrings to wear to a specific event, customizing the colour and style to match

Make multiple on-trend pieces in several different colours and materials for a fraction of the cost of purchasing just one at a store

Though, while everyone should have one or two trendy pieces in their accessory box to pull out on occasion, trends change so frequently that you can get exhausted just trying to keep up. You should consider making beaded jewelry that speaks to you on another level – not only in colour or style.

By choosing and creating pieces that can have a personal meaning, you can complement any outfit, while remaining true to your sense of creativity.

Materials You'll Need

Beads and beading materials come in so many different forms; you may want to experiment with several to discover what type you like best, regardless of trends or current style. Remember, trends come and go, and the skills and techniques you're learning now will serve you well for decades, so it doesn't matter if a colour or material that's hot right now isn't something you begin working with today.

It's also important to remember that beading and jewelry materials can vary, not only in trend but also in other ways. Beads themselves differ tremendously in terms of colour, pattern, size, shape, and material, but the stuff you can use to thread them can also vary. Different types of beads also sit differently within a pattern and move differently. At the same time, your different threading materials can also give you different results, even when using the same type and design of beads.

Therefore, it's essential to consider your materials and how they will affect your end project.

Colour and Bead Strings

While many specialty stores sell beads individually, it's a lot easier – and cheaper – to purchase beads by the string. Many pearls, including glass, stone, ceramic, and metal will be sold strung together on a piece of nylon. Buying your beads this way is an excellent way to see how the beads sit next to one another; round beads will sit very differently on a string than chips will, for example.

Some strings will also come with a variety of variegated colours mixed. If you're unsure about putting colours together, this can be an easy route to take. Otherwise, consider laying out whole strings of beads beside one another to start picking out the perfect colours for your design. Don't be afraid to select multiple beads of the same colour and change only things like texture or material to give your finished piece depth.

Irregular and Regular Beads

Beads come in multiple sizes and shapes, as well as colours and materials. The most significant difference you'll notice, however, is in the beads' regularity. Stone bead chips, shell beads, and some glass beads will come in varying sizes and shapes within one group or strand. These irregular beads won't function the same way "regular" beads will, beads that have been machined to be uniform in size and shape.

However, irregular beads can give you some fascinating looks by giving you randomness to the jewelry, even when using one bead or colour. They can also be the perfect fit in some stitching or loom beading; an irregular bead may fit the corner or turn of a piece better than a round or rectangular bead might.

Projects made with irregular beads tend to look a little more organic than those made with more uniform beads.

Wire

Many people prefer the use of thread, silk, or cord for beading, but you can get many different looks by using wire. There are three basic types of cable: memory wire, which is difficult to shape, but retains that shape once you achieve it, the standard wire which will bend more quickly, but unbends easily as well, and woven wire, which acts like a cord, but with a metallic sheen. This type of cable works best for pieces where the thread is visible between the beads.

The key to working with wire is the gauge. Each gauge or weight of the cable is assigned a number; the higher the number, the thinner and more pliable the wire. Look for 24 gauge wire for delicate wire wrapping or create multiple "strands" on a pair of earrings, or for 18 gauge wire to form a coil bracelet.

Jump Rings

Jump rings are fully formed circles of wire that are not easily unbent. You can join a bunch of them together to form a chain, hang several strands of beads of one ring, or use them as spacers between beads. You can usually find jump rings in two types: the first will require pliers to bend open and then shut again, while the second works more like a small key chain that you twist to attach to another.

Pliers

Prepare two pairs of pliers when working with beaded jewelry. One pair should have a flat nose, while the other should be rounded. Ideally, they should also be two different sizes to give you some more flexibility in this area. You'll need the pliers to hold small beads as you thread them, open jump rings, bend the end of a wire into a loop, or close a crimp bead.

Beading Needle and Thread

If you plan on using actual thread for your beads, rather than cord or wire, you should invest in a beading needle. Beading needles are thin, flexible pieces of metal with a large eye. To use them, you tie the end part of the thread to the needle, then use the stylus to string multiple beads onto your thread. Most of the time, you'll use a beading needle with thin cotton or silk thread. This is ideal for corralling, stitching, or any beading where you want to double back through a bead or around the outside of a bead.

Corralling

Corralling is a more advanced beading technique that can create all kinds of three-dimensional jewelry. It's usually a technique that many people master before they move onto stitching. It can be used to create necklaces, bracelets, and earrings that have multiple components joined together. You can use any bead size, but the majority of corralling projects are done either with small beads or seed beads.

When you're a beginner to coral, you may want to start with something abstract first. This is to get used to the technique of threading off several small branches that connect to the main trunk. Once you master this, you can start creating many very intricate patterns; the key is just in how you go in and out of the branches.

To learn how to coral properly, it's essential to start with seed beads. Larger beads may seem more comfortable to work with because they take up more space, but they can be more challenging to manipulate. Try this basic corralling technique using seed beads until you become comfortable. Then, you may want to try a simple project using larger beads, such as making a necklace with several "branches" coming off the main bib. In time, you may find that stitching will give you the versatility you're looking for, and you'll be able to combine techniques to get the final look that you're after.

CHAPTER 4:

Techniques For Knotting Cord Ends

Many Macramé tasks are easy to finish. Each job has a great deal of models to create it your own. At any time, you feel used to knotting, you are inclined to be in a position to produce your routines and make some genuinely exceptional cloths. Consider ways you can change a number of these Subsequent Macramé ideas:

- Wall-hangings
- Planters
- Crucial chains
- Hanging chairs
- Belts
- Antiques

Fringe on special fabrics

Button square knots: begin out with three square knots then keep onto screw pliers by the back amid the horn cables before their original. Publish a rectangle under the bottom of this button to finish.

Cosmetic Dentistry: used making jewelry or to get Special knots such as Celtic and Chinese. These two approaches go perfectly with handmade jewelry and precious stones, for example semi-precious stones, crystals, or pearls. These Macramé knots usually are intricate and could have a while to know.

Double-hitch knot: that Macramé knot is created by Generating two half hitch knots you afterward a second. Yank on the knots attentively.

Half Hitch knot: place Inch cable through your job Area (pin therefore that the cable will not proceed). At the finish of the cable that's been hauled across the unmoving cable is drawn under the cable and pulled the loop which has been shaped.

Half knot: One of the typical Macramé knots to create. A fifty% knot is an ordinary knot, you start with four strings. Put it using this loop produced by the center cable together with your hand cable. Tug to Fasten the knot.

Overhand knot: Just one of the Most Often used knots in Macramé. Start with developing a loop by way of one's cable. Pull the knot carefully.

Square knots: construct out of this fifty-five percent knot to produce the square knot. Take your righthand cable behind the center strings and then send it about the left-handed cable. Only choose the left-handed cable and place it throughout the ideal hand by merely moving the middle strings and pull.

Ever wanted to be able to make your bracelets & designer handbag, but did not comprehend just how or did not have the appropriate resources? You have probably experienced such a difficulty. Well, macramé design is precisely what the physician ordered.

Macramé is just a sort of fabric which works by using knotting. Materials that are utilized from the macramé process comprise jute, linen, strings got out of cotton twine, yarn, and hemp. It's a procedure for knotting ropes codes or strings collectively with one another to check something. This item might be described as a necklace jewelry, necklace, etc. Macramé designs can be made complicated if different knots have been united to produce one layout or complicated.

A macramé bracelet can be made under:

Desired materials a Razor-blade, a pencil or polyurethane Plank, or t-pin, a hemp cable, and sometimes some series of somebody else's taste.

Guidelines

Step 1: Measure Inch that the circumference of the wrist will probably soon be Measured. Afterward, cut two bits of this hemp rope together with the assistance of the scissors. The bits cut needs to be two times the magnitude of this wrist or the circumference measured initially. As an instance, when the dimension got was 5 inches, two strands measuring 15 inches per needs to be trimmed.

Step 2: Measure 2 strand is folded to around 30 minutes. Holding The pencil at a flat place, the strand is likely to probably be reverted onto the pen's cone to possess a loop just on the leading portion of stand, also, to guarantee loose finishes do hang. These ends ought to be passed via the loop and closely pulled. This procedure ought to be replicated with yet another strand too. In the very long term, you'll have to get four strands hanging this particular pencil. Mentally, you might label these strands from side to left side, only 1 2. It's likely to work with whatever tagging procedure you locate easily.

Step 3: Measure 3 strand Inch ought to be obtained, on the other hand, significantly more than just two strands 2 and strand 3 (that in personality will be stranded at the center), and then below strand 4.

Step 4: in This Time select strand 4 supporting the two Strands 3 and 2, throughout the loop that strand inch did form. To be certain a half square rectangle is achieved, carefully pull strand 1 and strand 4.

Step 5: now you need to know a strand Constituting process. Take with this particular strand crossing process until fundamentally the bracelet accomplishes this particular period which you can so desire. Spirals will probably be formed in both square knots because you carry on working out.

Step 6: the loops have been slid off the pen. After that, pull strand 2 and strand 3 to have the ability to lower the magnitude in these loops shaped only a small bit. Each of those four strands may then hold together along with two knots attached like a way of procuring the job. These knots are crucial. Those strings which you side-by-side should subsequently be trimmed, and this also should attentively be performed since close those knots as you possibly can.

Step 7 in the time you have obtained the bracelet set on your own wrist. The-knot needs to be passed via the fold, therefore to keep up the bracelet onto your wrist.

The measures above will allow you to design a really Straight-forward macramé bracelet. This macramé approach uses knotting instead of weaving or knitting process. You may utilize beads to craft a beaded macramé necklace. You'll design distinguishing forms of decorations with macramé strategy. This is dependent upon you personally.

Fantasy catchers have gotten Remarkably Popular and so they're extended in an enormous variety of styles and layouts. It's likely to uncover crotchet, woven or knotted dream-catchers. Macramé is really a material making procedure which is based on knotting in the place of knitting or weaving. It's a French saying that ostensibly means knot since it's on the list of very first art-forms there really is. The main knots within this procedure are square knots and hitching types that may possibly be twice or entire feasibility.

Macramé is a technique that's been used for its Maximum period to decorate and craft numerous goods. You'll detect magnificent among a sort macramé handbag, wall-hangings, fantasy catchers, and a good deal of longer. It isn't too complicated to produce your macramé dream house particularly the moment you have a couple of guides to take you through these knots. At any time, you have mastered the knotting, you're getting to be astounded by just how creative you can acquire.

The Strings

The strings are the most significant things you Are likely to have to generate your personal piece. Cotton twine strings would be one of the most common due to the complete appearance they furnish and you're getting to be in a posture to select unique colors to generate a design that fits with your taste. Besides cotton, then it's very likely to choose many substances for example cotton, linen, silk, and jute determined by the kind of structure that you would really like to realize. Numerous those cable chemicals are a ton easier for cosmetic purposes on the fantasy catcher than they truly are correct in creating a comprehensive slice.

Cord structure may potentially be 3-ply value it Consists of three different spans of fiber to produce a robust and superbly shaped fantasy catcher.

The Rings

Macramé fantasy catchers can be accomplished with just wooden joints nevertheless in some specific scenarios you could like to consider account a dowel determined by the dimensions of one's own thing. A decorative or metallic dowel may conduct the task well in offering you a fantastic surface to disperse a large number of strings and that means that you may readily control them to accomplish your favorite design in the very long haul. If you'd really like to produce smaller sized ones, a push board, maybe whatever you need to begin on work.

Decorations

Despite macramé fantasy catchers, it's extremely potential that you simply incorporate jewelry along with other cosmetic capabilities in the own piece. You're able to tie the ribbons using Different strand colors or maybe you include different necklaces, beads, and Cubes to make points of interest inside your design. It's likely to utilize right Hooks, u-pins or upholstery to preserve the decorations and strings put up. If You Would like to use beads as Well as another accessory, then you should pick strand thickness attentively; preferably thick strand can Not provide this alluring appearance using attachments. Thinner strings make it to Be potential for the decorations to stick out from elegance.

Mix and Match Knots to Create All Kinds of Patterns

The Square Knot and Square Knot Variations

The square knot is often used in macrame. Square knots can be tied in a sennetto (a length of knots tied one after the other) or through many lengths of ropes to create solid or mesh patterns as patterns. Each node is made with two passes and requires a minimum of three cables. Two cables are needed to tie the knots and an additional cable to tie. The following tutorial shows how to tie a basic square knot using four ropes and then how to use the knot in various shapes. Beads can be added to the knotting cords as you tie. They can also be threaded onto the central cords and then the knotting cords can be carried around them. For very large holed beads all the cords can be passed through the beads. The square knot can be tied individually or in sennets. Using two different colored cords will produce a simple pattern through the sennet. This knot can also be tied in various formations to achieve decorative and more complex looking patterns for jewelry making and other items. This guide contains photographs showing how to tie a basic square knot and then illustrates four further ways in which square knots can be used.

These steps can now be repeated to create as many knots as desired.

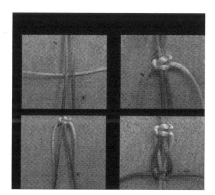

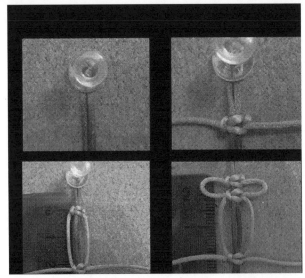

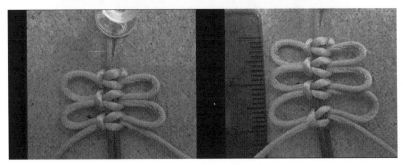

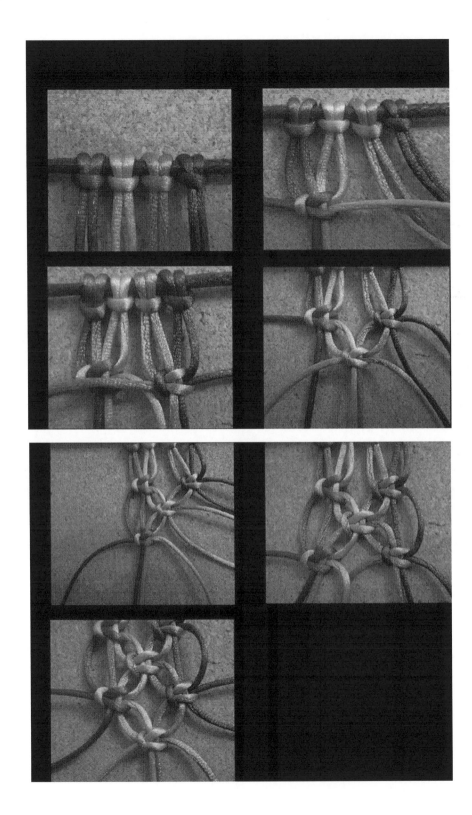

The Half Hitch Knot and Half Hitch Variations

The half hitch knot is another very common and versatile knot that is used in macramé. Like the square knot it is fairly easy to learn and can be used to create a variety of designs. Beads and other items can easily be added to either the central or knotting cords to embellish your designs.

Half hitch knots can be tied in two different ways. The knotting cord can be tied either over-under-over the holding cord or alternately it can be tied under-over-under the holding cord. I have included photographs showing both on the following pages. Either of these half hitch knots can be used to tie a variety of formations and I have included step by step photographs for four of these in the following part.

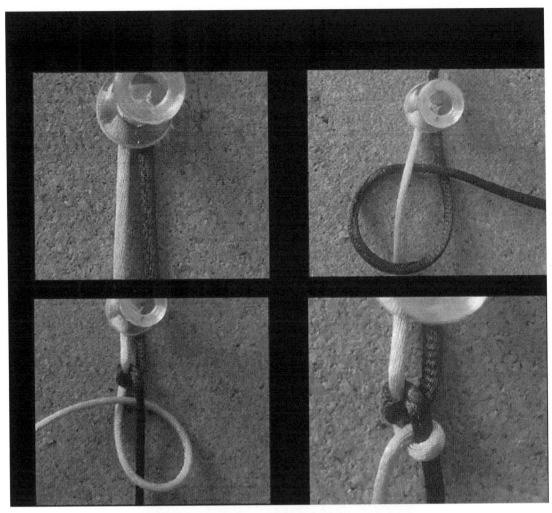

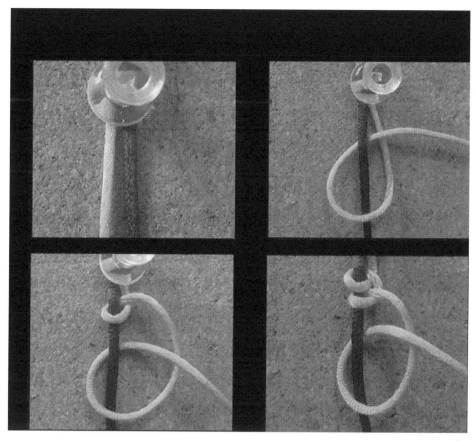

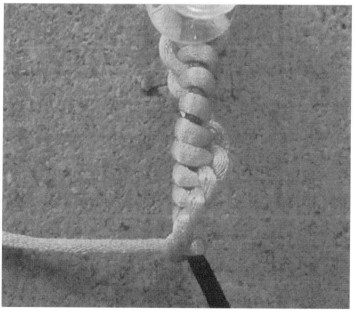

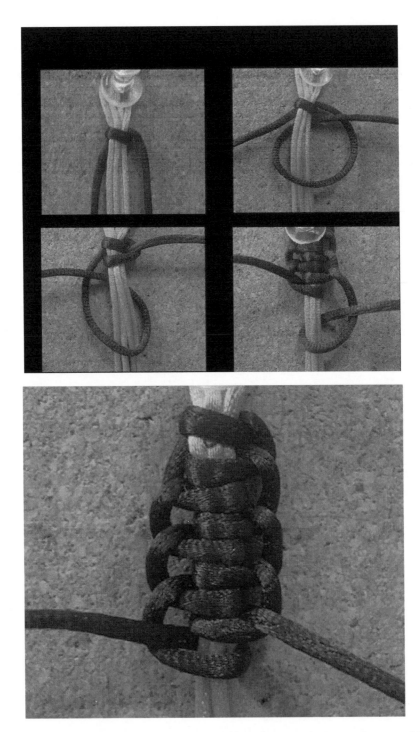

This is a vintage knot that can be used to create wide flat knotted pieces that would be suitable for bracelets, belts, bag straps, and similar. The width of the finished piece is based on the number of central cords used.

CHAPTER 5:

How to start a Macrame Project

Studying the knots

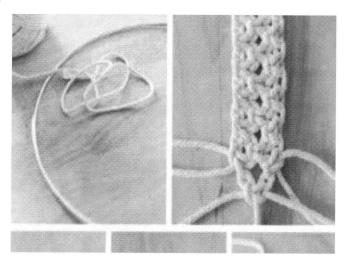

Before you are ready to begin learning the way to Macramé, gather your gear, and familiarize yourself with a few regular Macramé requirements, you will need to grasp.

Provides and substances

Here's what you are going to have to know and work out your Macramé knots:

- Macramé cable can be any cord, twine, or strand made from cotton, jute, or synthetic substance. It arrives in various sizes, colors, and spins. Within this tutorial, we found that a 3/16" cotton string provided that rope acquires clotheslines.
- Service: you could require something to link to. Popular choices comprise dowel sticks, branches, hoops, or bands. We used a dowel rod for all these knots.

Crucial Macramé States

- Macramé requirements you ought to know before its potential to start.
- Working string: either the cable or pair of ropes you utilize to create the real knots.
- Filler cable: either the cable or pair of wires your knots wrapping around.

- Senet: some knot or collection of knots which can be functioned in replicate.

Cord Measurement

Before you can embark on a macramé project, it is essential that you determine the amount of chord you will need. This includes knowing the length of the required cord and the total number of materials you have to purchase.

Equipment: to measure, you will need a paper for writing, pencil, tape rule and calculator. You would also need some basic knowledge of unit conversion as shared below:

· 1 inch = 25.4millimeters = 2.54 centimeters

· 1 foot =12 inches

· 1 yard = 3 feet = 36 inches

· 1 yard = 0.9 meters

Note: The circumference of a ring = 3.14 * diameter measured across the ring

Measuring Width

The first thing to do is determine the finished width of the widest area of your project. Once you have this width, pencil it down.

Next, determine the actual size of the materials, by measuring its width from edge to edge.

You can then proceed to determine the type of knot pattern you wish to use with the knowledge of the knot pattern. You must know the width and spacing (if required) of each knot. You should also determine if you want to add more cords to widen an area of if you would be needing extra cords for damps.

With the formula given above, calculate and determine the circumference of the ring of your designs.

Determine the mounting technique to be used. The cord can be mounted to a dowel, ring or other cord. Folded cords affect both the length and width of the cord measurement.

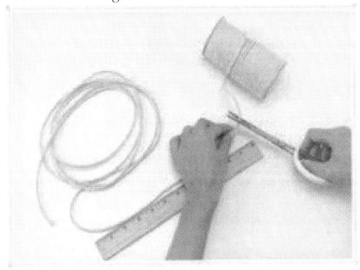

Cord Preparation

Though usually rarely emphasized, preparation of the cords and getting them ready for use in Macramé projects is one of the core pillars of the art of Macramé. At times, specialized processes such as conditioning and stiffening of cords need to be carried out before Macramé projects can be begun. In general, however, cord preparation in Macramé is mainly concerned with dealing with cut ends and preventing these ends from unraveling during the course of the project. During the course of a project, constant handing of materials can cause distortion in the ends which can end up having disastrous consequences on your project. Before starting your project, if you do not appropriately prepare special kinds of cords, like ones that were made by the twisting of individual strands, that cord is likely to come apart, effectively destroying your project completely.

Therefore, cord preparation is extremely and incomparably important to the success of any Macramé project, the preparation of each cord is meant to be done during the first step of making any knot, which is the step where you cut out your desired length of cord from the larger piece.

For cord conditioning, experts recommend rubbing beeswax along the length of the cord. To condition your cord, simply get a bit of beeswax, let it warm up a bit in your hands, and rub it along the cord's length. This will help prevent unwanted tight curls on your cord. Note that beeswax may be applied to both natural and synthetic materials. For synthetic materials however, only Satin and fine Nylon beading cords actually compulsorily require conditioning. After conditioning, inspect your cords for any imperfections and discard useless pieces to ensure the perfection of your project. After conditioning, then comes the actual process of cord preparation. Cords can be prepared (i.e. the ends can be prevented from fraying) through the use of a flame, a knot, tape and glue.

To prevent unraveling of your cord using a flame, firstly test a small piece of the material with the flame from a small lighter. The material needs to melt, not burn. If it burns, then such a cord is not suitable for flame preparation. To prepare using a flame, simply hold the cord to the tip of the flame for 2 to 5 seconds, make sure the cord does not ignite, but melts. Flame preparation is suitable for cords made from olefin, polyester and nylon, and the process is compulsory for the preparation of parachute cords.

Tying knots at the end of the cord is another effective method to prevent fraying. The overhand knot is an all-time favorite, but knots such as the figure 8 knot which is best suited to flexible cords can be used if you think the knot might have to be undone at some point of your project. The Stevedore knot can be used to prevent fraying when using slippery materials.

Glue is another priceless alternative that can be used to prevent fraying at the ends of cords efficiently. However, not all kinds of glue may be used in cord preparation. Only certain brands, such as the Aleen's Stop Fray may be used in cord preparation. Household glue might also be used, but only when diluted with water. TO prepare your cord, simply rub the glue on the ends of the material and leave it to dry. If you intend to pass beads over the glued end, roll the cord's end between your fingers to make it narrower as it dries. Nail polish may also be used as an alternative to glue.

Finishing Techniques

Finishing techniques refer to how the ends of cords after knots have been created may be taken care of to give a neat and tidy project. Finishing is often referred to as tying off. Several finishing knots are available and are incredibly effective methods for executing finishing processes. Steady finishing knots include the overhand knot and the barrel knot.

Folding techniques are also dependable finishing techniques. For flexible materials like cotton, all you need to do is fold the ends flat against the back surface and add glue to the ends to hold them in place. For less flexible materials, fold the cords to the back, pass them under a loop from one or more knots, apply glue, allow it to dry, and cut off excess material.

Finally, you can do your finishing with the aid of fringes. You may choose between a brushed fringe and a beaded fringe.

Adding Cords

During Macramé projects, you would continuously be faced with adding a cord to an existing cord or any other surface such as a ring or a dowel. The process of adding cords to surfaces is usually called mounting. The most common technique to use is the Reverse Larks Head Knot to add extra cords to a ring or dowel. However, when adding cords to already existing cords in use, the new cords must blend into the overall design. To prevent the pattern's lopsidedness, it is also essential to add an equal number of cords to both sides in some projects. It is also necessary to avoid gaps when adding new cords. You can add new cords to an already existing cord using the square knot, the linked overhand knot, and the regular overhand knot. Other techniques used for adding cords include the diamond stitch and the triangle knot.\

CHAPTER 6: **Macrame Patterns**

Capuchin Knot

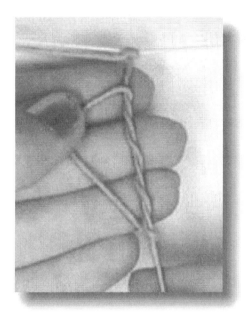

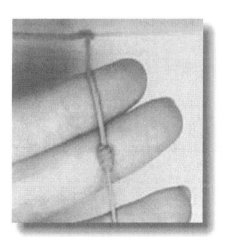

This is a great beginning knot for any project and can be used as the foundation for the base of the project. Use lightweight cord for this – it can be purchased at craft stores or online, wherever you get your macramé supplies.

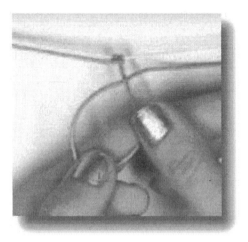

Watch the photos very carefully as you move along with this project and take your time to make sure you are using the right string at the right point of the project.

Don't rush, and make sure you have even tension throughout. Practice makes perfect, but with the illustrations to help you, you'll find it's not hard at all to create.

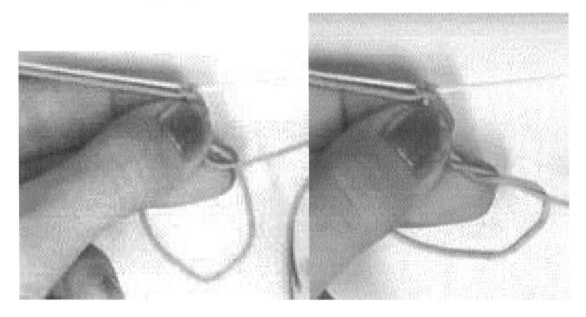

Start with the base cord, tying the knot onto this, and working your way along the project.

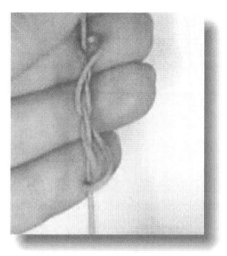

Twist the cord around itself 2 times, pulling the string through the center to form the knot.

For the finished project, make sure that you have all your knots secure and firm throughout, and do your best to make sure it is all even. It is going to take practice before you can get it perfectly each time, but remember that practice does make perfect, and with time, you are going to get it without too much trouble.

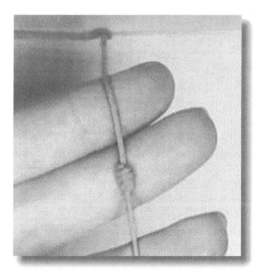

Make sure all is even and secure and tie off. Snip off all the loose ends, and you are ready to go!

Crown Knot

This is a great beginning knot for any project and can be used as the foundation for the base of the project. Use lightweight cord for this – it can be purchased at craft stores or online, wherever you get your macramé supplies.

Watch the photos very carefully as you move along with this project and take your time to make sure you are using the right string at the right point of the project.

Don't rush, and make sure you have even tension throughout. Practice makes perfect, but with the illustrations to help you, you'll find it's not hard at all to create.

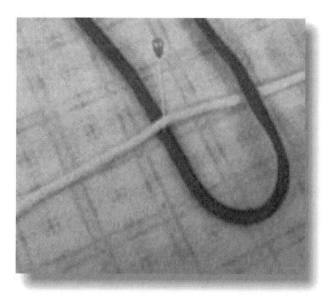

Use a pin to help keep everything in place as you are working.

Weave the strings in and out of each other as you can see in the photos. It helps to practice with different colors to help you see what is going on.

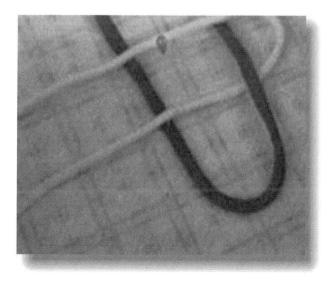

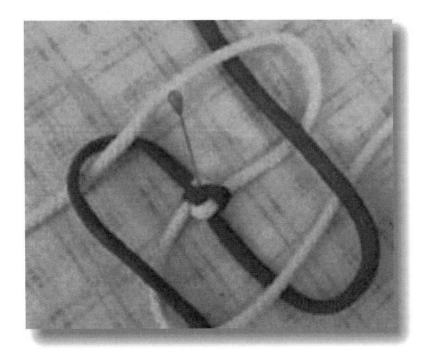

Pull the knot tight, and then repeat for the row on the outside.

293

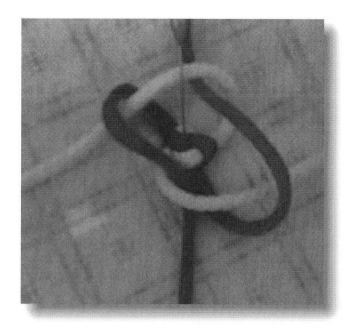

Continue to do this as often as you like to create the knot. You can make it as thick as you like, depending on the project. You can also create more than one length on the same cord.

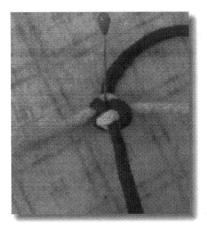

For the finished project, make sure that you have all your knots secure and firm throughout, and do your best to make sure it is all even. It is going to take practice before you can get it perfectly each time, but remember that practice does make perfect, and with time, you are going to get it without too much trouble.

Make sure all is even and secure and tie off. Snip off all the loose ends, and you are ready to go!

Diagonal Double Half Knot

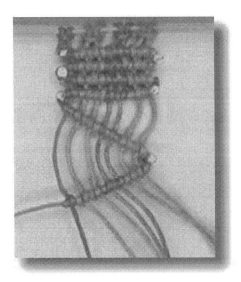

This is the perfect knot to use for basket hangings, decorations, or any projects that are going to require you to put weight on the project. Use a heavier weight cord for this, which you can find at craft stores or online.

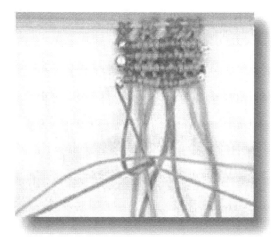

Watch the photos very carefully as you move along with this project and take your time to make sure you are using the right string at the right point of the project.

Don't rush, and make sure you have even tension throughout. Practice makes perfect, but with the illustrations to help you, you'll find it's not hard at all to create.

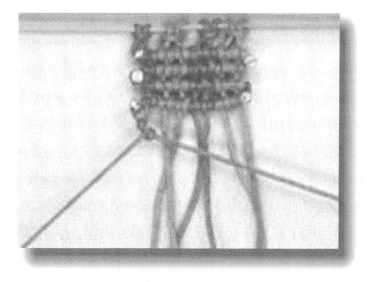

Start at the top of the project and work your way toward the bottom. Keep it even as you work your way throughout the piece. Tie the knots at 4-inch intervals, working your way down the entire thing.

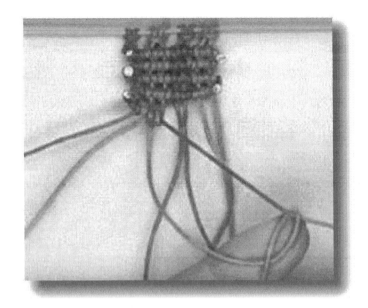

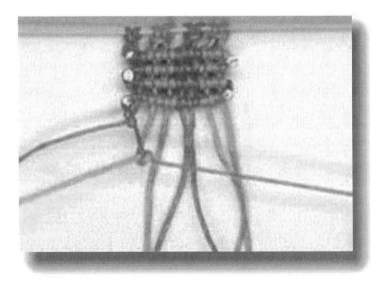

Weave in and out throughout, watching the photo as you can see for the right placement of the knots. Again, it helps to practice with different colors, so you can see what you need to do throughout the piece.

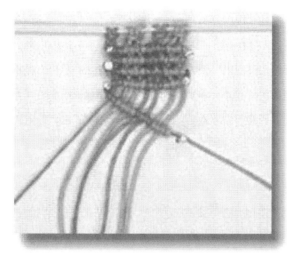

For the finished project, make sure that you have all your knots secure and firm throughout, and do your best to make sure it is all even. It is going to take practice before you can get it perfectly each time, but remember that practice does make perfect, and with time, you are going to get it without too much trouble.

Make sure all is even and secure and tie off. Snip off all the loose ends, and you are ready to go!

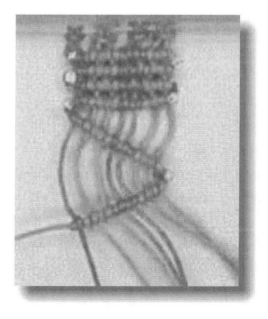

Frivolite Knot

This is a great beginning knot for any project and can be used as the foundation for the base of the project. Use lightweight cord for this – it can be purchased at craft stores or online, wherever you get your macramé supplies.

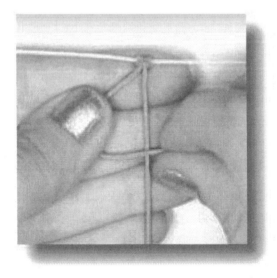

Watch the photos very carefully as you move along with this project and take your time to make sure you are using the right string at the right point of the project.

299

Don't rush, and make sure you have even tension throughout. Practice makes perfect, but with the illustrations to help you, you'll find it's not hard at all to create.

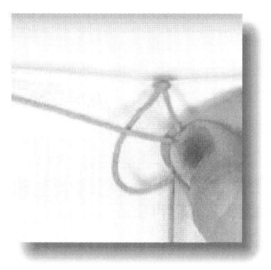

Use the base string as the guide to hold it in place, and then tie the knot onto this. This is a very straightforward knot; watch the photo and follow the directions you see.

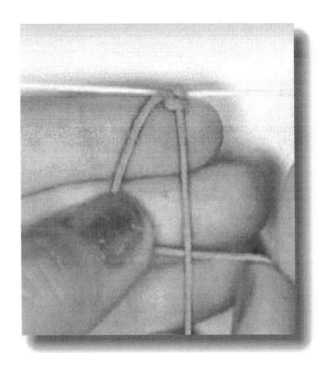

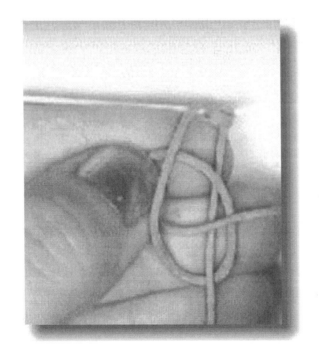

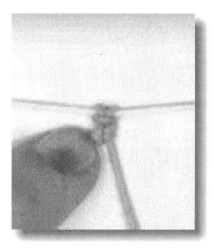

Pull the end of the cord up and through the center.

For the finished project, make sure that you have all your knots secure and firm throughout, and do your best to make sure it is all even. It is going to take practice before you can get it perfectly each time, but remember that practice does make perfect, and with time, you are going to get it without too much trouble.

Make sure all is even and secure and tie off. Snip off all the loose ends, and you are ready to go!

Horizontal Double Half Knot

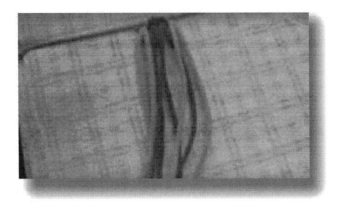

This is a great beginning knot for any project and can be used as the foundation for the base of the project. Use lightweight cord for this — it can be purchased at craft stores or online, wherever you get your macramé supplies.

Watch the photos very carefully as you move along with this project and take your time to make sure you are using the right string at the right point of the project.

Don't rush, and make sure you have even tension throughout. Practice makes perfect, but with the illustrations to help you, you'll find it's not hard at all to create.

Start at the top of the project and work your way toward the bottom. Keep it even as you work your way throughout the piece. Tie the knots at 4-inch intervals, working your way down the entire thing.

For the finished project, make sure that you have all your knots secure and firm throughout, and do your best to make sure it is all even. It is going to take practice before you can get it perfectly each time, but remember that practice does make perfect, and with time, you are going to get it without too much trouble.

Make sure all is even and secure and tie off. Snip off all the loose ends, and you are ready to go!

Josephine Knot

This is the perfect knot to use for basket hangings, decorations, or any projects that are going to require you to put weight on the project. Use a heavier weight cord for this, which you can find at craft stores or online.

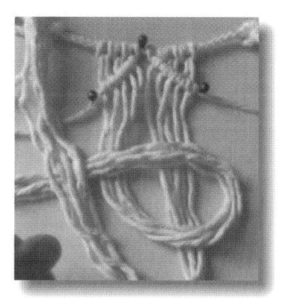

Watch the photos very carefully as you move along with this project and take your time to make sure you are using the right string at the right point of the project.

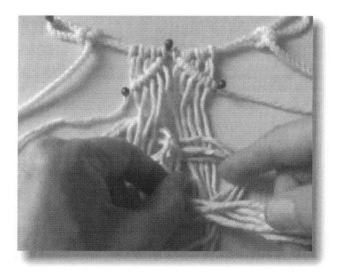

Don't rush, and make sure you have even tension throughout. Practice makes perfect, but with the illustrations to help you, you'll find it's not hard at all to create.

Use the pins along with the knots that you are tying, and work with larger areas all at the same time. This is going to help you keep the project in place as you continue to work throughout the piece.

Pull the ends of the knots through the loops and form the ring in the center of the strings.

For the finished project, make sure that you have all your knots secure and firm throughout, and do your best to make sure it is all even. It is going to take practice before you can get it perfectly each time, but remember that practice does make perfect, and with time, you are going to get it without too much trouble.

Make sure all is even and secure and tie off. Snip off all the loose ends, and you are ready to go!

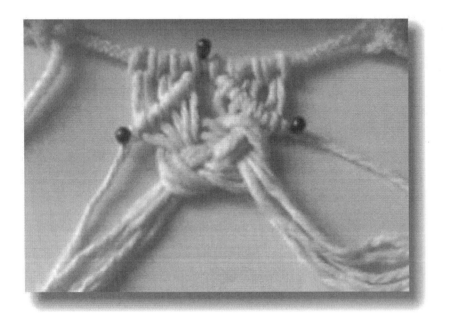

CHAPTER 7:

Sennit Patterns

Square Knots and Half Knot

Macrame knots mostly used, and it might be made as left or right facing.

A half knot is half of a square knot. It might be right facing or left facing; this relies upon the specific side you start from.

Square knots need to have on any occasion four ropes (2 working strings and two filler lines) anyway can have more. The first and last ropes are the working lines. We'll call them working string 1 and 4. The inside edges are filler strings, and we'll number those 2 and 3. These strings will switch puts anyway will regardless keep their one of a kind numbering.

·   Left Facing Half Knot and Square Knot

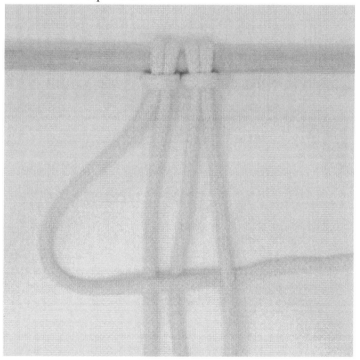

Take working rope four and move it aside under the two filler lines and overworking line 1. .

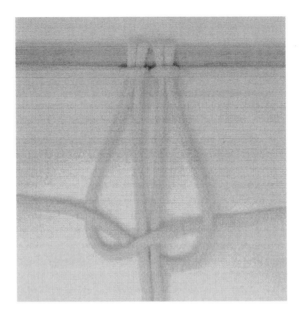

Pull both working lines to fix, keeping the filler ropes straight. This is how to accomplish the left confronting half square knot.

The working lines have now traded spots with working string one on the benefit and working string four on the left. Take working rope one and move it aside over the two filler lines and underworking line 4.

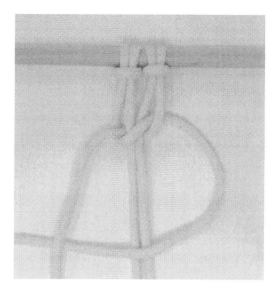

Take working rope four and move it aside under the two filler lines and overworking rope 1.

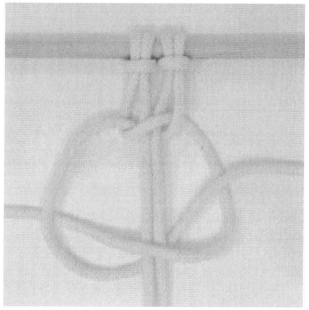

Pull both working strings to fix. Keeping the filler strings straight. This finishes your left facing square knot.

Right Facing Half Knot and Square Knot

Half knot and square knot involving different levels of thump on the right half of the finished knot.

Take the last string (working line 4) and move it aside, over the filler (ropes 2 and 3) and under the mainline (working string 1).

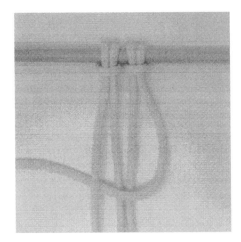

Take working rope 1 and take it aside, under the filler strings and over working rope 4.

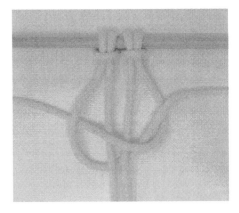

Pull the two ropes to fix, keeping everything straight. A right facing half square knot is exactly what you have here.

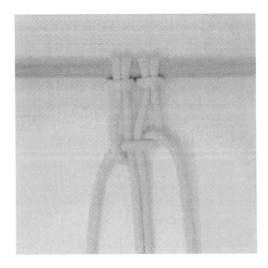

The working ropes have now traded places and working rope 1 is on the benefit and working string 4 is on the left. Take working line 4 over aside, over the filler ropes and under working line 1.

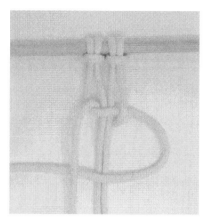

Take working line 1 and move it aside, going under the filler ropes and over working rope 4.

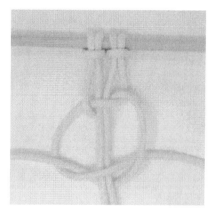

Pull both working lines to fix. This is a correct facing square knot.

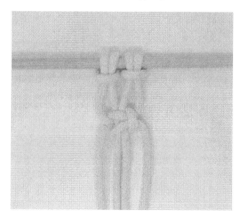

Half Hitch

HISTORY

The Half Hitch's exact history has never been recorded, mainly because it has been around for centuries and is one of the most natural knots to tie. Nevertheless, its form and application mark it out very much as a hitch, and it has a lot of use as a strengthening knot when used in combination with other knots.

BEST USES

While easy to tie in almost any line, the Half Hitch is not particularly strong when used on its own, and tends to unravel in all but the best conditions. However, it is beneficial as a fortifying knot when applied to the working end of another hitch. Thus, it can either hold the other hitch in place or make it's a bond stronger, depending on the circumstances. The Clove Hitch knot is one example of a glitch that can benefit from the addition of a Half Hitch (although it can also be applied to any knot where there is the leftover length in the working end). The Half Hitch is also a beautiful knot and is widely used to create French Whipping and other creative pursuits. The knot can be tied as either a single knot or as Two Half Hitches, with the latter being significantly more durable.

HOW TO MAKE A HALF HITCH

The Half Hitch is exceedingly simple to tie—so much so that many people will have used it countless times in the past without even knowing its name. When using it to anchor a line directly to a bar or similar object, it is tied as follows (to add it to another knot, omit to loop the line around the bar):

STEP 1

Pass your line over the bar. Bring the working end over the standing part.

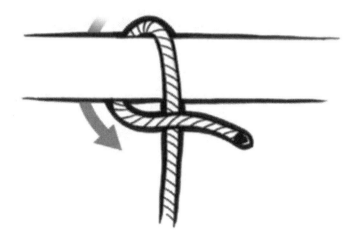

STEP 2

Tuck the working end through the turn formed by the line and pull tight.

STEP 3

To form Two Half Hitches, tie as above, pass the working end around the standing part again, take it first over, then under the standing character, and finally give it back over itself. Pull to tighten.

Double half hitch

The Dual Half-hitch can knot, horizontally, diagonally, or curved. The Macramé knot is generally initiated by lifting the substances on the dowel; another strategy is to join an overhand knot at each strand, which is subsequently glued into aboard. In producing the simple amount double half hitch, a flat cable is put across the hanging strands. Moving left-to-right, the vertical strand intact is subsequently made up, and above the strand together side, its ending is pulled out of its loop.

The Wrapped Knot

A vintage knot technique, the wrapped knot, is seen frequently in plant hangers made from Macramé. The process of making a Wrapped Knot is called lashing in some vintage textile crafts. The wrapped knot is used for securing the bundle of numerous cords that require being grouped. To finish the wrapped knot, cut off the bottom and top ends of the working cord. The wrapped knot is closely related to another pattern known as the linen stitch. The wrapped knot may be used for bracelets, necklaces, the branches of tree decorations. Getting the knots long is quite challenging. It is difficult for practical decorative purposes; as such, it is usually a fantastic challenge to use the wrapped to execute real Macramé projects. Creating the wrapped knots requires a minimum of three cords for holding the knots. The material for the working cord is separate and measures a minimum of 30 inches in length. The knot itself must measure between 1 and 2 inches.

Method

Vertically arrange the cords that hold the knot. At the end of the working cord, tie an overhand knot. Secure this knot to the other cords, on their left. Determine the area to be wrapped and fold the working cord a little beyond this area. Bring the other end of the working cord back to the direction of the knot. Proceed to secure the area folded. Now, wrap the returning working end around the holding cords, allowing it to pass beneath the secured end. Tug it to the left gently.Again, wrap the returning end around the holding cord as described above, making the second wrap to snug close to the first wrap, under the first wrap. Continue this until you have covered the desired area, leaving the working cord's folded end in a loop. Slot the end of the working cord into the loop and pull it all through. Ensure to hold the bundle tight while doing this. At the other end, tug the secured end just at the top. This would pull the folded area in, and with it, the working end. Keep pulling the secured end until the cord goes about halfway through the knot. Cut the bottom and top end of the working cord off at the ends of the knot. If it's only practicing and you would like to reuse your cord, you can skip cutting the ends off.

Alternating Square Knots

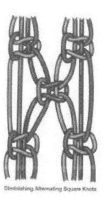

Diminishing Alternating Square Knots

Basic Macramé knots that are extremely popular and common and are considered one of Macramé's most critical basic knots. For perfection to be achieved in constructing this knot, however, constant practice and time are needed.

316

In a simple context, creating a Knots is to tie Square Knots in a vertical row such that in the other rows, you merely alternate the cords to form knots. From two knots, different knots, select two cords to shift the alternating square knots' position. This creates a woven and interconnected design. Before attempting to make a pattern, it is essential for you first to learn how to make Square Knots. A necessary application is in the production of striped clutches. Practicing requires about six 36 inches cords or more.

Before you begin making your knots, fold the six (or more) cords into 12 by folding each cord into halves. For this manual, we would be considering the use of six cords, which is the minimum number of cords required for this pattern. Fasten your cords to the board where the folds are and number the cords from left to right.

Tie each of the square knots using four cords; two will act as working cords while the other two act as fillers. It is also important to note, as would be described in this procedure, that each row must be created to move the cord on your extreme left to the one your absolute right.

Now, let's get down the business of creating our pattern.

Forming groups of four chords, tie square knots to create the first rows of two fillers and two working cords. We have square knots 1—4, 5—8, and 9—12.

Combine cord three and four from knot 1—4 with cord five and six knots 5—8 to create the second row. Tie the remaining square knot with cord 7—10. At most times, you would tie square knots alternate to each other together tightly. Some space may be needed in some different patterns; so, this depends on the exact kind of results you hope to achieve. Most importantly, though, maintain even row spaces.

Do step 1 again, creating the ASK's third row with the 1—4, 5—8, and 9—12 cords.

Now, redo steps two and three once or more.

Lark's Head Knot

This is an excellent beginning knot for any project and can be used as the foundation for the project's base. Use lightweight cord for this – it can be purchased at craft stores or online, wherever you get your macramé supplies. Oversee the photos as you move along with this project, and take your time to make sure you are using the right string at the right point of the project.

Don't rush, and make sure you have even tension throughout. Practice makes perfect, but with the illustrations to help you, you'll find it's not hard to create.

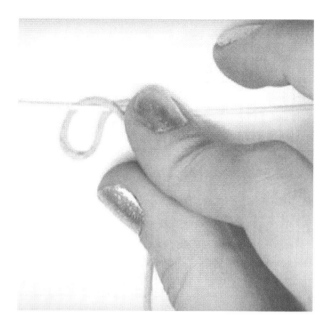

Use the base string as the core part of the knot, working around the string's end with the cord. Make sure all is even as you loop the string around the base of the cord.

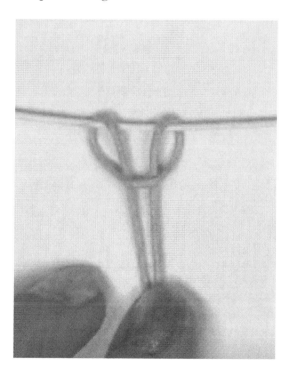

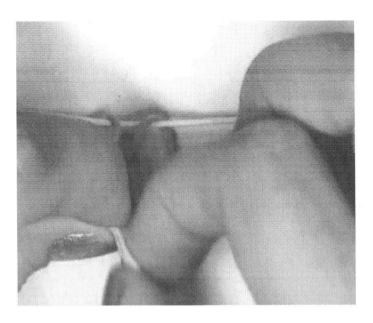

Create a slip knot around the base of the string and keep both ends even as you pull the cord through the center of the piece.

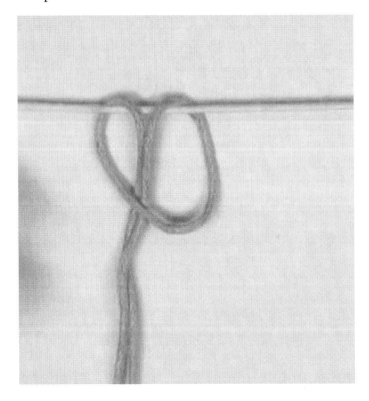

For the finished project, make sure that you have all your knots secure and firm throughout, and do your best to make sure it is all even. It is going to take practice before you are able to get it perfectly each time, but remember that practice does make perfect, and with time, you are going to get it without too much trouble.

Make sure all is even and secure, and tie off. Snip off all the loose ends, and you are ready to go!

CHAPTER 8:

Spiral Knots

Spiral Stitches

This is the perfect knot to use for basket hangings, decorations, or any projects that are going to require you to put weight on the project. Use a heavier weight cord for this, which you can find at craft stores or online.

Watch the photos very carefully as you move along with this project, and take your time to make sure you are using the right string in the right point of the project.

Don't rush, and make sure you have even tension throughout. Practice makes perfect, but with the illustrations to help you, you'll find it's not hard at all to create.

Use different colors to start so you can find it easy to see where you should be on the project. Take your time and don't rush it – go slow at first and find where you should be on the project before you move on to the next step.

Go through one row at a time, following the photos as you work each set of knots. Move on to the next one after you get through the first set.

Once you go through the set of knots on one side, you are going to come back and do it on the next. Then, take the center of these knots and work through that to create a new set.

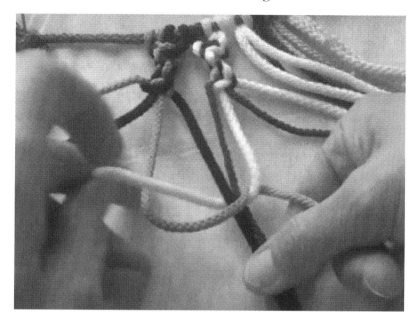

Next, you are going to work through the same sequence on the other side.

Keep the stitches even until you get to the bottom.

For the finished project, make sure that you have all your knots secure and firm throughout, and do your best to make sure it is all even. It is going to take practice before you are able to get it perfectly each time, but remember that practice does make perfect, and with time, you are going to get it without too much trouble.

Make sure all is even and secure, and tie off. Snip off all the loose ends, and you are ready to go!

This is a great beginning knot for any project, and can be used as the foundation for the base of the project. Use lightweight cord for this – it can be purchased at craft stores or online, wherever you get your macramé supplies.

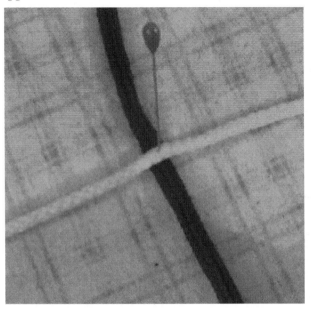

Watch the photos very carefully as you move along with this project, and take your time to make sure you are using the right string in the right point of the project.

Don't rush, and make sure you have even tension throughout. Practice makes perfect, but with the illustrations to help you, you'll find it's not hard at all to create.

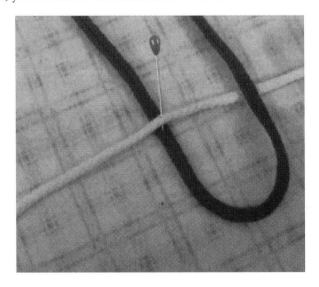

Use a pin to help keep everything in place as you are working.

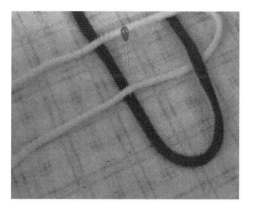

Weave the strings in and out of each other as you can see in the photos. It helps to practice with different colors to help you see what is going on.

Pull the knot tight, then repeat for the next row on the outside.

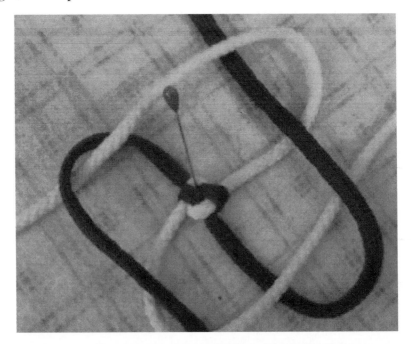

Continue to do this as often as you like to create the knot. You can make it as thick as you like, depending on the project. You can also create more than one length on the same cord.

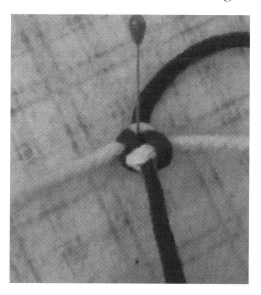

For the finished project, make sure that you have all your knots secure and firm throughout, and do your best to make sure it is all even. It is going to take practice before you are able to get it perfectly each time, but remember that practice does make perfect, and with time, you are going to get it without too much trouble.

Make sure all is even and secure, and tie off. Snip off all the loose ends, and you are ready to go!

Half-square Spiral Knot

They also called as helix knots, the spirals of the half square, are simple to create, solid and decorative.

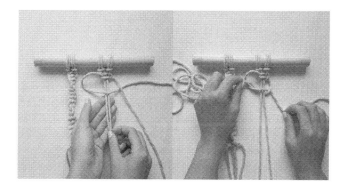

1 Attach step 1 of a knotted square, pick the two cord pairs you choose to use, and take the left cord above the two Middle cords and below the right cord to make a D-shaped curve backward.

First, take the right-hand tail of the chord and move it into the D-shaped backward, passing through the two cords in the Middle and above the left string.

2 Not like the square knot, you don't need to duplicate or switch the sides that you're focused on to proceed to build a series of knots. Do Phase 1 several times, instead. The macramé knots, of course, continue spiraling.

Winding Or Spiral Stitch

A winding fasten needs at any rate 4 ropes, 2 working and 2 filler lines, however more can be utilized. Intellectually number these lines 1-4 moving left to right. Lines 1 and 4 are your working strings and lines 2 and 3 are your filler lines.

These headings are the manner by which to make a left facing winding fastens, yet you can likewise begin the correct side and utilize good facing half knots.

Take working line 1 and move it to one side, over the filler lines yet under working string 4.

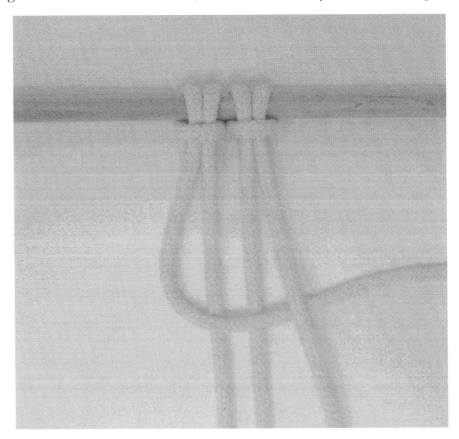

Move working rope 4 to one side, going under the filler ropes yet over working string 1.

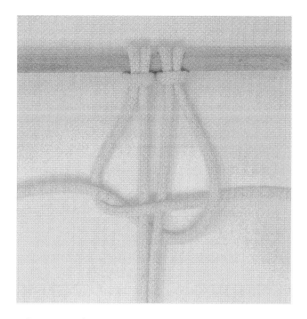

Pull both working ropes to fix around the filler lines.

Continue making all the more half knots a similar path as above. As you work, your strings will begin to winding.

Clove Hitch

A Clove Hitch, likewise called a Double Half Hitch, makes lines in your ventures. They can be worked on a level plane, askew or diagonally, and now and again, vertically.

Horizontal Clove Hitch

This makes a progression of knots that go over your macrame venture. In this knot, the primary string is the filler line and rest of the lines is working ropes.

Take your left rope, the filler string, and hold it on a level plane over different ropes.

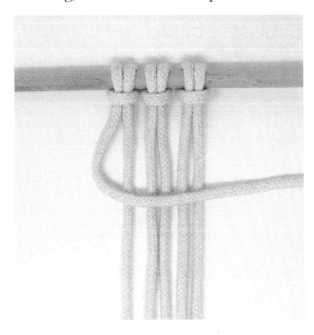

Take the following rope (your first working line) and present it, up, and around the filler rope towards the left to shape a counter-clockwise circle.

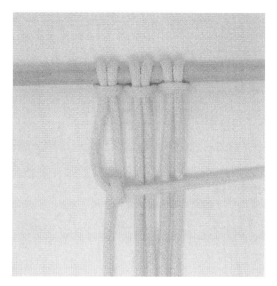

Take a similar working rope and to one side of the main knot, take it up, finished, and through the circle. There should now be two knots sitting close to one another.

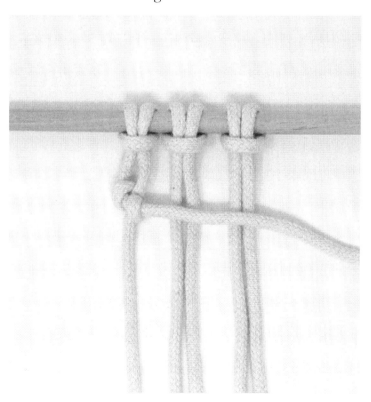

Continue the clove hitch knots by utilizing the following working rope around a similar filler line. Keep making hitches until you have the look you need.

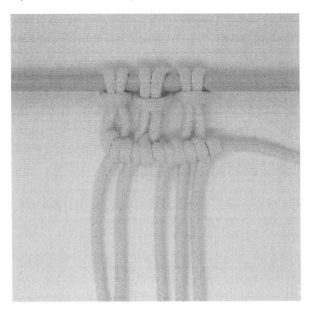

Diagonal Clove Hitch

This makes a progression of corner to corner knots in your venture.

Take the line on the left, the filler string, and hold it askew over different ropes.

Replicate stages 2 through 4 of the level clove hitch, descending slantingly rather than straight over.

Replicate until you have the look you need.

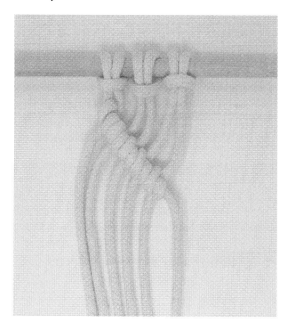

Overhand Knot

The Overhand Knot is an essential knot that integrates various ropes. It very well may be finished with numerous lines or only one rope.

Overlay the line into a circle.

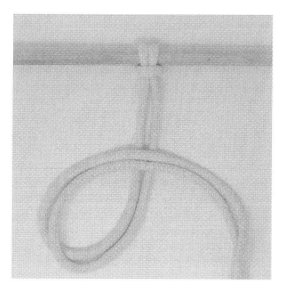

Pass the finishes of the lines through the circle to fix or tighten.

CHAPTER 9:

Panel Patterns

Hanging Macramé Vase

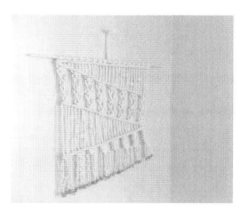

Supplies:

- **Masking tape**
- **Tape measure or ruler**
- **30 meters thick nylon cord**
- Small round vase (with around 20 cm diameter)

Cut eight cords measuring 3.5 yards or 3.2 meters each and set aside one of them. Cut a cord that measures 31.5 inches and set it aside, as well. Then, cut one cord that measures 55 inches.

Now, group eight lengths of cord together—the ones you did not set aside, of course, and mark the center with a piece of tape.

Wrap the cords by holding them down together and take around 80 cm of it to make a tail—just like what you see below.

Wrap the cord around the back of the long section and make sure to keep your thumb on the tail. Then, wrap the cord around the main cord group. Make sure it is firm, but do not make it too tight. If you can make the loop bigger, that would be good, too.

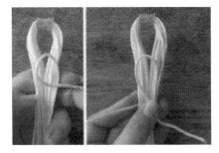

Do it 13 more times through the loop and go and pull the tail down so the loop could soften up. Stop letting the cords overlap by pulling them whenever necessary and then cut both ends so they would not be seen anymore.

Divide the cords into groups of four and secure the ends with tape.

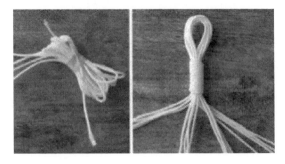

Get the group of cords that you have not used yet and make sure to measure 11.5 inches from the beginning—or on top. Do the overhand knot and get the cord on the left-hand side. Fold it over two of the cords and let it go under the cord on the right-hand side.

Fold the fourth cord and let it pass under the leftmost cord then up the loop of the first cord. Make sure to push it under the large knot so that it would be firm.

Make more half-hitches until you form more twists. Stop when you see that you have made around 12 of them and then repeat with the rest of the cords.

Now, it is time to make the basket for the vase. What you must do here is measure 9 centimeters from your group of cords. Tie an overhand knot and make sure to mark with tape.

Let the two cord groups come together by laying them side by side.

Tie the cords down but make sure to keep them flat. Make sure that the knots will not overlap, or else you would have a messy project—which is not what you would want to happen. Use two cords from the left as starting point and then bring the two cords on the right over the top of the loop. Loop them together under the bottom cords and then work them back up once more.

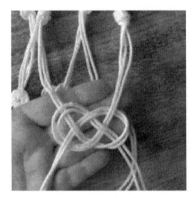

Now, find your original loop and thread the same cords behind them. Then, let them pass through the left-hand cords by making use of the loop once more.

Let the knot move once you already have it in position. It should be around 3 inches or 7.5 cm from the overhand knots. After doing so, make sure that you flatten the cords and let them sit next to each other until you have a firm knot on top. Keep dividing and letting cords come together.

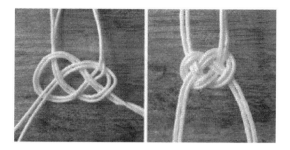

Next, get the cord on the left-hand side and let it go over the 2nd and 3rd cords before folding the fourth one under the first two cords. You would then see a square knot forming between the 2nd and 3rd cords. You should then repeat the process on the right-hand side. Open the cord on the right side and let it go under the left-hand cord. Repeat this process thrice, then join the four-square knots that you have made by laying them out on a table.

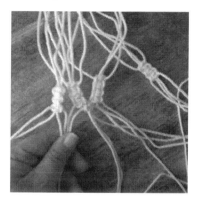

You will then see that the cords have come together at the base. Now, you must start wrapping the base by wrapping a 1.4-meter cord and wrap around 18 times.

To finish, just cut the cords the way you want. It is okay if they are not of the same length so that there would be variety—and they would look prettier on your wall. Make sure to tie overhand knots at the end of each of them before placing the vase inside.

Copper Pipe Wall Hanging DIY

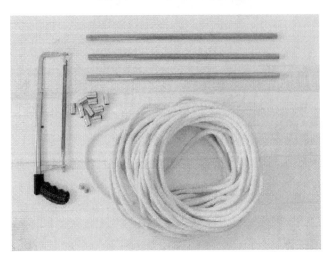

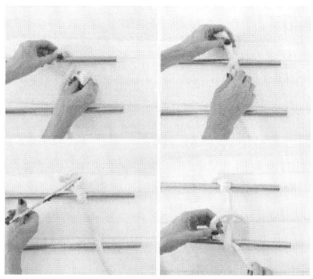

Supplies needed for this DIY are:
- 25 yards of 1/2" (size 5) Cotton Piping
- 3 copper pipes measuring 1/2" x 2'
- 19 copper couplings 1/2"
- 4 copper tube caps 1/2"
- scissors
- a hack saw
- a file

Begin cutting off length of cotton, and then tie knot onto one of the bars. Then cut off the excess. Next tie another knot around the second pipe so that the two copper pipes were apart.

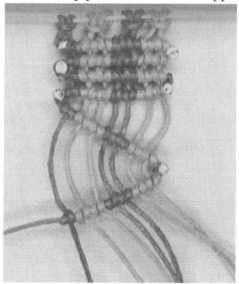

Frivolite knot

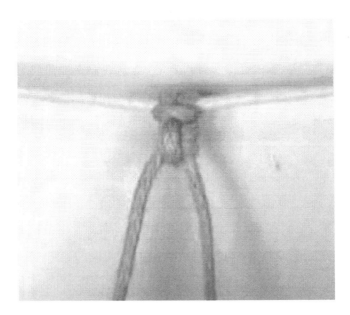

This is a great beginning knot for any project, and can be used as the foundation for the base of the project. Use lightweight cord for this – it can be purchased at craft stores or online, wherever you get your macramé supplies.

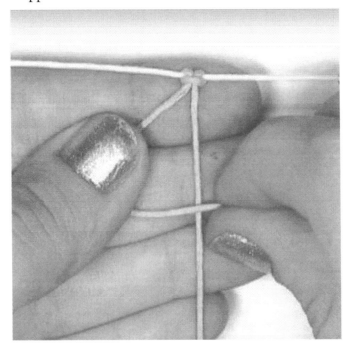

Watch the photos very carefully as you move along with this project, and take your time to make sure you are using the right string in the right point of the project.

Don't rush, and make sure you have even tension throughout. Practice makes perfect, but with the illustrations to help you, you'll find it's not hard at all to create.

Use the base string as the guide to hold it in place, then tie the knot onto this. This is a very straightforward knot, watch the photo and follow the directions you see.

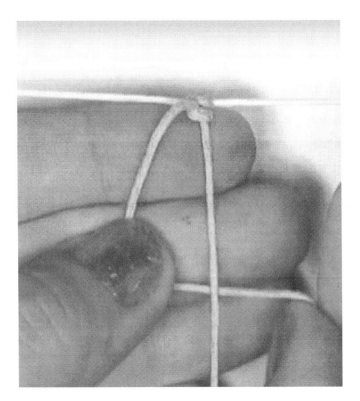

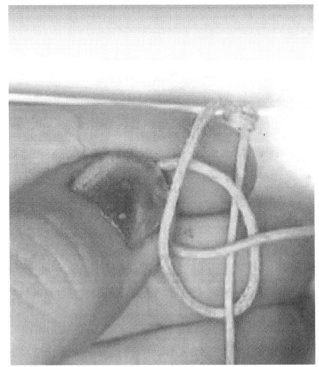

Pull the end of the cord up and through the center.

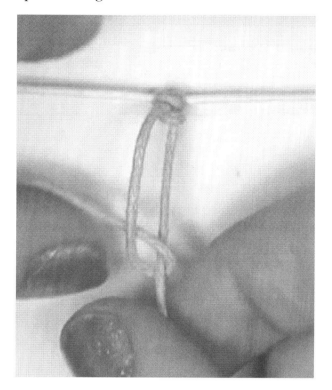

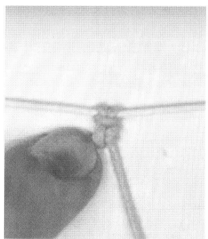

For the finished project, make sure that you have all your knots secure and firm throughout, and do your best to make sure it is all even. It is going to take practice before you are able to get it perfectly each time, but remember that practice does make perfect, and with time, you are going to get it without too much trouble.

Make sure all is even and secure, and tie off. Snip off all the loose ends, and you are ready to go!

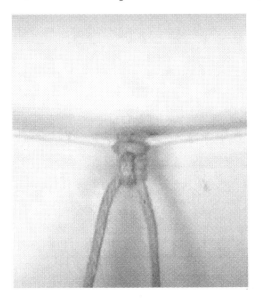

Single Half Stitch

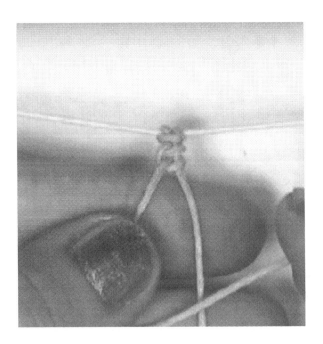

This is a great beginning knot for any project, and can be used as the foundation for the base of the project. Use lightweight cord for this – it can be purchased at craft stores or online, wherever you get your macramé supplies.

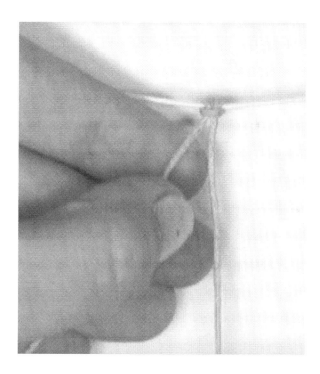

Watch the photos very carefully as you move along with this project, and take your time to make sure you are using the right string in the right point of the project.

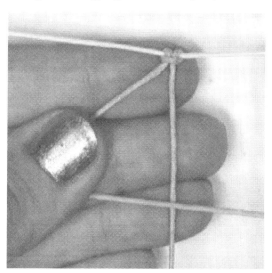

Don't rush, and make sure you have even tension throughout. Practice makes perfect, but with the illustrations to help you, you'll find it's not hard at all to create.

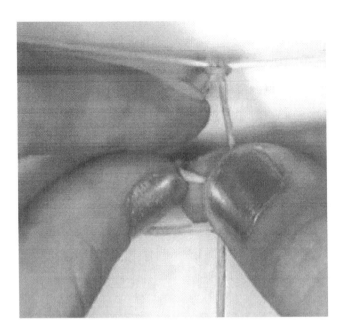

Use both hands to work around the cord, and make sure you follow each loop before you put on the next loop. One step at a time as you see in the photo, and you're going to be fine.

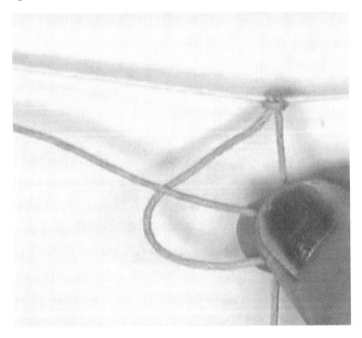

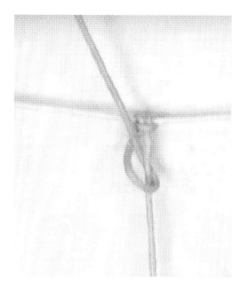

For the finished project, make sure that you have all your knots secure and firm throughout, and do your best to make sure it is all even. It is going to take practice before you are able to get it perfectly each time, but remember that practice does make perfect, and with time, you are going to get it without too much trouble.

Make sure all is even and secure, and tie off. Snip off all the loose ends, and you are ready to go!

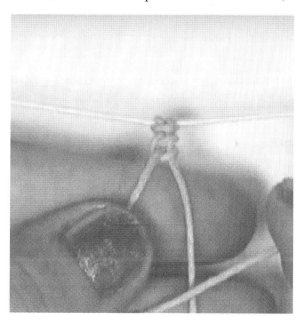

Reverse Lark's Head Knot

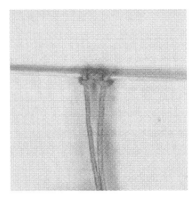

This is a great beginning knot for any project and can be used as the foundation for the base of the project. Use lightweight cord for this – it can be purchased at craft stores or online, wherever you get your macramé supplies.

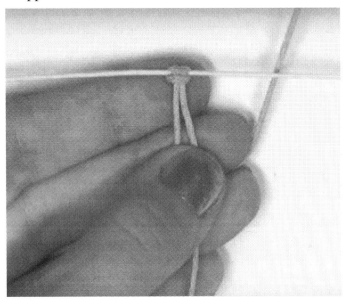

Watch the photos very carefully as you move along with this project, and take your time to make sure you are using the right string in the right point of the project.

Don't rush, and make sure you have even tension throughout. Practice makes perfect, but with the illustrations to help you, you'll find it's not hard at all to create.

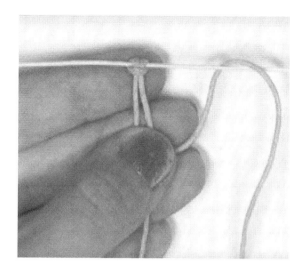

Use two hands to make sure that you have everything even and tight as you work. You can use tweezers if it helps to make it tight against the base of the string.

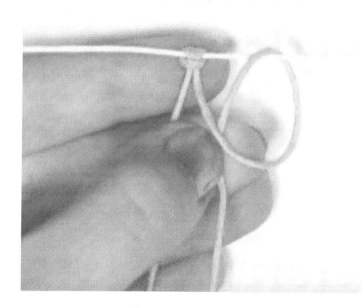

356

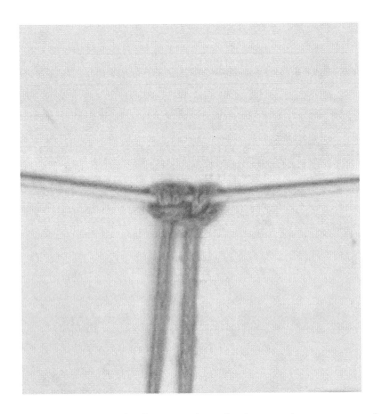

Use both hands to pull the string evenly down against the base string to create the knot.

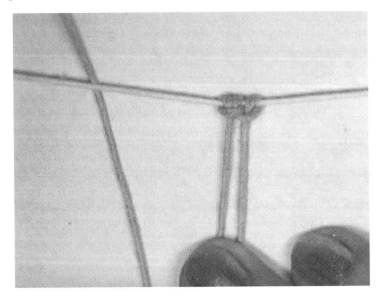

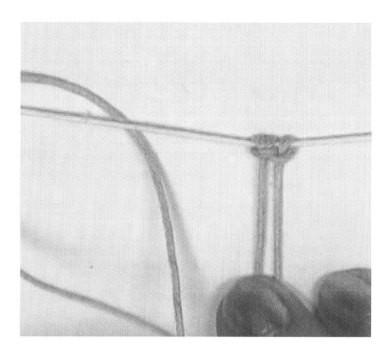

Again, keep the base even as you pull the center, creating the firm knot against your guide cord.

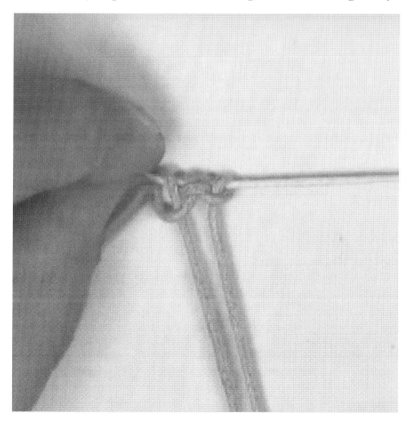

For the finished project, make sure that you have all your knots secure and firm throughout, and do your best to make sure it is all even. It is going to take practice before you are able to get it perfectly each time, but remember that practice does make perfect, and with time, you are going to get it without too much trouble.

Make sure all is even and secure, and tie off. Snip off all the loose ends, and you are ready to go!

CHAPTER 10:

Panel Patterns

Dream Catcher

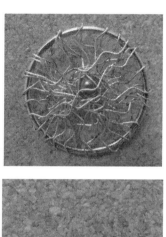

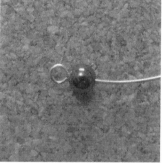

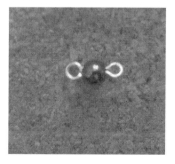

Step 1 - First, we will create the dream catcher centerpiece for the bracelet.
Push the 6mm hematite bead into the center of the wire shape and move the wire wraps over and around it to secure it in place.
Step 2 - Cut a 5cm length of 6mm wire.

Make a small loop in one end of the wire using the ends of the round-nosed pliers. Thread on 4mm hematite bead onto the wire.

Step 3 - Make a second small loop to match the first, after the hematite bead. Trim off any excess wire as needed.

Step 4 - Create two more hematite bead components to match the one created in steps 2 and 3.

Step 5 - Using three 4mm jump rings, attach the feathers to one loop on each hematite bead component.

Step 6 - Attach three further 4mm jump rings to the opposite ends of the hematite bead component. These will be the dream catcher tails.

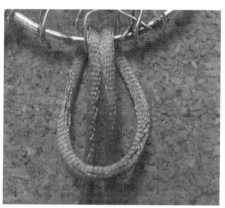

Step 7 - Use the last three 4mm jump rings to connect the tails to the wrapped wire shape. You may find it easier to use both pairs of pliers to close the jump rings in this step.

Step 8 - Gently heat the ends of all the rattail cords to seal them and prevent fraying.

Using a lark's head knot, attach one of the 40-inch cord to the center of one side of the dream catcher.

A lark's head knot is created by folding the cord in half and then threading the loop formed in the middle over the dream catcher's rim. The long cord ends are threaded through the loop and pulled until the loop closes around the metal rim.

The loop can be threaded through either direction, but you will need to do all three the same way as doing so front to back creates a knot that looks different from threading the cord back to front.

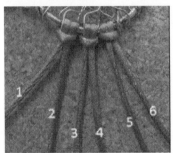

Step 9 - Attach the other two 40-inch cords to the dream catcher, in the same way, one of each side of the first.

Step 10 - Spread out the cords and mentally number them from 1 to 6.

Step 11 - Thread one 8mm hematite bead onto thread 2. Using threads 1 and 3 ties one square knot underneath the bead.

Step 12 - Thread one 8mm hematite bead onto thread 5. Using threads 4 and 6 ties one square knot underneath the bead.

Step 13- Separate the cords, so that cord 1 and 6 are laid out to the side; cords 3 and 4 are straight down in the center, and cords 2 and 5 are in between.

Step 14 - Using cords 2 and 5 ties two square knots around cords 3 and 4.

Step 15 - Separate the cords into two sets of three. Thread an 8mm hematite bead onto cord 1. Using cords 1 and 3 and tie one square knot around cord 2.

Step 16 - Repeat step 15 using the second set of three cords. The bead is threaded onto cord six, and then cords 4 and 6 are used to tie a square knot around cord 5.
Steps 11 to 16 form the pattern of the bracelet.

Step 17 - Repeat steps 11 - 16 once one so that there are four rows of beads.

Step 18 - Use cords 1 and 6 to tie a square knot around the four remaining cords.

Step 19 - Carefully cut off the remaining lengths of cords 2 and 5 leaving a 3mm tail. Gently heat the ends, so they melt slightly. Press this melted end against the two spare central cords (cords 3 and 4). Take your time completing this step so as not to damage any of the other cords.

The rat tail cord's melted end gets quite hot and can stick to skin so it best to use the point of your scissors or a needle to complete this step.

Step 20 - Tie another square knot directly below the last knot.

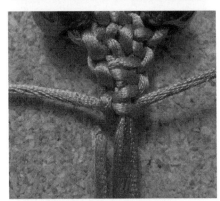

Step 21 - Measure down 1.5 inches and fold the central rattail cords in half.

Step 22 - Hold the central cords between two fingers to meet the square knots and trim off the excess cord. Gently heat the edges to stop them fraying.

Step 23 - Tie a square knot around the folded over cords to hold them in place.

This creates a loop that will become part of the bracelet's fastener.
Pull this knot tight.

Step 24 - Continue tying square knots until there is only 1 cm of the loop left showing.
This loop needs to be sized so that it is a tight fit for the disk bead to fit through. Test with your
bead and adjust as needed before moving on to step 25.

Step 25 - Cut off the excess cords leaving a 3mm tail. Gently heat the ends, so they melt slightly. Press this melted end against the final square knot. Take care of completing this step so as not to damage any of the other cords.

The melted end of the rat tail cord gets quite hot and can stick to skin so it best to use the point of your scissors or a needle to complete this step.

Step 26 - Repeat steps 8 and 9 to attach the three 20 lengths of rattail cord to the dream catcher's opposite side.

Take care to form the lark's heads knot the same as you did on the other side.

Step 27- Repeat steps 10 - 16 to create hematite beads to match the one already built.

Step 28 - Use cords 1 and 6 to tie a square knot around the four remaining cords.

Step 29 - Carefully cut off the remaining lengths of cords 2 and 5 leaving a 3mm tail. Gently heat the ends, so they melt slightly. Press this melted end against the two spare central cords (cords 3 and 4). Take care of completing this step so as not to damage any of the other cords.

The melted end of the rat tail cord gets quite hot and can stick to skin so it best to use the point of your scissors or a needle to complete this step.

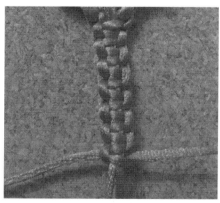

Step 30- Tie another square knot directly below the other knot.

Step 31 - Continue tying square knots until you have a Sennett measuring 2cm long.

Step 32- Trim off the excess knotting cords leaving a 3mm tail. Gently heat the ends, so they melt slightly. Press this melted end against the two remaining central cords (cords 3 and 4).

Take your time completing this step so as not to damage any of the other cords.

The melted end of the rat tail cord gets quite hot and can stick to skin so it best to use the point of your scissors or a needle to complete this step.

Step 33 - Now trim off one of the central cords in the same way described in step 32.

Step 34 - Thread the hematite disk bead on the remaining central cord.

Step 35- Leave a 3mm gap between the final square knot and the bead, tie one overhand knot to secure it on the cord.

Step 36 - Trim off the remaining cord and melt the end to prevent fraying.

Lark's Head Half Stitches Knot

This is a great beginning knot for any project, and can be used as the foundation for the base of the project. Use lightweight cord for this – it can be purchased at craft stores or online, wherever you get your macramé supplies.

Watch the photos very carefully as you move along with this project, and take your time to make sure you are using the right string in the right point of the project.

Don't rush, and make sure you have even tension throughout. Practice makes perfect, but with the illustrations to help you, you'll find it's not hard at all to create.

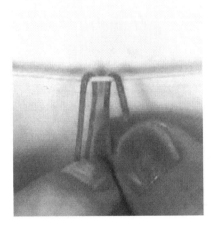

You are going to work this the same as the lark's head, just going in the opposite direction. Make sure you keep it firm against the base of the cord and work through the steps as you did with the last.

Watch the photos as a guide, following each step as you see them outlined there.

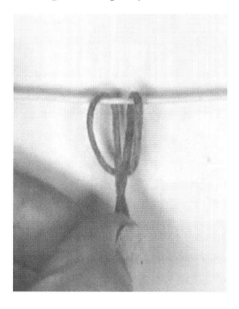

For the finished project, make sure that you have all your knots secure and firm throughout, and do your best to make sure it is all even. It is going to take practice before you are able to get it perfectly each time, but remember that practice does make perfect, and with time, you are going to get it without too much trouble.

Make sure all is even and secure, and tie off. Snip off all the loose ends, and you are ready to go!

Diagonal Double Half Knot

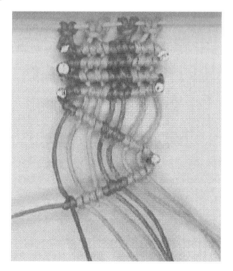

This is the perfect knot to use for basket hangings, decorations, or any projects that are going to require you to put weight on the project. Use a heavier weight cord for this, which you can find at craft stores or online.

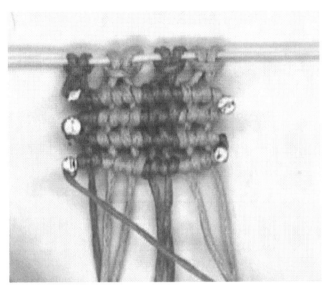

Watch the photos very carefully as you move along with this project, and take your time to make sure you are using the right string in the right point of the project.

Don't rush, and make sure you have even tension throughout. Practice makes perfect, but with the illustrations to help you, you'll find it's not hard at all to create.

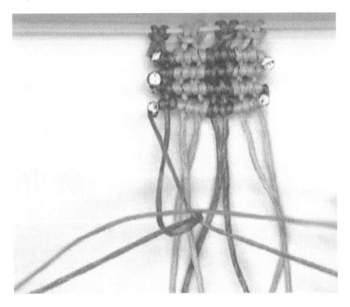

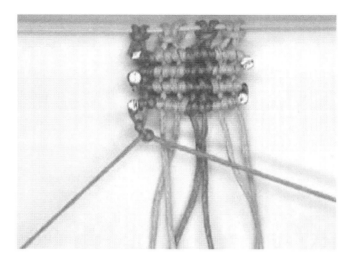

Start at the top of the project and work your way toward the bottom. Keep it even as you work your way throughout the piece. Tie the knots at 4 inch intervals, working your way down the entire thing.

Weave in and out throughout, watching the photo as you can see for the right placement of the knots. Again, it helps to practice with different colors so you can see what you need to do throughout the piece.

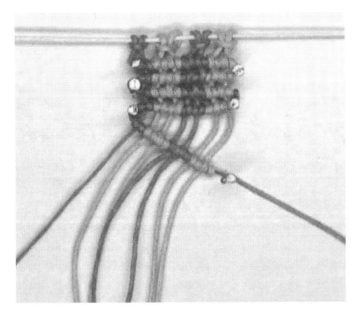

For the finished project, make sure that you have all your knots secure and firm throughout, and do your best to make sure it is all even. It is going to take practice before you are able to get it perfectly each time, but remember that practice does make perfect, and with time, you are going to get it without too much trouble.

Make sure all is even and secure, and tie off. Snip off all the loose ends, and you are ready to go!

CHAPTER 11:

Projects

DIY Macramé Wall Hanging:

Amacramé wall suspended in a home A macramé wall hanging is an easy DIY project that adds a handmade touch to every room. Given its size, this is a simple project that takes you an hour or two to finish. It gets together quickly, and you will find many ways of adding your style.

This is only one of many free macramé patterns, including plant hangers, bookmarks, curtains, etc.

The knots you use to mount this macramé wall include the head knot, the spiral knot, and the square knot.

What you will need to finish this macramé DIY hanging wall:

Cotton Macramé cord (200 feet) and 61 meters (3/4-inch circumference, 24) "wooden dwell (3/4, "24-inch) I've been using cotton clothesline on my macramé string. It looks entirely natural and is quite cheap.

The wooden dowel must not be such exact measurements and use whatever scale you like in the wood dowel as long as all ropes are placed over it. If you want to give it an outdoor experience, you can use a tree branch about the same height.

Make a hanger for your wooden dowel.

Cut a piece of macramé cord that is three feet (1 meter) and tied to a wooden dowel. Connect the two sides of the wooden dowel to each end of the thread. You are going to use this to mount your macramé project when it is over. In the beginning, I like to attach it, so I can hang up the macramé project when I tie knots. It is much easier to work this way than to determine it.

Cut your macramé rope into 12 string lengths 15 feet (4.5 meters) long. It might sound like a lot of rope, but knots take up more cord than you expect. If you need it, there's no way to make the rope thicker, so you better cut it than you will.

Fold one of the macramé cores in half on the wooden dowel and use a ladle's head knot to tie it to a wooden dowel.

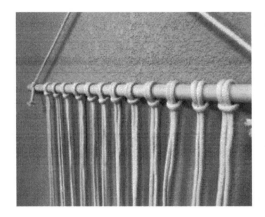

Join the other cords in the same way Take the first four strings and make left facing spiral Knot (also referred to as a half-knot Lynton) by tying 13 half knots.

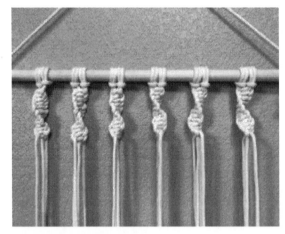

Using four rope to make a further spiral knot of 13 half knots using the same pair of four ropes. Continue to work in four-chord. You should have a minimum of six spiral knots before you finish.

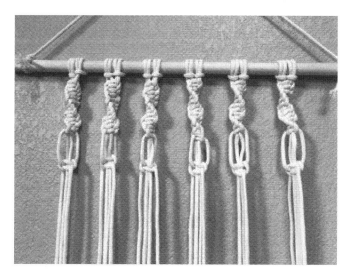

Scale about two inches down from the last knot in a spiral point.

Make a right knot profile with the first four strings. Continue to make the correct knots face throughout this row. Do your best to keep them all even horizontally. You're going to end up with six knots together.

The second row of square knots now is the time to start the square knots so we can have the knots "V" shape

Set open the first two strings and the last two strings. Consider each group of four right-facing square knots. You now have a second line with the first two and last two unknotted cords and five square knots. It doesn't matter how you space them; just keep them for each row together.

Keep Decreasing the Square knots A "V" formed from the square knots in the third row, the first four strings and the last four strings will be left out. You're going to have four knots together. For the fourth row at the top, leave six cords and at the end six cords. You're going to have 3 square ties. In the fifth row, in the beginning, you'll have eight cords and at the end eight cords. Now you're going to have two square ties. For the sixth and final row, ten cords at the beginning and ten cords at the end are to be released. It lets you make a last square knot with four strings.

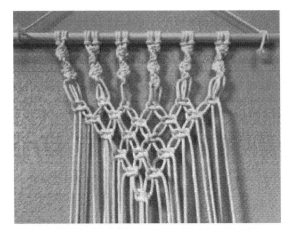

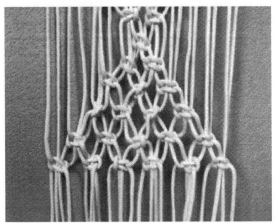

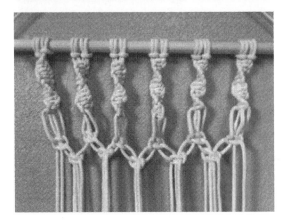

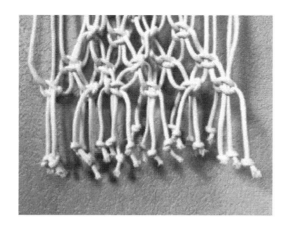

DIY Macramé Feathers:

Delightful, wispy macramé feathers have been stopping up my online life takes care lately — however, I'm not frantic about it. They're unimaginably lovely, and I've certainly gotten myself bookmarking them to buy later, to hang in the children's room. I was likewise curious to know how they were made.

You'll Need:

1) 5mm single wind cotton string

2) Texture stiffener

3) Sharp texture shears

4) Feline brush

5) Ruler

For a medium measured plume, cut:

1) 1 32" strand for the spine

2) 10-12 14" strands for the top

3) 8-10 12" strands for the center

4) 6-8 10" strands for the base

Steps:

Overlap the 32" strand into equal parts. Take one of the 14" strands, overlap it down the middle, and fold it under the spine.

Take another 14" strand, crease it down the middle, and supplement it into the big strand circle. Pull it through and lay it horizontally on the restricting strand.

Presently pull the base strands all the path through the top circle. This is your knot!

Pull the two sides firmly. On the following line, you'll interchange the beginning side. If you laid the even strand from left to right the first time, you'd put the level strand from options right to left straightaway.

Lay the first collapsed strand under the spine, string another collapsed strand into its circle. Pull the lower strands through the top circle. Also, fix.

Continue onward and work gradually down in size.

Make sure to push the strands up to fix - snatch the base of the center (spine) strand with one hand and with another, push the strands up. When you're set, drag the fringe downwards to meet the base of the center strand.

At that point, could you give it a rough trim? This helps direct the shape as well as assists with brushing the strands out. The shorter the strands, the simpler, to be completely honest. It likewise helps to have a sharp pair of texture shears!

After a rough trim, place the quill on a stable surface as you'll be using a feline brush to brush out the cording. The brush will harm any fragile or wood surface, so I recommend using a self-mending cutting mat or even a smoothed out cardboard box.

When your plume has hardened up a bit, you would now be able to return and give it the last trim. This, I would state, is the most challenging part. Relax. It's smarter to trim just a little more! What's more, you may need to modify your trim contingent upon how regularly you're moving the piece. When you're ended cutting, you can even give it another wanderer of texture stiffener for good measure. And afterward, you'll be ready to hang your piece!

DIY Macrame Keychains

1) Update the keychain you've had since before you can remember
2) Make a charming ring
3) Give a lot of keys, so when you lock yourself out you don't need to break into your place
4) Embellish your ruck bag
5) Embellish your satchel
6) Make the snazziest gear tag on the baggage claim

7) Get sorted out by making a different key ring for all those small rewards cards

8) Stocking stuffers, birthday presents, present wrap additional items

Supplies for DIY Tassel and Macramé Keychains:

1) 1 ring

2) 3/16 natural cotton piping cord

3) Beads

4) Weaving floss or yarn

5) Small Rubber Band (Keychain Only)

6) Scissors

Steps:

1) For both, you'll start with two 50 or so bits of line. Circle each through the loop with a larkspur hitch, making the outside strands go around 2/3 the string's length. (See the free download for step by step photographs.)

2) For the keychain, make around five square knots, include the globule, make a half square knot underneath it, and tie the rest off in a decoration.

3) For the keychain, create around 16 half square knots and end it off with an embellishment.

4) To give your decoration the extravagant ideal shaft, use your preferred colors of yarn.

5) Separate the rope at the closures, trim it up, and you're done!

Expert tip:

To cut the tuft base impeccably straight, press it levels and wrap it with a bit of tape. Cut the tape down the middle, expel it, and ponder about the ideal fringe.

Make Keychains with Beads and Tassels:

Keychains (beneath left) and (above) use a similar method, yet change up the quantity of dots and length of the tuft.

1) For both, you'll start by tying a 10-16 piece of yarn to your loop with a larkspur hitch.

2) Include the beads.

3) Cut yarn for a tuft—we used around 20 bits of wool. (You pick the length and softness. Make it twice the length you need your clump.) Center it under the dot and tie it on with a square knot. Take care of your dabs and decoration and double the knot.

4) Overlap the tuft into equal parts and wrap the neck with yarn or dental floss using the means in our printed guidelines or this video.

5) Trim the closures. That is, it!

Make A Striped Clove Hitch Keychain:

A keychain may look extravagant and cluttered—however, it takes two fundamental knots to get its attractive custom colored palette.

1) Start with two 20 or so bits of string (you can generally cut them shorter, so it's smarter to begin long). Circle each through the keyring with a larkspur hitch, making the outside strands somewhat longer than the ones within.

2) Include vertical clove knots with a couple of different shades of yarn. This video has simple guidelines to kick you off, including how to gauge your wool. We completed two columns, each in the original two colors, and one line in the third color.

3) Make a full square knot in the center.

4) Include another arrangement of vertical clove hitch, turning around what you did on the top.

5) A quick trim of the closures polishes it off.

6) Interlaced and macramé keychains

Make A Folded Braid Keychain:

This Keychain making is effortless.

1) Cut three bits of rope somewhat more than twice the length you need for the completed key holder.

2) Stack them, even the strands, and wrap one end with a small elastic band a couple of inches from the ends.

3) Do a straightforward mesh. Stop when you are the same distance from the closures as the elastic band is.

4) Circle one end through the keychain. If you'd like, but the elastic band around the two
 Closures to hold them erect. 5) Tie knots in the part of the bargains to wrap it up.

DIY Macramé Necklace:

Macramé has gotten uncontrollably mainstream over the last few years for its uniqueness, high quality, and tasteful look. Making macramé yourself gives you an excellent opportunity to create unique pieces. As of late, we shared an instructional exercise for some lovely macramé wall artistry structures that you can add to your home or office style. Here we present an instructional practice for a straightforward DIY macramé necklace, ideal for matching with all of your mid-year outfits!

Making Your Necklace:

You will need a chain and decorative discoveries. We found our copper chain at our nearby jewelry store and afterward used a lobster fastener with two-hop rings

Ensure that the beads are a similar thickness as your string or the beads will fall off!

DIY Wreath of Nature

Just imagine having a Macramé wreath in your home! This one is inspired by nature and is one of the most creative things you could do with your time!

What you need:

Clips or tape

Fabric glue

Wreath or ring frame

80 yards 12" cords

160 yards 17-18" cords

140 yards 14-16" cords

120 yards 12-13" cords

Instructions:

Mount the cords on top of the wreath and make the crown knot folding one of the cords in half. Let the cords pass through the ring and then wrap a knot and make sure to place it in front of the ring. Let the loops go over the ring and pull them your way to pass the area that has been folded.

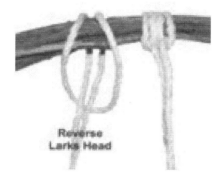

Let the ends pass over the first loop so you could make way for some half-hitches. Let them go over and under the ring, and then tightly pull it over the cord. This way, you'd get something like the one below. Repeat these first few steps until you have mounted all the cords on

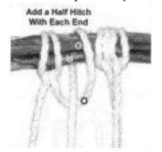

top of the ring. Organize them in groups of ten.

Now, you can make leaf-like patterns. To do this, make sure to number the first group of cords on the right side and make half-hitches in a counter-clockwise direction. Take note that you have to place the holding plate horizontally. If you see that it has curved slightly, make sure to reposition it and then attach cords labeled 5 to 7. Move it to resemble a diagonal position and then attach cords 8 to 10.

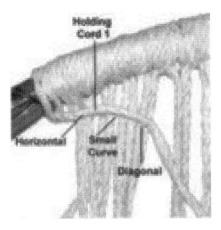

Make sure knots have been pushed close together and then use the cord on the leftmost corner to lower the leaf-like portion. The first four cords should be together on the handle and then go and attach cords labeled 3 to 6 to the holding cord. Move the cords so they'd be in a horizontal position.

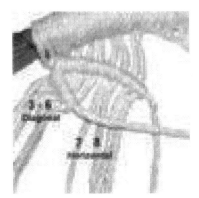

Now, move the cord upwards so that the center would not curve unnecessarily. Repeat the process for the cords on the bottom part of the frame and then start making the branches by selecting 2 to 4 cords from each of the leaves. Don't select the first and second row's first and last leaves.

Hold the cords with tape or clips as you move them towards the back of the design and decide how you want to separate—or keep the branches together. Secure the cords with glue after moving them to the back.

Wrap the right cords around the ones on the left so that branches could be joined together. Make sure to use half-hitches to wrap this portion and then use a set of two cords to create a branch.

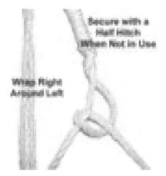

Together with your wrap, make use of another wrap and make sure they all come together as one.

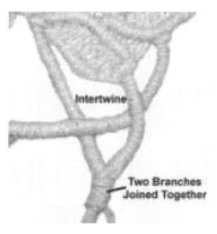

Secure the bundle by wrapping a 3-inch wrap cord around it and then let it go over the completed knot.

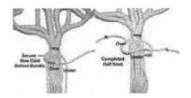

As for the fringe, you have to divide the knots into groups of two and make sure to tie a half-hitch on the rightmost cord on the left, and then let them alternate back and forth continuously under you have managed to cover your whole wreath. Let each sent slide under the whole wreath and then attach each cord to the ring itself.

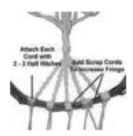

Make sure to divide the cords into small groups and then use the cords so you could tie the overhand knots. Unravel the fibers so you could form a wavy fringe.

That's it! You now have your own Macramé Wreath of Nature!

DIY Macramé Curtain

Macramé Curtains give your house the feel of that beach house look. You don't even have to add any trinkets or shells—but you can, if you want to. Anyway, here's a great Macramé Curtain that you can make!

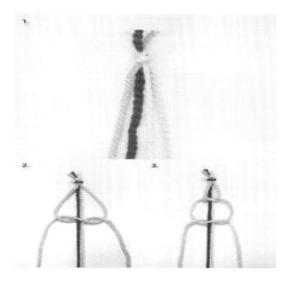

What you need:

Laundry rope (or any kind of rope/cord you want)

Curtain rod

Scissors

Pins

Lighter tape

Instructions:

Tie four strands together and secure the top knots with pins so they could hold the structure down.

Take the strand on the outer right part and let it cross over to the left side employing passing it through the middle. Tightly pull the strings together and reverse.

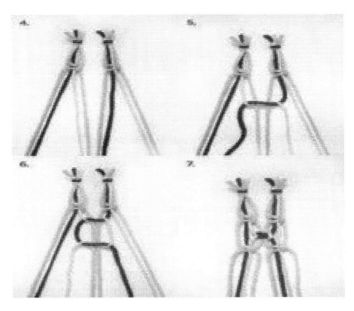

Repeat crossing the thread over four more times for the thread you now have in front of you. Take the strand on the outer left and let it pass through the middle, and then take the right and let it cross over the left side. Repeat as needed, then divide the group of strands to the left, and also to the right. Repeat until you reach the number of rows you want.

You can now apply this to the ropes. Gather the number of ropes you want—10 to 14 is okay, or whatever fits the rod, with good spacing. Start knotting at the top of the curtain until you reach your desired length. You can burn or tape the ends to prevent them from unraveling.

Braid the ropes together to give them that dreamy, beachside effect, just like what you see below.

That's it, you can now use your new curtain!

Macramé Wall Art

Adding a bit of Macramé to your walls is always fun because it livens up the space without making it cramped—or too overwhelming for your taste. It also looks beautiful without being too complicated to make. You can check it out below!

What you need:

Large wooden beads

Acrylic paint

Painter's tape

Scissors

Paintbrush

Wooden dowel

70 yards rope

Instructions:

Attach the dowel to a wall. It's best just to use removable hooks so you won't have to drill anymore.

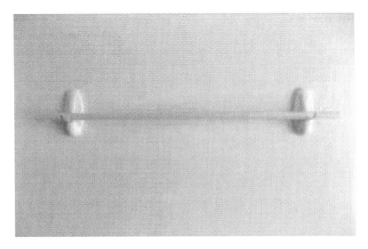

Cut the rope into 14 x 4 pieces, as well as 2 x 5 pieces. Use 5-yard pieces to bookend the dowel with. Continue doing this with the rest of the rope.

Then, start making double half-hitch knots and continue all the way through, like what's shown below.

Once you get to the end of the dowel, tie the knots diagonally so that they wouldn't fall down or unravel in any way. You can also add the wooden beads any way you want, so you'd get the kind of décor that you need. Make sure to tie the knots after doing so.

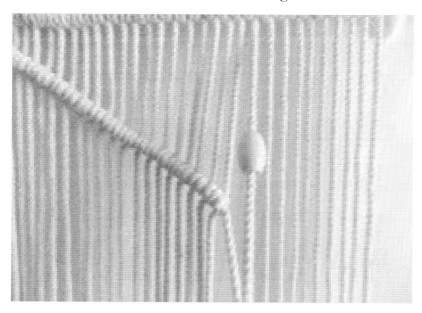

Use four ropes to make switch knots and keep the décor all the more secure. Tie around 8 of these.

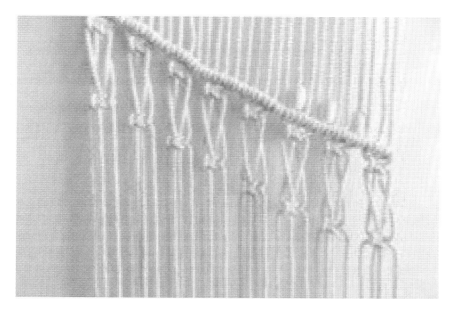

Add a double half hitch and then tie them diagonally once again.

Add more beads and then trim the ends of the rope.

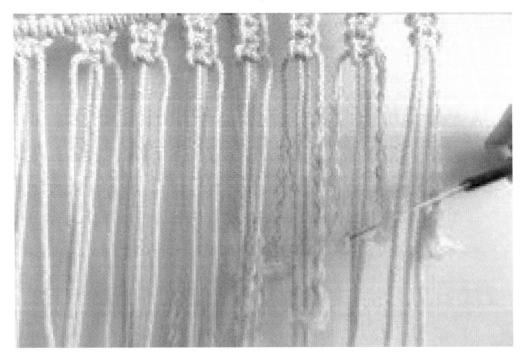

Once you have trimmed the rope, go ahead and add some paint to it. Summery or neon colors would be good.

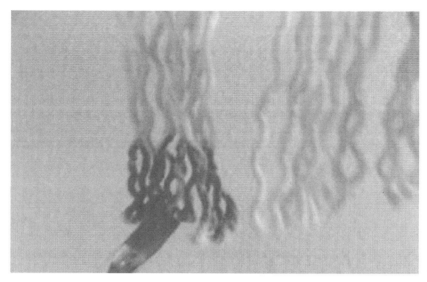

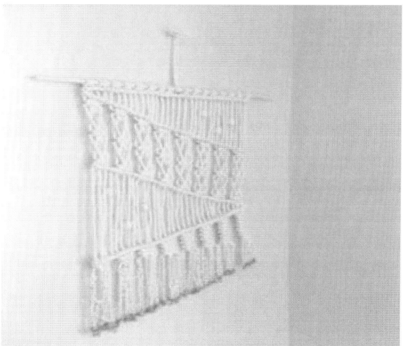

That's it! You now have your own Macramé Wall Art!

Hanging Macramé Vase

To add a dainty, elegant touch to your house, you could create a Macramé Vase. With this one, you'll have to make use of basket stitches/knots—which you'll learn about below. It's also perfect for those who really love flowers—and want to add a touch of nature at home!

What you need:

Masking tape

Tape measure or ruler

30 meters thick nylon cord

Small round vase (with around 20 cm diameter)

Instructions:

Cut eight cords measuring 3.5 yards or 3.2 meters each and set aside one of them. Cut a cord that measures 31.5 inches and set it aside, as well. Then, cut one cord that measures 55 inches.

Now, group eight lengths of cord together—the ones you didn't set aside, of course, and mark the center with a piece of tape.

Wrap the cords by holding them down together and take around 80 cm of it to make a tail—just like what you see below.

Wrap the cord around the back of the long part and make sure to keep your thumb on the tail. Then, wrap the cord around the main cord group. Make sure it is firm, but don't make it too tight. If you can make the loop bigger, that would be good, too.

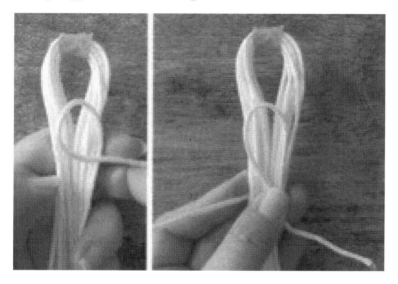

Do it 13 more times through the loop and go and pull the tail down so the loop could soften up. Stop letting the cords overlap by pulling them whenever necessary and then cut both ends so they would not be seen anymore.

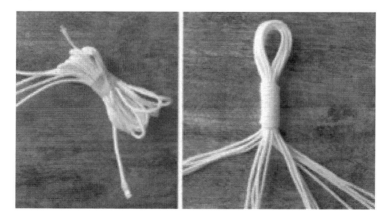

Divide the cords into groups of four and secure the ends with tape.

Get the group of cords that you have not used yet and make sure to measure 11.5 inches from the beginning—or on top. Do the overhand knot and get the cord on the left-hand side. Fold it over two of the cords and let it go under the cord on the right-hand side.

Fold the fourth cord and let it pass under the leftmost cord then up the loop of the first cord. Make sure to push it under the large knot so that it would be really firm.

Make more half-hitches until you form more twists. Stop when you see that you have made around 12 of them and then repeat with the rest of the cords.

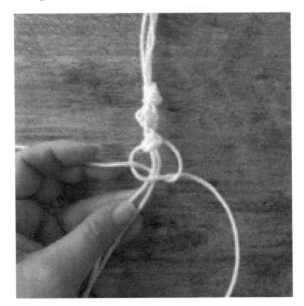

Now, it's time to make the basket for the vase. What you have to do here is measure 9 centimeters from your group of cords. Tie an overhand knot and make sure to mark with tape.

Let the two cord groups come together by laying them side by side.

Tie the cords down but make sure to keep them flat. Make sure that the knots won't overlap, or else you'd have a messy project—which isn't what you'd want to happen. Use two cords from the left as a starting point and then bring the two cords on the right over the top of the loop. Loop them together under the bottom cords and then work them back up once more.

Now, find your original loop and thread the same cords behind them. Then, let them pass through the left-hand cords by making use of the loop once more.

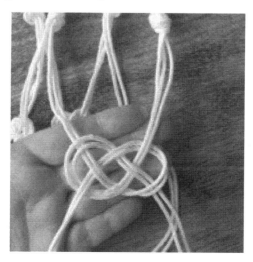

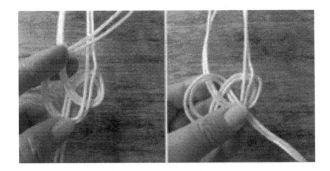

Let the knot move once you already have it in position. It should be around 3 inches or 7.5 cm from the overhand knots. After doing so, make sure that you flatten the cords and let them sit to each other until you have a firm knot on top. Keep dividing and letting cords come together.

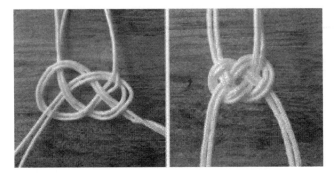

Get the cord on the left-hand side and let it go over the 2nd and 3rd cords before folding the fourth one under the first two cords. You'd then see a square knot forming between the 2nd and 3rd cords. You should then repeat the process on the righthand side. Open the cord on the right side and let it go under the left-hand cord. Repeat this process thrice, then join the four-square knots that you have made by laying them out on a table.

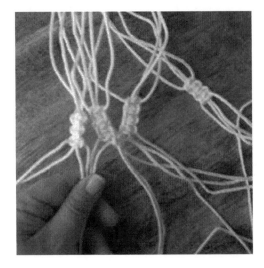

You'll then see that the cords have come together at the base. Now, you have to start wrapping the base by wrapping a 1.4-meter cord and wrap around 18 times.

To finish, just cut the cords the way you want. It's okay if they're not of the same length so that there'd be variety—and they'd look prettier on your wall. Make sure to tie overhand knots at the end of each of them before placing the vase inside.

Enjoy your new hanging vase!

Black and Red Macramé Bracelet

Steps:

Step 1 - Fold the shorter red cord in half and lay it flat in front of you. These are the designs central cords.

Step 2 - Fold the black cord in half and tie one square knot around the red central cords.

This knot needs to be positioned so that it creates a loop that the bead/flat button can pass through tightly. This forms the bracelets fastener.

Step 3 - Fold the longer red rattail cord in half and tie one half knot around the red central cords underneath the black square knot.

Step 4 - Tie a further four half knots always starting with the same side cord so that the knots begin to form a spiral.

Step 5 - Carry the black cords over the red and tie one square knot underneath the half knots.

Step 6 - Pass the red cords under the black and tie five half knots.

Step 7 - Continue in this way until you have tied 18cm of knots.

If you have the bracelet pinned to a board or solid surface the bracelet will twist as the spirals forms so you may find it easier to unpin and re-pin it as you work. The black cords should be flat, only the red knotting cords form the spiral.

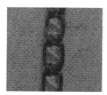

Step 8 - Turn the bracelet over and trim away all the excess knotting cords leaving 3mm ends.

Step 9 - Gently melt the cord end with the lighter and press them against the knots.

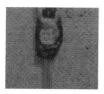

Heated rattail cord becomes very hot and can stick to your skin and burn so this step is safest carries out using a needle or scissors point to press on the melting cord.

Step 10 - Thread the flat bead/button onto the central cords. Push it up to the knots and leaving a 3mm gap tie an overhand knot to secure the bead. Cut off any excess cord and gently melt the ends to prevent fraying.

Macrame Shopping Bag

Materials:

Jute Rope

Bag Handles

Steps:

1. Split 2.3-meter long rope into 10 lengths. Fold them in half and thread through the gap on the bag handle to the folded middle. Take the ends of the rope and move through the loop you made in this earlier stage. Tight drive. Repeat this until 5 pieces of rope are attached to the handle of each bag.

2. Starting at one end, separate two pieces of rope from each other and push the rest sideways. With those two pieces, we will make the first knot. This is the knot that we will use in the tutorial, so keep moving to the next few steps if you get confused.

Make a right strand bend, so it crosses the right angle over the left rope.

Take the rope on the left (which is still straight) and thread that you made with the two ropes through the gap. Push both ends of the rope away before the knot is shaped and is in the right position. You want the handle to be about 5 cm forward.

Take the left-hand rope to complete the knot, and this time bring it over the right.

This time the right-hand rope is threaded through the gap. Push the tight knot over again. This is a double half hitch knot now complete.

3. Use the remaining ropes on the handle to make four more of those knots in a line. Then continue again but skip the first rope this time, and the second and third knot. Move on down the line. This time, you'll make four knots, and there's no knotting of the first and last rope.

4. Make the third row the same as the first one (thus five knots, without losing any ropes) once you have completed the second row.

5. Repeat steps 2-4 on the second handle once the third row is done. If that's finished, but the two handle facing each other together with the backsides.

6. Keep knotting in this pattern until you are left with around 10 cm of rope on the ends.

7. Cut rope length 4 meters long. Using the same method as you used for handles to tie this into the last side knot.

8. Take one front and one back string and wrap the rope around them. Then take another two knots (one from the front and one from the back) and do the same again. Act before you make it to the top.

9. Draw the rope which hangs down. Connect these strands together to stay in place in knots. To strengthen these, you should apply some glue. Combine it to form a fringe.

Macrame Sunscreen Holder

Materials:

Line

Carabiner Cer

Sun screen

Large empty bottle

Manager

Scissors

Candle

Steps:

1. Cut 5 pieces of string about 20cm long.

2. Fold one big knit in half and tie in the middle. Type the knot down to keep it.

Group the string into 5 pairs and each pair into 1" knot. Take another 1" down and tie the next set line.

4. Use this for about four rows of knots or span the length of your bottle. Glide into your bottle to test the fitness and number of knots required. Put the bottle down in the cap side for easy use.

5. Once the fit is correct, tie a big knot to hold the bottle with the strands.

6. Place each chord over the heat to melt the ends of the candle to prevent sprays.

7. Add a carabiner to your knot and add it to your curtain.

Macrame Guitar Strap

Materials:

Macrame List

Active Clasps

Nice areas.

Industrial resistance to adhesive

Scissors

Steps:

Step 1: Cut 2 macrame cord lengths, every 4 yards.

Step2: Fold the length of each string so that one yard is on one side, and three yards on the other side. Insert the centers on the thread outside, which leave the long ends, in the flat part of the swivel handle.

Step 3: Push each cord into its own circuit and close its knot.

Step 4: begin making a knot of a square. Take the longest left string and cross the middle of each string and underneath the left string. Take the right cord under the center two and the left cord up and down. Pull this taut. That's half your knot square.

Step 5: Complete square knot with reverse step 4. Intersect the right cord over the center two and the bottom left; then, under the center two, across the center and over the left cord. A quick pull and a square knot was completed.

Step 6: Keep adding your square knots for your camera strap to the right length.

Step 7: Trim all four ends of the thread. In a pivoting knot, join all four cords. At the end of each string, put a dollop of adhesive, fold the strings and hold clothespins in put until the adhesive is soft.

Replace the clips until the glue is dry and pop your strap!

Macramé Top

Materials:

Plain white cotton T-shirt (long is better than short)

Dylon Pink Flamingo Dye

Salt

Bucket

Spoons/stick for stirring

Small container for mixing dye

Rubber gloves

Hanger

Steps:

Step one

Mix the dye as per the manufacturer's Steps: and thoroughly wet the T-shirt. We used half a packet of dye, as we were only dyeing a couple of T-shirts. Choose a 100% cotton garment or one with as high a cotton percentage mix as possible, as human-made fibres such as polyester or viscose won't absorb the dye.

Step two

Put your T-shirt on a hanger (it's the easiest way to control the dyeing process) and dip it into the dye bath, approximately two thirds of the way up the shirt, for 30 seconds. This first dip needs to be really quick.

Step three

For the second dip, put the T-shirt back into the dye bath two thirds up the dyed section. This time leave for a minute or two. Keep an eye on the colour – once you're happy with the ombré effect that's starting to appear, take the T-shirt out of the bath and rinse the dyed section with warm water. Be careful not to get any pink dye on the white section.

Step four

Add another tablespoon of dye to the bath and mix thoroughly. Put only the lower third of your T-shirt back in for three or four minutes. Check the ombré effect – if you think the base needs to be darker, leave in the bath for a few more minutes. Once happy, rinse the dyed part until the water runs clear and leave to dry.

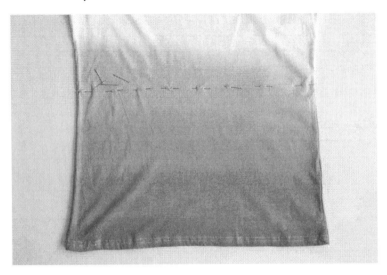

Step five

Give the T-shirt a good press as you need it to be flat for the next steps. Run a line of pins where you want the top of the macramé section to start – ours began 26cm (10¼") up from the hem.

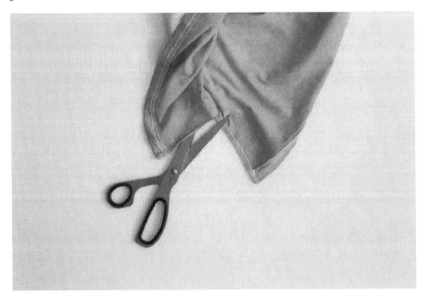

Step six

Remove the seams up to where you've pinned by cutting very closely to the edge of the stitching. This gives a neat finish.

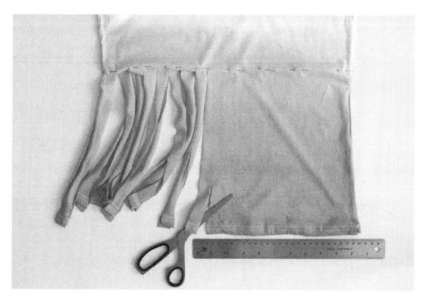

Step seven

Measure the T-shirt's width and divide by two – this will give you the number of strips you need to cut. If the number is odd, then round down to the nearest even number (you need an equal number of strips and it's better if they're thicker rather than thinner). Cut the strips up to the pinned line.

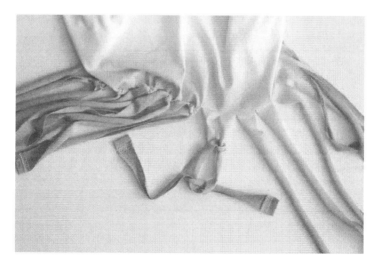

Step eight

Take the first two strips on the outside edge (we worked left to right) and tie together in a double knot. You want the tension to be firm but not over-pulled. Continue knotting in pairs along the whole of the T-shirt front and back.

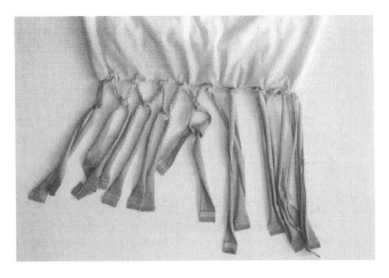

Step nine

For the next row, take two strips from the next-door knots and knot together 2.5cm (1") below the first row. Continue front and back. You should start to see a triangular shape forming.

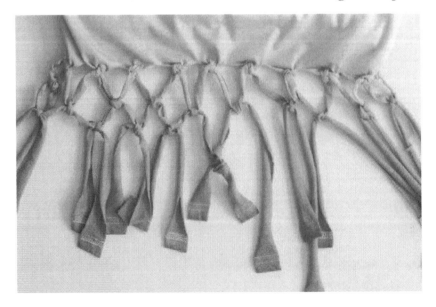

Step ten

Repeat the above step to create another row of knots. This time a diamond shape will have formed. If you're working with a really long T-shirt then you could add a few more rows of knots – we liked the cropped effect we created, so have kept to just three.

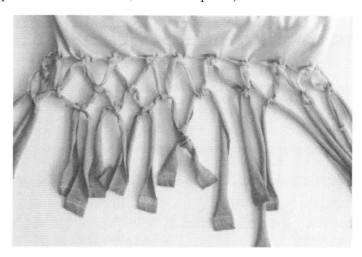

Step 11

To finish, cut off the over locked hem from the bottom of each strip so they curl up neatly. Now all you need is a sunny day to show it off.

Conclusion

The beauty of Macramé as a vintage art that has survived extinction for centuries and has continued to thrive as a technique of choice for making simple but sophisticated items is simply unrivalled. The simple fact that you have decided to read this manual means that you are well on your way to making something great. There is truly a certain, unequaled feeling of satisfaction that comes from crafting your own masterpiece. The most important rule in Macramé is the maxim: "Practice makes perfect". If you cease to practice constantly, your skills are likely to deteriorate over time. So, keep your skills sharp, exercise the creative parts of your brain, and keep creating mind-blowing handmade masterpieces. Jewelry and fashion accessories made with even the most basic Macramé knots are always a beauty to behold, hence they serve as perfect gifts for loved ones on special occasions. Presenting a Macramé bracelet to someone, for instance passes the message that you did not just remember to get them a gift, you also treasure them so much that you chose to invest your time into crafting something unique specially for them too, and trust me, that is a very powerful message. However, the most beautiful thing about Macramé is perhaps the fact that it helps to create durable items. Hence you can keep a piece of decoration, or a fashion accessory you made for yourself for many years, enjoy the value and still feel nostalgic anytime you remember when you made it. It even feels better when you made that item with someone. This feature of durability also makes Macramé accessories incredibly perfect gifts. Macramé can also serve as an avenue for you to begin your dream small business. After perfecting your Macramé skills, you can conveniently sell your items and get paid well for your products, especially if you can perfectly make items like bracelets that people buy a lot. You could even train people and start your own little company that makes bespoke Macramé fashion accessories. The opportunities that Macramé presents are truly endless. Remember that each of these knots is going to be the foundation of the other projects that you create, so you are going to have to take the time to get familiar with each of them – and practice them until they are what you need them to be. You are not likely going to get them perfectly right away – so take the time to make sure you do it right before you move on to the succeeding one. So, what are you waiting for? All It is going to take is your time and effort, and you are going to get just what you are after with your macramé projects. From now on, you are on the path to be a macramé master, and you are going to fall in love with everything macramé. The world of macramé awaits, just begging you to dive in and get started. Good luck and create to your heart's content. So, stay sharp, keep practicing and keep getting better. Welcome to a world of infinite possibilities!

Stop reading, start doing!

MACRAMÉ PATTERNS:

The Easy Beginner's And Intermediate Guide To The Ancient Art Of Macramé. Including Step-By-Step Projects For All Levels And High-Quality Images.

EMILY SENRA

Table Of Contents

Introduction

In old times Knots and knot lore were closely associated with magic, medication, religious views for much of history. Knots also acted as bases for mathematical structures (for example, by the Mayans), before writing skills were introduced; and string games and other alternate uses were and are still numerous, of course. All these things have been carried out in one way or another and by all races since ancient times. They are even being taught all over the world nowadays. Additionally, it is safe to say that it will continue to follow until the day comes that humankind no longer exists.

Macramé as an aspect of decorative knots permeates nearly every culture, but within those cultures, it can manifest in different directions. The carefully braided strings, with the assistance of a needle-like tool, became the item for shaping fishnets. Their use in the fashion industry has been spectacular and influential among the youth in making sandals, shoes, jewelry, etc. It is now used also with other products to fashion all kinds of beautiful works of art.

Macramé is closely associated with the trendy youth due to its rapid growth, quick adaptability, and extensive uses. Concerning its use for fashion items, macramé exercised in the textiles became an essential focus on the creation of each decorative piece of clothing, particularly on the fringes of each tent, clothing, and towel. In this, macramé became a synonym for hanging planter. In its traditional forms, Macramé (is an Italian name given in Genoa-its home and place of birth) became one of the most common textile techniques.

Knots are used for the passage of time for several practical, mnemonic and superstitious reasons. Knotting dates back to early Egyptian civilization in Africa, where knots were used in fishnet and decorative fringes. The Peruvian Incas used a Quip, made from mnemonic knot (Basically, overhand knots) to help them record and convey information. The use of ties, the knot size, rope color, and knot both helped to communicate complicated messages Knots were used in surgery (as slings for broken bones) and in games in ancient Greece (one such mystery was the Gordian knot). In the early Egyptians and Greek times,' Hercules ' knot (square knot) was used on clothes, jewelry, and pottery, which had a spiritual or religious meaning.

The near association between contemporary crafts and macramé has led to the discovery of a range of methodologies and integrative methods, common in most cases, in the content and the adapted techniques. Such advanced methods and integrative techniques reflect the accomplishment of macramé art and its development.

As a product of the artistic intervention of scholarly artisans, this human intellectual accomplishment became necessary to incorporate modern architecture requiring the use of other materials for trendy artifacts. While macramé art has been created and used for onward creation in most cultures aimed at achieving both practical and artistic appeal, their end products vary from one culture to the next. These innovations, however, are, by definition, integral parts of cultural growth and are the results of the macramé artisans ' revolutionary accomplishments over the years. The use of adornment knotting distinguishes early cultures and reflected intelligence creation. It is an art that fits all ages and abilities. Today, macramé is experiencing a Revival of the 20th century. Both men and women transition to work with their hands and build not just utilitarian pieces but also decorative ones.

CHAPTER 1:

Types of Cord

Cord Preparation

Though usually rarely emphasized, preparation of the cords and getting them ready for use in Macramé projects is one of the core pillars of the art of Macramé. At times, specialized processes such as conditioning and stiffening of cords need to be carried out before Macramé projects can be begun. In general, however, cord preparation in Macramé is mainly concerned with dealing with cut ends and preventing these ends from unraveling during the project. During a project, constant handing of materials can distort the ends which can end up having disastrous consequences on your project. Before starting your project, if you do not appropriately prepare special kinds of cords, like ones that were made by the twisting of individual strands, that cord is likely to come apart, effectively destroying your project completely.

Therefore, cord preparation is extremely and incomparably important to the success of any Macramé project, the preparation of each cord is meant to be done during the first step of making any knot, which is the step where you cut out your desired length of cord from the larger piece.

For cord conditioning, experts recommend rubbing beeswax along the length of the cord. To condition your cord, simply gets a bit of beeswax, let it warm up a bit in your hands, and rub it along the cord's length. This will help prevent unwanted tight curls on your cord. Note that beeswax may be applied to both natural and synthetic materials. For synthetic materials, however, only Satin and fine Nylon beading cords compulsorily require conditioning. After conditioning, inspect your cords for any imperfections and discard useless pieces to ensure the perfection of your project. After conditioning, then comes the actual process of cord preparation. Cords can be prepared (i.e. the ends can be prevented from fraying) through the use of a flame, a knot, tape, and glue.

To prevent unraveling of your cord using a flame, firstly test a small piece of the material with the flame from a small lighter. The material needs to melt, not burn. If it burns, then such a cord is not suitable for flame preparation. To prepare using a flame, simply hold the cord to the tip of the flame for 2 to 5 seconds, make sure the cord does not ignite but melts. Flame preparation is suitable for cords made from olefin, polyester, and nylon, and the process is compulsory for the preparation of parachute cords.

Tying knots at the end of the cord is another effective method to prevent fraying. The overhand knot is an all-time favorite, but knots such as the figure 8 knot which is best suited to flexible cords can be used if you think the knot might have to be undone at some point in your project. The Stevedore knot can be used to prevent fraying when using slippery materials.

Glue is another priceless alternative that can be used to prevent fraying at the ends of cords efficiently. However, not all kinds of glue may be used in cord preparation. Only certain brands, such as the Aleen's Stop Fray may be used in cord preparation. Household glue might also be used, but only when diluted with water. TO prepare your cord, simply rub the glue on the ends of the material and leave it to dry. If you intend to pass beads over the glued end, roll the cord's end between your fingers to make it narrower as it dries. Nail polish may also be used as an alternative to glue.

The tape is also a reliable method to prepare your cords. Simply wrap the tape around the end of the cord where you want to prevent fraying of your material. Make sure the end of the cord remains narrow by squeezing it between your fingers. It is advisable to use masking tape or cellophane tape for your preparations.

A special class of Macramé cords, known as a parachute cord requires a special form of preparation. Parachute cords are composed of multiple core yarns surrounded by a braided sleeve. To prepare a parachute cord (also called a Paracord), pull out the core yarns from the sleeve, and expose the yarns by about half an inch. Now cut the core yarns back, so that they become even with the outer sleeve, and then push the sleeve forward till the yarns become invisible. To complete the preparation, apply flame to the outer sleeve till it melts, and then press the handle of your lighter onto the sleeve while it's still warm to flatten the area and keep it closed up. The melted area will look darker and more plastic than the rest of the material.

Finishing Techniques

Finishing techniques refer to the methods by which the ends of cords after knots have been created may be taken care of to give a neat and tidy project. Finishing is often referred to as tying off. Several finishing knots are available and are extremely effective methods for executing finishing processes. Reliable finishing knots include the overhand knot and the barrel knot.

Folding techniques are also dependable finishing techniques. For flexible materials like cotton, all you need to do is fold the ends flat against the back surface and add glue to the ends to hold them in place. For less flexible materials, fold the cords to the back, then pass them under a loop from one or more knots, and then apply glue, allow it to dry, and cut off excess material.

Finally, you can do your finishing with the aid of fringes. You may choose between a brushed fringe and a beaded fringe.

CHAPTER 2:

Essential and Useful Tools

The Essential Project Board

There are several different kinds of padded board designs available on the internet. Some are made of foam and others of cork. There are also some available for purchase in bead stores that are not foam, but instead have a scalloped edge that allows you to wedge your cord in between the scallops, provided your cords are long enough to reach the edge of the board.

I prefer to use thick foam which gives me the ability to push my straight pin all the way in, using the head to hold the cord tightly when necessary. A feature I used often when I was first learning. I also often pin horizontally across a cord to give it some tension without piercing the cord itself.

To make my board, I started with a leftover piece of foam that was lying around. (Ok, it was lying around at my mom's house, but it was in the attic, so it is fair game, right?). As you can see, I made a rough cut that is a bit larger than my clip board. This is about 12in x 13in. Where the top clip will be, I cut out a slope.

I added about 4 inches to each side and cut out my fabric. Choose wisely here. On my first try, I used a very light, soft pink fabric that was a flannel type of material. When I worked on a project though, especially picking up beads to string onto the cords, I was forever having little bits of fluff on my fingers and in my way. Cotton is a better choice. Cover the foam with your fabric. Turn to the back and safety pin it in place. I like to be able to take the cover off to wash it (there may be a coffee spill in the future) or just change it out if it does not work (like the pink stuff).

Turn to the front and fit onto your clipboard.

I keep straight pins in the top corners of my board, which I use to pin cords, hold the fastenings (closures), or keep a focal bead.

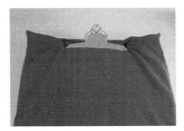

Tools

Reaming tools

The right beads can really complement your project. What fun it is finding the perfect shape and color, then rushing home to work it into your creation – and what disappointment if you then spend hours wrestling with the tiny bead opening which is stubbornly refusing to go on to your cord.

So, what is the solution? A simple set of bead reamers. I most often use the smallest one, but I have had occasion to reach for the subsequent size up also. My reamers are for use on glass, ceramic, pearl, and stone beads. This tool can literally smooth the way with tricky beads.

Beading tools

It is a good idea to have some basic beading tools on hand. Several patterns have jump rings or ribbon clasp closures, which would benefit from the use of (shown from left to right) needle nose pliers, round nose pliers, a crimp tool and wire cutters. You will also need a pair of small, sharp scissors. And I do mean sharp; if they are dull, they will fray the cord when you cut it.

Glue

Often in micro-macramé, your only loose ends are at the end of the project when you tie it all off. In my experience, this is your weakest link. So why not strengthen it as best as you can? Many people use nail polish; I prefer glue. One type of glue you can use is E6000. It works well on leather and many jewelry makers prefer to use it.

Another good choice is Beacon 527 multi-purpose glue. It dries clear, though shiny. Usually I leave it to dry well (often overnight) then trim my cords and apply a second coat.

Note: Some crafters use a singeing tool to fuse the ends of nylon cords, melting them together. This leaves a bit of black residue, so use this technique only on dark cords, or where it will not show like behind a focal bead or button.

Pins

Straight pins are significant in micro-macramé design work. Some people prefer T-pins. Either way, a long shank is more comfortable to work with. Pins are vital when it comes to holding cords in place, and useful for teasing out a mistake without unraveling your cord.

Cords and Beads

Types of cording

C-Lon - My patterns use a cord called C-Lon Bead Cord. It is a 3-ply nylon cord comparable to Conso and Mastex Nylon #18 but offers a much larger range of color options and a smaller price per spool. This cord is the standard size for micro macramé jewelry. It is also available in smaller diameters.

Tuff - Also a 3-ply nylon cord, it is available in 16 colors and has several size options. It does not stretch or stain, and resists fraying. Size 5 is comparable to C-Lon Beading Cord.

D&E (formerly Mastex no. 18) – nylon cord originally designed for the upholstery industry, it is soft and pliable. Available in about 17 colors.

Types of beads

Metal – These are non-precious metals, which offer a less expensive alternative to silver and gold.

Crystal – It is the refraction created by the many cuts in a glass surface that gives crystal it is fancy shine.

Glass – This category is where you will find flame work and lamp work beads. Versatile and affordable, glass bead is an excellent choice for novice beaders.

Semiprecious (or gemstone) – These beads are a popular choice as they offer a large variety of options. The list is extensive, so here are a just a few: agate, amber, garnet, jade, malachite, and onyx.

Clay - These beads can be made of ceramic clay, which is fired in a kiln and glazed, or made of porcelain, which generally involves a potter's wheel, a kiln, and hand painting. There is also polymer clay, which is not technically a clay at all, but a plastic. This material is an oven- baked clay that can be used at home to make your own unique beads and is very versatile.

Other - There are also beads made from shell, such as mother of pearl, tiger shell, abalone, and conch shells. You may also come across wooden beads which come from the bark, roots, or branches of many types of trees. Some wooden beads are carved and have been popular for generations.

Cord Measurement

Before you can embark on a macramé project, it is essential that you determine the amount of chord you will need. This includes knowing the length of the required cord and the total number of materials you must purchase.

Equipment: to measure, you will need a paper for writing, pencil, tape rule and calculator. You would also need some basic knowledge of unit conversion as shared below:

- 1 inch = 25.4millimeters = 2.54 centimeters

- 1 foot =12 inches

- 1 yard = 3 feet = 36 inches

- 1 yard = 0.9 meters

Note: The circumference of a ring = 3.14 * diameter measured across the ring

Measuring Width

The first thing to do is determine the finished width of the widest area of your project. Once you have this width, pencil it down.

Determine the actual size of the materials, by measuring its width from edge to edge.

You can then proceed to determine the type of knot pattern you wish to use with the knowledge of the knot pattern. You must know the width and spacing (if required) of each knot. You should also determine if you want to add more cords to widen an area of if you would be needing extra cords for damps.

With the formula given above, calculate and determine the circumference of the ring of your designs.

Determine the mounting technique to be used. The cord can be mounted to a dowel, ring, or other cord. Folded cords affect both the length and width of the cord measurement.

CHAPTER 3:

Technique for Knotting Cord Ends

1.) Strategy ahead

Try to design all your style before making the first knot. This consists of the length of your final piece, the number of knots you will use, and how you will complete the piece.

Record all of these things before you start to make sure you start with a fairly long cable.

2.) Identify your 'knot factor'. If you prepare your style as much as possible and understand the knot aspect of your cable, it will be a more detailed action to understand the amount of cable needed for each task. Each product has what I call a 'knot element', which suggests how much wire each knot uses

How to find out what your cable knot looks like: I run an area of wire that is a large even number, like 4 inches. Tie a knot in the wire. Example: With the 8mm waxed wire I like to use, starting with a 10cm piece: After making a knot, the wire determines 3.75cm. The knot aspect for this cable is 25 inches.

3.) Mathematic

Pivotal: This essential rule uses to littler estimated strings and links principally, for example, 1 mm link or littler measured. Longer pendants would require longer links to start out with this rule is basically a guide for the commonplace size pendant which is around 16-18 inches in length. I would incredibly prompt using the equation I brought up however much as could be expected.

As I call attention to in the video, there is a fundamental general principle that works fairly well for littler measured size links.

I don't absolutely like doing science - all things considered, I'm a craftsman notwithstanding, I moreover don't savor the experience of lacking link in an errand. (Too deplorable face).

Since you have the hitching component, and an estimate of the quantity of bunches you wish to make, you can expand the bunch angle by the assortment of bunches and discover exactly how much space you require to remember for to your starting length.

The no-math technique for doing it.

For a hitched link arm band: (using a solitary link, not collapsed like frequently used in pearl tying) is, in the first place, a piece that is the length of your arm (from underarm to wrist). In the event that you are managing a multiplied link, you will require to twofold the length, so start with a piece multiple times as long as your arm.

For a tied link pendant: multiple times the length of your arm for a solitary link, multiple times the length of your arm in the event that you are multiplying the string over.

You can find the equation I use here, along with some elaboration on pointers 1 and 2.

4.) Utilize a drawbore or a tying device.

A hitching apparatus is somewhat harder to ace at first; be that as it may, it is phenomenal help with working quickly and is a beneficial money related venture on the off chance that you get ready to do a lot of tying. The essential advantage of using a hitching device instead of a drill is the best thought and the thumb discharge, which gets the bunch off the instrument as it fixes it into area, allowing you to work quicker and put less exertion into each bunch. The introduction is coming rapidly.

Using a sharp thing like a drawbore or a tying instrument is the main technique I comprehend to get those bunches to go absolutely where you want them as well! A borer is an essential pointed steel device with an arrangement with. The tightened, pointed end is the mystery, so you may in like manner use a security pin or extraordinary tweezers to help with your bunches when there's no other option, however they are somewhat increasingly undesirable and awkward to use for a bunch overwhelming assignment.

On the off chance that you've endeavored tying before, in any case, have really been disturbed by endeavoring to cajole the bunches into the best area, straight up versus the globule, at that point this is the absolute best strategy of all! You comprehend it's commonly hard to get a bunch to 'land' essentially where you expect it to by simply interfacing a bunch with your fingers and pulling it tight.

A bit is a reasonable apparatus that can be used for various different capacities other than hitching (I in like manner use my own to make openings in calfskin and as a mandrel for making little jump rings). You would then be able to use the borer to move the bunch along the link into position when you straighten out the bunch around the drawbore.

5. Twofold bunch and triple bunches.

On the off chance that you require a greater or all the more impressive bunch (like toward the finish of your beading or up versus a dab with a greater opening), interfacing one bunch over another bunch doesn't definitely work to make one gigantic solid bunch. You essentially get two average estimated ties one next to the other, which may absolutely be a style alternative; in any case, it won't prevent those dabs from moving over.

To frame a twofold bunch, make one overhand bunch as typical, at that point pass culmination of the link around and up through the bunch by and by before pulling it tight. For a triple bunch, finish through the underlying bunch 2 additional occasions.

6.) Conserve the pieces.

I educate monitoring your pieces concerning link (or at least a couple of them) that are 5 or 6 inches and more. This length is perfect for making customizable moving bunches to finish your hitched design gems styles. A solitary customizable moving bunch is made around two finishes of the link by using an alternate length of link that has to do with 6 inches in length.

7.) Beeswax is your mate.

Beeswax can be used on fruitions of your links and string to help abstain from fraying as you're beading. Just drag culmination of the link all through some beeswax, and from that point forward, turn the link in the middle of your thumb and index finger in exactly the same directions as it is at present bent. This will tame those flyaway closures, and you should be able to curve by and by various more occasions varying while at the same time beading without expecting to utilize more beeswax each time.

Links are involved bunches of little hairs that are turned together solidly to incorporate quality and flexibility to the item. The 'utilize' of the link is the quantity of littler estimated links it is comprised of. A 3 employ link is comprised of 3 littler estimated hairs bent into the one essential hair.

In case you're not using a beading needle, the particular hairs toward the finish of a link can catch on the dot as it travels through, activating fulfillments to shred and making it an uneasiness to endure that next dot

CHAPTER 4:

Macramè Troubleshooting

Macramé is the art of knotting threads or cords to create a decorative or useful object. To start your project off right, choose the right materials, and a suitable workspace. First, you need to learn the easy knots of macramé. You will start most of your projects with an inverted lark's head knot. The flat knot and the half knot are used in the manufacture of all kinds of objects, scarves, or wall decorations, for example. Then, when you master the flat knot, you can enrich your creations by incorporating beads. With diagonals of half-key knots, you will be able to create patterns for your achievements.

Prepare and gather the material.

Choose your material. This choice depends on the object you want to make. There are different kinds of cords for making macramé. For example, you can use wool, string, cotton ropes, leather, or any other material in the form of sufficiently flexible threads. Leather is perfect for making jewelry. Cotton cords are well suited for making wall decorations, and you can choose woolen threads to make a blanket or scarf. Take some sewing pins. Depending on the type of knots you use, they will be used to hold your threads. Sewing pins are well suited for this purpose, but you can also use thumbtacks. Make a macramé board. There is no need to take sophisticated items. The board simply needs to be practical and soft enough for the pins to pierce through it. You can stick a gardening cushion or an old foam mattress on a clip holder. You can also use expanded polystyrene or balsa wood. Choose a knot holder. It is a piece of wood, plastic, or metal to which you attach your wires. You will place it at the top of your macramé board, and you will build your project from this anchor point. You will choose your knot holder according to your project. If you make a key ring or jewelry, take a key ring as a knot holder, it is undoubtedly the most suitable one. If your project is larger, take a rod.

Start with A Reverse Lark's Head Knot

Fold your thread in half. The two parts must be exactly the same. You will use this thread to tie other knots and if it is not properly bent this can create difficulties for the rest of your project Put the loop under your knot holder. Your folded thread now forms a circle. Wrap it around the knot holder so that the loop is below and the ends of the thread above. If your knot holder is a ring, pass the loop under part of the circle so that it is found in the center of it.

Thread the ends of the wire through the loop. Pull it under the stick or the edge of the ring. Then slide your fingers into it to catch the two halves of the wire above it. Then, pull the cord down to pass it inside the loop. In the end, you will get a shape similar to that of a pretzel.

Pull the thread down to tighten the knot. Hold the rod or ring with one hand. On the other, pull the two halves of the wire down. Thus, the loop will go up towards the rod or the ring as you tighten the knot.

Install multiple wires for your new projects. Generally, you will need at least two sets of yarns to make macramé. Therefore, at least two reverse lark's head knots must be made with two different threads on the same knot holder before starting a project.

Create a model with half knots

Make two reverse lark's head knots. Instead, place them in the middle of your knot holder.

Distinguish between the working wires and the carrying wires. After making an inverted lark's head knot, two strands of thread remain hanging down. The working yarn is the strand that you will move to make the knot. The supporting thread is the strand around which you will wind the working thread to tie the knot.

Pass the right working thread over the supporting threads. Start at the top. Take the working thread on the right, fold it and pass it over the supporting threads located in the middle, then under the working yarn on the left.

Pass the left working thread under the carrying wires. Start at the same height as for the right ribbon. Pull the left working wire so that it goes under the supporting cables, then over the other working fence. Pull the two working threads to tighten the knot.

Create a spiral shape. Continue to make your half knots. A spiral will form naturally in your weaving. The number of knots necessary for the formation of a twist of the spiral depends on the thickness of the wire. When the number of twists suits you, knot the threads.

Make a flat knot. Make the first half-knot described above, then start again from the thread opposite your starting point. Take the working thread located on the left and pass it above the carrying wires located in the middle, then under the working yarn on the right. Then move the right working thread under the carrying wires, then over the left strand. Pull-on the working threads to finish the flat knot.

Make A Pattern By Alternating Flat Knots.

Make eight reverse lark's head knots. You will need at least eight different wires. When tying your threads to the knot holder, be sure to stick them to each other.

Divide your threads into groups of four strands. You will make a flat knot with each of these sets. You can tie more than eight threads to your knot holder, but the total number of strands must be a multiple of four.

Make flat knots. Proceed as previously described to tie each group of four threads. Start each flat knot at the same distance from the knot holder. Thus, they will be aligned horizontally.

Space the rows of knots. Choose where you will start the next row. If you want a tight weave, ideal for scarves and blankets, start the second row just below the first. If you prefer a more airy weaving or some kind of lace, keep a space of about 3 cm between your rows.

Let two wires hang on each side. By making the next row, you will not use the two wires located at each end of the knot holder. Then divide the number of strands remaining by four to determine the number of flat knots that will make up this row.

Divide the remaining strands into groups of four. Then tie a flat knot with each group. Start each knot at the same distance from the one before it to have a regular pattern.

Continue your rows. With each new row of flat knots, let two strands hang from each end of the knot holder until you run out of thread. When you can no longer divide your threads by four, repeat the process with the 16 strands (or more) that you had at the beginning. Then repeat this pattern on the desired length.

Make diagonals of knots in half key.

Tie four threads. A diagonal of half-key knots requires the use of a load-bearing thread and seven working threads. So you need to tie four threads with reverse lark's head knots to get the eight strands you need. Your four knots should be tight against each other on your knot holder.

Choose your work thread. You can start the right or left of the model. If you start on the left, the strand at the left end of the knot holder will be your main thread. Conversely, if you start on the right, the strand at the right end will become load-bearing.

Pin the carrier wire to the left of the working cables. Small pins like the ones you use to sew are perfect for this purpose. Plant one under the knot holder, just to the left of the wires. Pass the carrier wire around the pin, then pull it to the right so that it crosses the other wires diagonally. Secure the carrier wire with a second pin, about 3 cm lower than the first pin.

If you wish to obtain a more pronounced diagonal, fix the lower carrying wire.

Make two loops with the first working thread. It is located just to the right of the carrier wire. Pass it under it, then wrap it around. Then pull it so that it continues on its way under the carrier wire. Wrap it again around the carrier wire. After this second loop, you must pass the working cord through the small space that has formed between the two wires, under the carrier wire, following the first loop. Pull the thread and close the knot.

Repeat the operation with each working thread. Once you have made the first knot, go to the next strand on the right. Make two loops around the carrier wire, then pass the working cord through the small circle that has formed between the two wires. Pull the thread to finish the knot. Repeat these operations until the end of the diagonal.

Create a zigzag. When the first diagonal is finished, you can make a diagonal of half-key nodes in the opposite direction. So you will get a zigzag pattern. If the first diagonal starts on the left, start on the right. The wire at the right end of the knot holder becomes the carrier wire, and the other cables will be the working wires.

You can also repeat the diagonals of half keys starting on the same side. You will get a diagonal pattern with knots close to each other.

CHAPTER 5:

How to Start a Macramè Project

In case you have never touched a Macramé job earlier, it's ideal to begin with a blue print which is too straightforward. This endeavor from live beautiful will permit one to own a way for developing a plant holder silhouette, also it might potentially be performed in several moments the minute that you have the hang of it. Take this quick pattern in the event that you'd really like to produce a pair of several plant hangers.

02

Use a vibrant thread to Bring attention

Don't under estimate simple Macramé patterns. But, at the function you'd like your Macramé plant hanger to seem simpler, consider like an enjoyable pop of color like Lia Griffith neglected. This tutorial is straightforward and easy to follow with clear directions and pictures.

03

Use a classic shirt Together with your preferred

Traditionally, the Macramé is performed using a rope-like thread. But creatives are experimentation with many substances for centuries. Re-cycle one of one's old tops and attempt this tutorial in a magnificent jumble for an inch plant hanger.

04

Insert on a few Additional Pom-poms

When You get a fundamental downward routine, consider a few Of items it's very likely to add to create additional attention. Sarah hearts made a decision to hang a few colossal pom-poms for its Macramé plant holder. Have a gander at the tutorial to find additional info.

05

Use a mason jar along with your cherished vessel. Maybe not only is your Macramé pattern significant, however Take into account when choosing a planter. Mason jars work perfect for various non-invasive plants and also are small so you never need to generate an extremely fancy Macramé holder to reveal off it.

06

Create a contemporary looking plant holder Utilizing black

In most situations, Macramé appears very bohemian and varied. But you may put in a contemporary twist on your endeavor working with a straightforward, elongated design and black rope. This tutorial in deuce cities hen-house is the best position to follow along with.

07

Add a Gigantic team in the top

Many Macramé plant flashlights use a metallic jump Ring in the start of this product. Ordinarily, these rings are notably small compared to this hanger. Persia Lou chose to decide on an extremely major round focal point that balances nicely with the bigger planter. Understand tips on how to do precisely the same by minding their own tutorial.

08

Use beads Rather than knots

You can Encounter the Look and Feel of a Macramé Plant hanger without having to complete a whole lot of knots. This routine from born in a-day incorporates wooden beads which make this much quicker to finish. Mix your bead choice to add your private spin for this particular tutorial.

09

Insert Just a few bead accents

Should you enjoy the Thought of integrating Beads but do not require the whole planter to develop into beaded, have a good look at out the tutorial of makes perfect. The notion is the fact that the principal knots all over the planter are wrapped inside large wooden beads. Go for their page to really have a glimpse at the incremental guide.

10

Attempt outside a design into elongated planters

This Macramé pattern Should work nicely with lots of Measurements of planters, but in addition, it works well nicely with elongated replicas such as that. The thick, yet straightforward rope is easy to knot, that may get this kind of tutorial you might complete in less than one hour.

11

Lean twine Macramé pattern

This Macramé pattern carries a Great Deal of little Knots that look perfect with a slim, twine-like rope. In the event that you opted to come across a milder thread, then plant holder could seem too straightforward and rust. To make one similar, have a glimpse at the one-of-a-kind allow it to think it's great.

12

Master 1 knot because of its planter

After You've finished some plant baits, in order to May possibly be convinced enough to check a person with a protracted group of tips on each rope. Opt for a knot you are knowledgeable about and use that in your own most important sections. You will truly have a great deal of rope to maintain tabs with a blueprint this fashion, so it is ideal to follow along together with the tutorial.

13

Produce a category on a wall

1 way to make novice Macramé plant holders look More striking would be to put them together on the wall socket. Hang the holders from varying peaks and then use an range of blossoms. Pay attention to the manner at charlotte's house pulled this appearance with their own website.

14

Select a thick jute for outside usage

If You'd like on dangling from Your Macramé plant Holder out, it is ideal to choose a thick, thick durable rope on the endeavor. The motivated hive chose to get a natural-looking jute rope to obtain this very simple plant hanger guide. See how she achieved it today, and create one all on your own.

15

Wrap a planter Rather than knotting

This plant holder believed outside of Lia Griffith will be Ingenious because it hardly uses any flaws in any way. Discover ways to wrap a rope at the same manner by checking these out easy-to-follow directions.

Macramé knot directions

In this tutorial you will receive directions on the following Macramé knots.

Inch. Directions regarding the Best way to tie the fundamental 1 / 2 the knot. With special approaches to ensure it's fast and simple.

2. Directions concerning the Best way to tie some Very straightforward square knot.

3. Instructions for creating an essential overhand knot.

4. Directions for making the Macramé flat blueprint Design.

5. Directions for making the Macramé spiral Design.

6. Higher Level instructions for creating a more Josephine knot.

A quick background of Macramé. The contemporary artwork of Cosmetic Macramé knots will have originated using Arabian weavers sometime in the 13th century. Arabian weavers might knot the surplus threads at the border of hand loomed cloths to cosmetic knots.

Macramé is just a really versatile craft. It's Been used in the creation of several forms of jewelry such as necklace, bracelets and chokers. In addition, it's used to create ordinary everyday things such as vases, plant accessories and drapes.

Thus, let us produce any Macramé knots.

Inch. The Absolute Best method to Make a Fundamental half of an Evening.

A half knot is among those very fundamental Macramé knots There really is. It creates the cornerstone of a number of those advanced knots and layouts that are made from Macramé. To earn a half knot that you want three elements. A center cable which remains stationary and 2 outside knotting strings.

Suggestion - half of knot linking is a Fantastic deal simpler if the core series is protected and educated.

Now to make our half knot take one of these Knotting strings go inside the middle string and below the alternative knotting chain. Next choose a second knotting cord and after that move under the middle chain along with on the preliminary knotting chain. Now pull tight. You've finished a Macramé half daily.

Now that is a technical summary of the way by That the Half knot is attached but does a expert get it done? Whenever you're this professionally the secret will be speed.

Step inch. Only take the best hand knotting cord on your right place stick it throughout the middle collection. This produces a loop in regards to the perfect hand.

Measure two. Only choose the Lefthand knotting cable on the left hand and put it around the ideal hand cable.

Step 3. After placing the left-handed string series Over the perfect hand knotting cable flex, it beneath. As you are bending it upon push your righthand finger and then mind during the ideal hand loop catch onto the left-handed cord together with your index finger and thumb and pull the loop.

Measure 4. Tug tight. In case your midst series is tight Since I proposed before you are capable to pull the knot tight fast and it goes to be secure and comfy. If your middle string isn't tight then you definitely would like to conduct the knot right into position. Done right each and every knot needs just to have a few moments to tie.

2. Square knot creating.

Now You Know how to tie a half knot You're all Set to make a square knot. Contemplating that a square knot is only 2 half knots attached against still another. So first we'll earn a half chance since we mentioned earlier in the day. But for the following 1 / 2 the square knot we'll begin with the 2 nd safest cable rather than the specific first knotting series. Only choose still another knotting strand and scrutinize the middle chain and below the contrary knotting chain. Then pick the very first knotting cord and after that move under the middle chain and over a second knotting cord. Tug tight. You've just finished a square knot.

3. Guidelines for linking an overhand knot.

An overhand knot is an extremely basic simple Macramé knot. To generate an overhand knot need you rope. Start with making a loop interior Your personal series. Bring the end of the chain underneath the cable and also throughout the loop. Pull tight and you're finished.

4. Instructions for developing a Macramé flat pattern design. In Macramé the flat layout design is created when a streak of consecutive square knots is attached together.

5. Instructions for developing a Macramé spiral design. The Macramé spiral design was created when a selection of half knots are tied into a row. To watch the coil develop it's advised to tie at least four or even half knots.

6. Instructions for making a Josephine knot.

The Josephine knot is a somewhat complex advanced Macramé knot.

Measure 1. Take series a and sort it in a loop you'll placed along with series b.

Measure 2. Take string b and deliver this up and above the initial end of series a.

Measure 3. Proceed to manoeuvre cord b up and then send it under another end of strand a.

Measure 4. Now bring cable down b and over cord a.

Quantify 5. Continue transferring rope down b passing under cord b that's right it's going pass under itself.

Quantify 6. Next bring cable b inside the outside of cable a.

Quantify 7. Pull evenly onto all four cables to finish the Josephine knot.

CHAPTER 6:

Macramè Patterns Step By Step And Easy To Follow With Clear Images

Decorating your home is the dream of everyone. The inclusion of decorative items will re ally make your house look amazing and stylish. The right decoration items will bring tog ether all the components of your interior decor. One of the ways to decoate your walls with beautiful art is through Macrame. Macramé helps to create decorative items of versatile designs

Macramé Christmas Tree:

The macramé Christmas Tree Design is perfect for decorating your house, and it also makes a very good present. The piece's finished size will be around 31 inches in length, so pick a beautiful place on to the room wall to display the beauty!

Materials Required:

- 30, 20mm round redwood bead

- 7 ply 8mm of jute 41 yds in length.

- One dowel stick, 1.5" diameter 17" in length.

- One average sized bow tie and other ornament

- 1,1%" diameter ring or circle

Directions:

1. Cut fourteen strings of length 2 1/2 yds all.

2. Now cut two more ties. Their measures should be 3 yds both.

3. Wrap two of the 2 1/2 yds strings on the one and a half inch ring by the help of Lark's Head knots (LHK).

4. Move down to seventeen inches and wrap cords using Double Half Hitch knot (DHH) ties near the edge of the dowel.

5. Fold the two of three yards string. Strings in half now join 1 on every one of the external strings with Lark's Heads, near the top portion. Double Half Hitch (DHH) these tied strings to the inner ones.

6. Add one bead to two of your middle strings closest to the top edge, and then add one Square Knot (SK) underneath the bead with the help of the remaining four cords.

7. Wrap 2 two and a half yd strings, one on every exterior strings, with the help of a Lark's Heads knot (LHK), roughly an inch from the previous Lark's Head knot (as in step 3), now Double Half Hitch (DHH) these to the inner strings   as you have already done in stage 3.

8. Split strings into two sets: each group must have four wires. Two middle-cords are your filler cords (FC) of every group. Take the two of your filler cords (FC) from each set and slide a bead through it, and make one square knot (SK) under every bead.

9. Join 2 more strings, as done in the last step, on the external cords, and Double Half Hitch (DHH) it all to the underside of the ties as done earlier.

10. Split the cords among three sections, four wires in each section, and repeat as done in step no 6, but this time with three beads.

11. Attach two more strings as set out in phase no 7.

12. Split the cords into four sets, of four strings in each set, and redo as in stage 6 with four beads.

13. Take down about an inches and make up four Square Knots (SK) in a line.

14. Redo stage 7 by attaching two more cords to the existing set. Now split these cords into five groups of four ties each, and redo as is done in stage no 6, but with five beads this time.

15. Again redo stage 7 by adding two more cords to the existing group; split ties into six groups and redo as is done in stage 6. Redo this stage another time, the final time using seven beads.

16. Double Half hitch (DHH) all the cords to the rod of the dowel and put one bead at the ends of the dowel.

17. Collect all the cords and tie them up using a bow at about four inches underneath the dowel stick. Embed decoration into the bow, if necessary.

451

Simple Macramé Table Runner DIY

Consider them as layers which complement and contrasts when decorating any location. Whether it's color, shape, or size, these three elements will make a space feel less simple. The fourth piece of advice is on versatility! This Macramé table runner marks all the check boxes, and with its simple yet unique style has made this sleek breakfast nook much more unique.

All that is required to learn are three easy knots, and you have a charming table decoration at your hands. If you're aware with the knots mentioned here, then you can tailor your table runner that suits your table length, or alter it entirely and build a DIY wall hanging!

Materials Needed:

- 12 inch dowel

- Twenty-two strands of 16 inch cotton rope of length 3mm

- Scissors

- Over door handle

- 2 inch of cotton twine for the dowel hanger

Knots Used:

- the lark's head knot

- the half-hitch knot

- the square knot

Step by Step Instructions:

1. Tie cotton string to both the corners of your wooden dowel and suspend it using your over the door handle. Fold in half your 1st 16 inch rope loop, and build the head knot of a lark over your dowel. For more specific measures, please see this below.

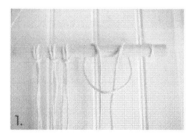

2. Continue to add up every 16' rope strand; use the head knot of a lark till you have a minimum of 22. That will send you 44 working strands.

3. Pull the right outer rope over the front side of all of your other ropes (to your left) and cover the end on the hook at your entrance. This will be the basis for the following row of knots called a half hitch knot which creates a straight row using the 2nd rope to tie a solo knot across the cord that you've just stretched over so that it's about 6" below your dowel.

4. Bind a second knot over the base strand using the same strand. This is considered a knot semi-hitch.

5. Assure they are clear and even.

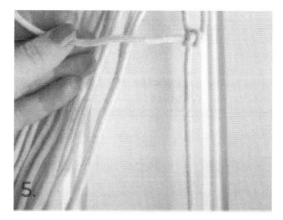

6. Repeat from the outside with the 2nd, 3rd, and 4th rope and add a new half hitch knot to keep it tight, etc. You're going to start looking at trends. That is a Half-Hitch horizontal.

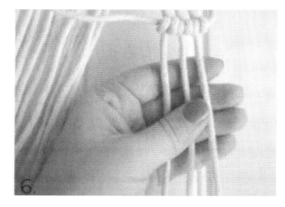

7. Continue to tie consecutive knots all around. Don't make this too close that the space at the sides is drawn in.

8. Using the outer four strands from your right side again, and make a square knot (SK) about 1.5" below the horizontal knots.

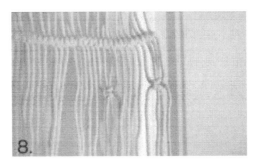

Miss the next 4 strands (five to eight) and use cords 9 through 12 to form another square knot. Start to skip four, linking up to four before you get through the whole way.

9. Using the 4 cords you missed (five to eight) and make a square knot (SK) around 3" under the dowel, beginning from the right side again.

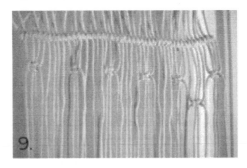

10. Keep ting the four- skipped sets in square knots (SK) until you end the sequence.

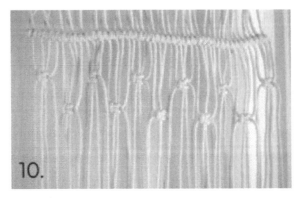

11. Move the two outer strands off to your left at the top. In step seven, we are using strands 3 to 6 to make another square knot (SK) about 11" below the

horizontal row of knots. Then use the next four strands to construct another square knot over the last square knot (SK), around 1.5".

12.　　　　Go all around, as shown. With the past two lines, you won't do anything.

13.　　　　Creates another series of straight half hitch knots beginning from the right side again by redoing phases from 3 through 7.

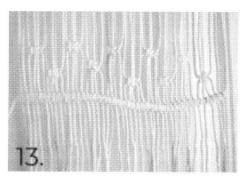

14. Using the similar base string of cord from the left side, then build a new horizontal half hitch line of knots about two and a half inch below the previous. On this one, you are going to be starting from left to right.

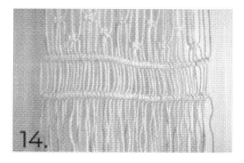

15. Build a line of square knots (SK) on the left side without missing any threads that lie around 1" below the horizontal row of knot. Now make a 2nd row of square knots (SK) by missing the 1st two threads on to the left before joining a complete line of square knots together. This is known as alternating square knot (ASK). You don't want a lot of space between those rows, and you can draw them together closely as every square knot (SK) is applied.

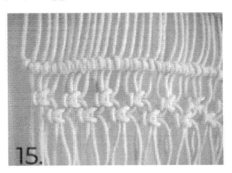

16. Redo until you have a limit of about thirteen rows of alternating square knots (ASK). This portion is the core of the table runner, and anything other after this stage should echo what you've already woven above.

17. Attach another half-hitch horizontal line of knots beginning from the outer left hand side and making the way to your right hand side.

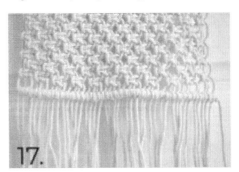

18. Dropdown another 2.5" and use the identical base rope to make another half-hitch horizontal line of knots going from right to left.

19. Miss the outermost 2 strands of the rope to the right for this part, and now tie a square knot (SK) by taking strands 3 to 6. Miss strands from seven to ten, then use strands from 11 to 14 to make a new square knot. Undo, so for every 4 strands, you missed. On to the left hand side, you will have six strings.

Miss 1 and 2 cords on the left hand side and tie three to six strands to make a square knot (SK) approximately 1.5" below the last row of square knots. Then miss the next 4 strands and end the pattern for the square knots second section. This would put you on the right hand side, with six extra strands.

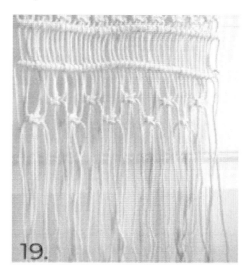

20. Measure 11" from the last created line of horizontal ties and make a square knot (SK) to the right using the four outer threads. Then tie the following 4 cords into a square knot (SK) over the previous knot, around 1.5".

21. Repeat the same, entire way

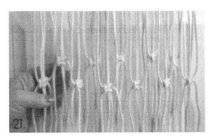

20.   Lastly, tie one last line of parallel half hitch knots around 1.5" under the alternating square knots (ASK) level. Trim the edges to be as lengthy as you wish, indicating how lengthy they are on the differing end. Clip the cotton string from the dowel and softly pull off all the knots of the lark's head. Now cut the head knot core of the lark, and shorten the ends.

Your table runner's center is the right place for a decoration, so put on a vase, and finds some fresh roses to support anchor your eye. You may also use it on a breakfast slab as your own giant place mat to ensure your kitchen looks its finest! You may also use the 3 basic knots you've mastered, the lark head knot (LHK), the half hitch knot and the square knot (SK) to make a number of layered wall hangings!

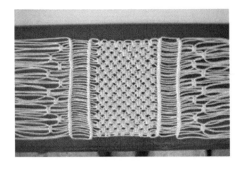

CHAPTER 7:

Sennit Patterns: Basic Knots And Their Uses

Capuchin Knot

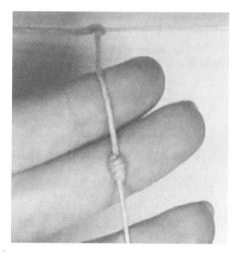

This knot for any project and can be used as the foundation for the base of the project. Use lightweight cord for this – it can be purchased at craft stores or online, wherever you get your macramé supplies.

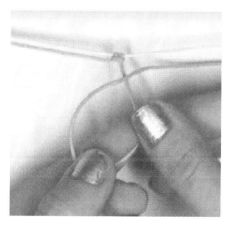

Watch the photos very carefully as you move along with this project, and take your time to make sure you are using the right string in the right point of the project.

Don't rush, and make sure you have even tension throughout. Practice makes perfect, but with the illustrations to help you, you'll find it's not hard at all to create.

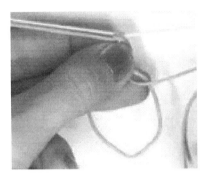

Start with the base cord, tying the knot onto this and working your way along the project.

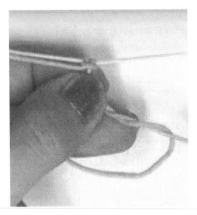

Twist the cord around itself 2 times, pulling the string through the center to form the knot.

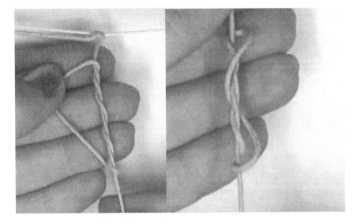

For the finished project, make sure that you have all your knots secure and firm throughout, and do your best to make sure it is all even. It is going to take practice before you are able to get it perfectly each time, but remember that practice does make perfect, and with time, you are going to get it without too much trouble.

Make sure all is even and secure, and tie off. Snip off all the loose ends, and you are ready to go!

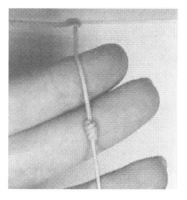

Crown Knot

This is a great beginning knot for any project, and can be used as the foundation for the base of the project. Use lightweight cord for this – it can be purchased at craft stores or online, wherever you get your macramé supplies.

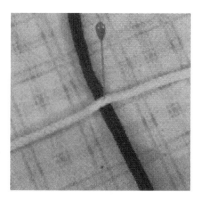

462

Watch the photos very carefully as you move along with this project, and take your time to make sure you are using the right string in the right point of the project.

Don't rush, and make sure you have even tension throughout. Practice makes perfect, but with the illustrations to help you, you'll find it's not hard at all to create.

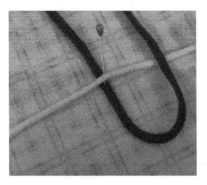

Use a pin to help keep everything in place as you are working.

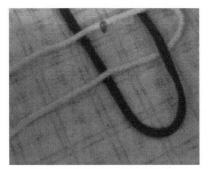

Weave the strings in and out of each other as you can see in the photos. It helps to practice with different colors to help you see what is going on.

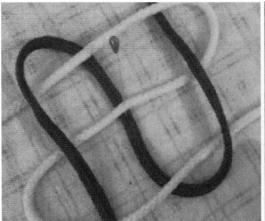

Pull the knot tight, then repeat for the next row on the outside.

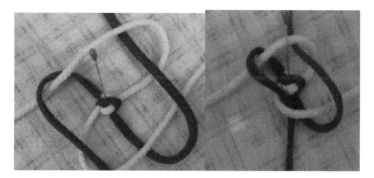

Continue to do this as often as you like to create the knot. You can make it as thick as you like, depending on the project. You can also create more than one length on the same cord.

For the finished project, make sure that you have all your knots secure and firm throughout, and do your best to make sure it is all even. It is going to take practice before you are able to get it perfectly each time, but remember that practice does make perfect, and with time, you are going to get it without too much trouble.

Make sure all is even and secure, and tie off. Snip off all the loose ends, and you are ready to go!

Diagonal Double Half Knot

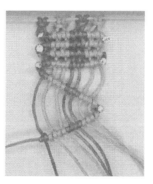

This is the perfect knot to use for basket hangings, decorations, or any projects that are going to require you to put weight on the project.

Use a heavier weight cord for this, which you can find at craft stores or online.

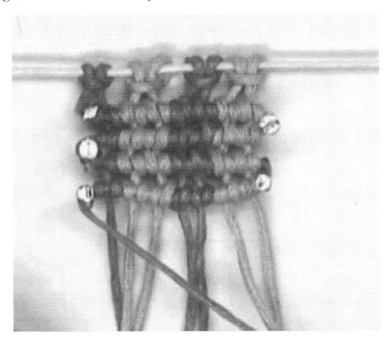

Watch the photos very carefully as you move along with this project, and take your time to make sure you are using the right string in the right point of the project.

Don't rush, and make sure you have even tension throughout. Practice makes perfect, but with the illustrations to help you, you'll find it's not hard at all to create.

Start at the top of the project and work your way toward the bottom. Keep it even as you work your way throughout the piece.

Tie the knots at 4 inch intervals, working your way down the entire thing.

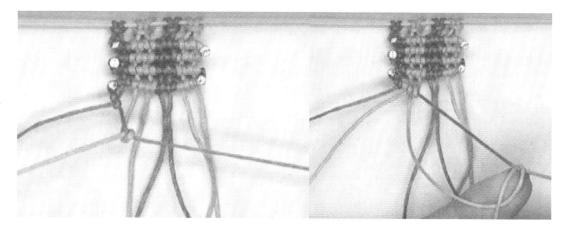

Weave in and out throughout, watching the photo as you can see for the right placement of the knots. Again, it helps to practice with different colors so you can see what you need to do throughout the piece.

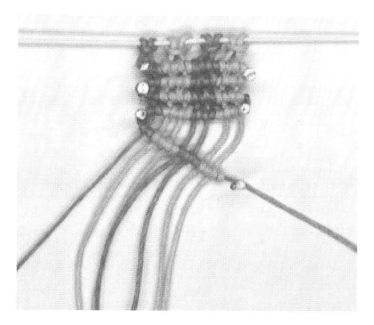

For the finished project, make sure that you have all your knots secure and firm throughout, and do your best to make sure it is all even. It is going to take practice before you are able to get it perfectly each time, but remember that practice does make perfect, and with time, you are going to get it without too much trouble.

Make sure all is even and secure, and tie off. Snip off all the loose ends, and you are ready to go!

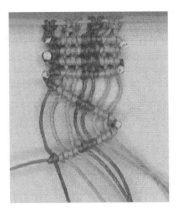

Frivolite Knot

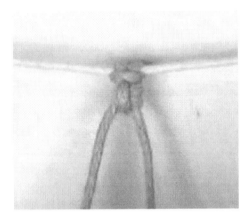

This is a great beginning knot for any project, and can be used as the foundation for the base of the project. Use lightweight cord for this – it can be purchased at craft stores or online, wherever you get your macramé supplies.

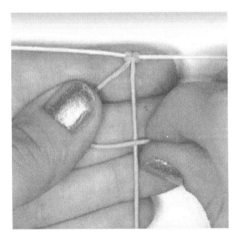

Watch the photos very carefully as you move along with this project, and take your time to make sure you are using the right string in the right point of the project.

Don't rush, and make sure you have even tension throughout. Practice makes perfect, but with the illustrations to help you, you'll find it's not hard at all to create.

Use the base string as the guide to hold it in place, then tie the knot onto this. This is a very straightforward knot, watch the photo and follow the directions you see.

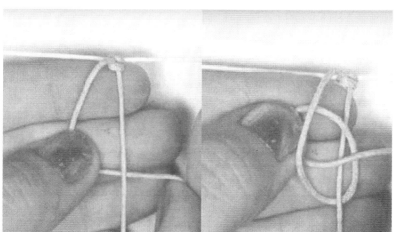

Pull the end of the cord up and through the center.

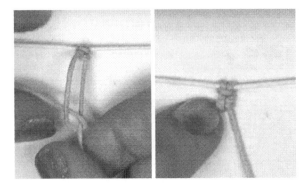

For the finished project, make sure that you have all your knots secure and firm throughout, and do your best to make sure it is all even. It is going to take practice before you are able to get it perfectly each time, but remember that practice does make perfect, and with time, you are going to get it without too much trouble.

Make sure all is even and secure, and tie off. Snip off all the loose ends, and you are ready to go!

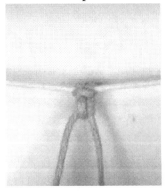

Horizontal Double Half Knot

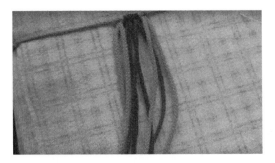

This is a great beginning knot for any project, and can be used as the foundation for the base of the project.

Use lightweight cord for this — it can be purchased at craft stores or online, wherever you get your macramé supplies.

Watch the photos very carefully as you move along with this project, and take your time to make sure you are using the right string in the right point of the project.

Don't rush, and make sure you have even tension throughout. Practice makes perfect, but with the illustrations to help you, you'll find it's not hard at all to create.

Start at the top of the project and work your way toward the bottom. Keep it even as you work your way throughout the piece. Tie the knots at 4 inch intervals, working your way down the entire thing.

For the finished project, make sure that you have all your knots secure and firm throughout, and do your best to make sure it is all even. It is going to take practice before you are able to get it perfectly each time, but remember that practice does make perfect, and with time, you are going to get it without too much trouble.

Make sure all is even and secure, and tie off. Snip off all the loose ends, and you are ready to go!

Josephine Knot

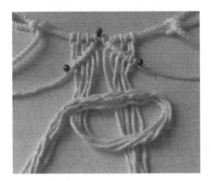

This is the perfect knot to use for basket hangings, decorations, or any projects that are going to require you to put weight on the project. Use a heavier weight cord for this, which you can find at craft stores or online.

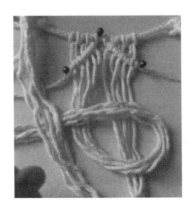

Watch the photos very carefully as you move along with this project, and take your time to make sure you are using the right string in the right point of the project.

Don't rush, and make sure you have even tension throughout. Practice makes perfect, but with the illustrations to help you, you'll find it's not hard at all to create.

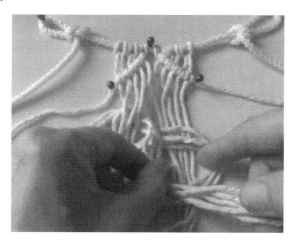

Use the pins along with the knots that you are tying, and work with larger areas all at the same time. This is going to help you keep the project in place as you continue to work throughout the piece.

Pull the ends of the knots through the loops, and form the ring in the center of the strings.

For the finished project, make sure that you have all your knots secure and firm throughout, and do your best to make sure it is all even.

It is going to take practice before you are able to get it perfectly each time, but remember that practice does make perfect, and with time, you are going to get it without too much trouble.

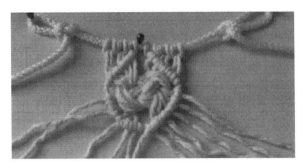

Make sure all is even and secure, and tie off. Snip off all the loose ends, and you are ready to go!

Lark's Head Knot

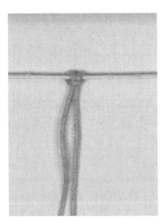

This is a great beginning knot for any project, and can be used as the foundation for the base of the project. Use lightweight cord for this – it can be purchased at craft stores or online, wherever you get your macramé supplies.

Watch the photos very carefully as you move along with this project, and take your time to make sure you are using the right string in the right point of the project.

Don't rush, and make sure you have even tension throughout. Practice makes perfect, but with the illustrations to help you, you'll find it's not hard at all to create.

Use the base string as the core part of the knot, working around the end of the string with the cord. Make sure all is even as you loop the string around the base of the cord.

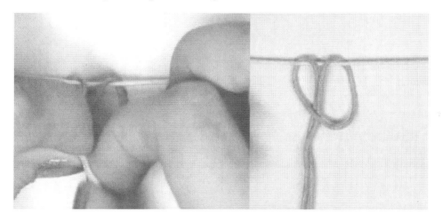

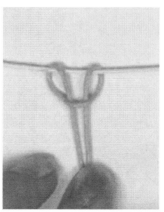

Create a slip knot around the base of the string and keep both ends even as you pull the cord through the center of the piece.

For the finished project, make sure that you have all your knots secure and firm throughout, and do your best to make sure it is all even. It is going to take practice before you are able to get it perfectly each time, but remember that practice does make perfect, and with time, you are going to get it without too much trouble.

Make sure all is even and secure, and tie off. Snip off all the loose ends, and you are ready to go!

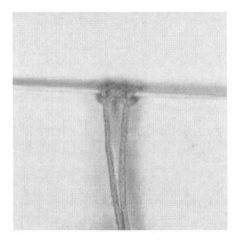

Reverse Lark's Head Knot

This is a great beginning knot for any project, and can be used as the foundation for the base of the project. Use lightweight cord for this – it can be purchased at craft stores or online, wherever you get your macramé supplies.

Watch the photos very carefully as you move along with this project, and take your time to make sure you are using the right string in the right point of the project.

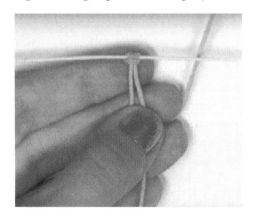

Don't rush, and make sure you have even tension throughout. Practice makes perfect, but with the illustrations to help you, you'll find it's not hard at all to create.

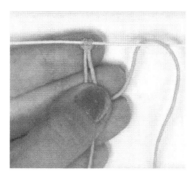

Use two hands to make sure that you have everything even and tight as you work. You can use tweezers if it helps to make it tight against the base of the string.

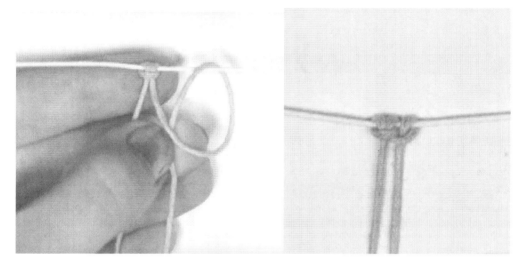

Use both hands to pull the string evenly down against the base string to create the knot.

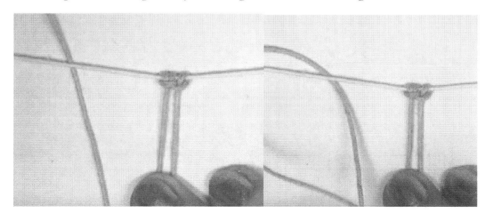

Again, keep the base even as you pull the center, creating the firm knot against your guide cord.

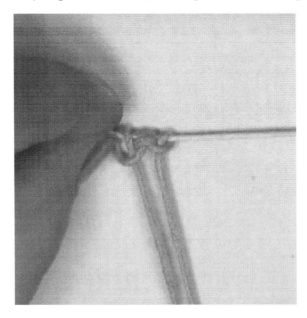

For the finished project, make sure that you have all your knots secure and firm throughout, and do your best to make sure it is all even. It is going to take practice before you are able to get it perfectly each time, but remember that practice does make perfect, and with time, you are going to get it without too much trouble.

CHAPTER 8:

Macrame knots and Pattern Techniques

Many Macramé tasks are easy to finish. Each job has a great deal of models to create it your own. At any time, you feel used to knotting, you are inclined to be in a position to produce your routines and make some genuinely exceptional cloths. Consider ways you can change a number of these Subsequent Macramé ideas:

- Wall-hangings

- Planters

- Crucial chains

- Hanging chairs

- Belts

- Antiques

Fringe on special fabrics

Millennials might have attracted Macramé past, but individuals of ages can indeed love and fall in love for this particular craft.

Button square knots: begin out with three square knots Then keep onto screw pliers by the back amid the horn cables before their original. Publish a rectangle under the bottom of this button to finish.

Cosmetic Dentistry: used making jewelry or to get Special knots such as Celtic and Chinese. These two approaches go perfectly with handmade jewelry and precious stones, for example semi-precious stones, crystals, or pearls. These Macramé knots usually are intricate and could possibly have a while to know.

Double-hitch knot: that Macramé knot is created by Generating two half hitch knots you afterward a second. Yank on the knots attentively.

Half Hitch knot: place Inch cable through your job Area (pin therefore that the cable will not proceed). At the finish of the cable that's been hauled across the unmoving cable is drawn under the cable and pulled the loop which has been shaped.

Half knot: One of the normal Macramé knots to create. A fifty% knot is really an ordinary knot, you start with four strings. Put it using this loop produced by the center cable together with your hand cable. Tug to Fasten the knot.

Overhand knot: Just One of the Most Often used knots in Macramé. Start out with developing a loop by way of one's own cable. Pull the knot carefully.

Square knots: construct out of this fifty-five percent knot to Produce the square knot. Take your righthand cable behind the center strings and then send it about the left-handed cable. Only choose the left-handed cable and place it throughout the ideal hand by simply moving the middle strings and pull.

Ever wanted to be able to make your own bracelets & designer handbag, but did not comprehend just how or did not have the appropriate resources? You have probably experienced such a difficulty. Well, macramé design is exactly what the physician ordered.

Macramé is just a sort of fabric which works by using knotting. Materials that are utilized from the macramé process comprise jute, linen, strings got out of cotton twine, yarn, and hemp. It's a procedure for knotting ropes codes or strings collectively with one another to check something. This item might be described as a necklace jewelry, necklace, etc. Macramé designs can possibly be made complicated if different knots have been united to produce one layout or complicated.

A macramé bracelet can be made under:

Desired materials a Razor-blade, a pencil or polyurethane Plank, or t-pin, a hemp cable, and sometimes some series of somebody else's taste.

Guidelines

Step 1: Measure Inch that the circumference of the wrist will probably soon be Measured. Afterward, cut two bits of this hemp rope together with the assistance of the scissors. The bits cut needs to be two times the magnitude of this wrist or the circumference measured initially. As an instance, when the dimension got was 5 inches, two strands measuring 15 inches per needs to be trimmed.

Step 2: Measure 2 strand is folded to around 30 minutes. Holding The pencil at a flat place, the strand is likely to probably be reverted onto the pen's cone to obviously possess a loop just on the leading portion of stand, also, to guarantee loose finishes do hang. These ends ought to be passed via the loop and closely pulled. This procedure ought to be replicated with yet another strand too. In the very long term, you'll have to get four strands hanging this particular pencil. Mentally, you might label these strands from side to left side, only 1 2. It's likely to work with whatever tagging procedure you locate easily.

Step 3: Measure 3 strand Inch ought to be obtained, on the other hand, significantly more than just two strands 2 and strand 3 (that in personality will be stranded at the center), and then below strand 4.

Step 4: in This Time select strand 4 supporting the two Strands 3 and 2, throughout the loop that strand inch did form. To be certain a half square rectangle is achieved, carefully pull strand 1 and strand 4.

Step 5: now you need to know a strand Constituting process. Take with this particular strand crossing process until fundamentally the bracelet accomplishes this particular period which you can so desire. Spirals will probably be formed in both square knots because you carry on working out.

Step 6: the loops have been slid off the pen. After that, pull strand 2 and strand 3 to have the ability to lower the magnitude in these loops shaped only a small bit. Each of those four strands may then hold together along with two knots attached like a way of procuring the job. These knots are crucial. Those strings which you side-by-side should subsequently be trimmed, and this also should attentively be performed since close those knots as you possibly can.

Step 7 in the time you have obtained the bracelet set on your own wrist. The-knot needs to be passed via the fold, therefore to keep up the bracelet onto your wrist.

The measures above will allow you to design a really Straight-forward macramé bracelet. This macramé approach uses knotting instead of weaving or knitting process. You may utilize beads to craft a beaded macramé necklace. You'll design distinguishing forms of decorations with macramé strategy. This is dependent upon you personally.

Fantasy catchers have gotten remarkably popular and so they're extended in an enormous variety of styles and layouts. It's likely to uncover crotchet, woven or knotted dream-catchers. Macramé is really a material making procedure which is based on knotting in the place of knitting or weaving. It's a French saying that ostensibly means knot since it's on the list of very first art-forms there really is. The main knots within this procedure are square knots and hitching types that may possibly be twice or entire feasibility.

Macramé is a technique that's been used for its maximum period to decorate and craft numerous goods. You'll detect magnificent among a sort macramé handbag, wall-hangings, fantasy catchers, and a good deal of longer. It isn't too complicated to produce your macramé dream house particularly the moment you have a couple of guides to take you through these knots. At any time, you have mastered the knotting, you're getting to be astounded by just how creative you can acquire.

The Strings

The strings are the most significant things you Are likely to have to generate your personal piece. Cotton twine strings would be one of the most common due to the complete appearance they furnish and you're getting to be in a posture to select unique colors to generate a design that fits with your taste. Besides cotton, then it's very likely to choose many substances for example cotton, linen, silk, and jute determined by the kind of structure that you would really like to realize. Numerous those cable chemicals are a ton easier for cosmetic purposes on the fantasy catcher than they truly are correct in creating a comprehensive slice.

Cord structure may potentially be 3-ply value it Consists of three different spans of fiber to produce a robust and superbly shaped fantasy catcher.

The Rings

Macramé fantasy catchers can be accomplished with just wooden joints nevertheless in some specific scenarios you could like to consider account a dowel determined by the dimensions of one's own thing. A decorative or metallic dowel may conduct the task well in offering you a fantastic surface to disperse a large number of strings and that means that you may readily control them to accomplish your favorite design in the very long haul. If you'd really like to produce smaller sized ones, a push board, maybe whatever you need to begin on work.

Decorations

Despite macramé fantasy catchers, it's extremely potential that you simply incorporate jewelry along with other cosmetic capabilities in the own piece. You're able to tie the ribbons using Different strand colors or maybe you include different necklaces, beads, and Cubes to make points of interest inside your design. It's likely to utilize right Hooks, u-pins or upholstery to preserve the decorations and strings put up. If You Would like to use beads as Well as another accessory, then you should pick strand thickness attentively; preferably thick strand can Not provide this alluring appearance using attachments. Thinner strings make it to Be potential for the decorations to stick out from elegance.

Mix and Match Knots to Create All Kinds of Patterns

The Square Knot and Square Knot Variations

The square knot is a very common and versatile knot that is used in macramé. Square knots can be tied in a sennet (a length of knots tied one after the other) or across many lengths of cords to create solid or netting like patterns. Each knot is made using two steps and needs a minimum of three cords. Two cords are needed for tying the knots and a further cord is needed to knot around. The following tutorial shows you how to tie a basic square knot using four cords and then how to use the knot in various forms.

Beads can be added to the knotting cords as you tie. They can also be threaded onto the central cords and then the knotting cords can be carried around them. For very large holed beads all the cords can be passed through the beads. The square knot can be tied individually or in sennets. Using two different colored cords will produce a simple pattern through the sennet. This knot can also be tied in various formations to achieve decorative and more complex looking patterns for jewelry making and other items. This guide contains photographs showing how to tie a basic square knot and then illustrates four further ways in which square knots can be used.

These steps can now be repeated to create as many knots as desired.

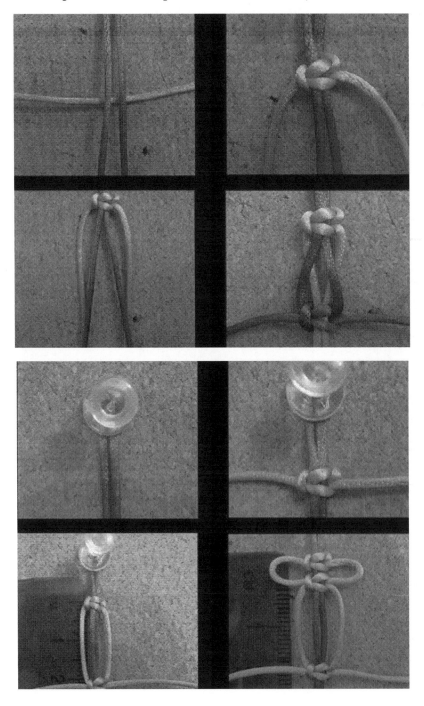

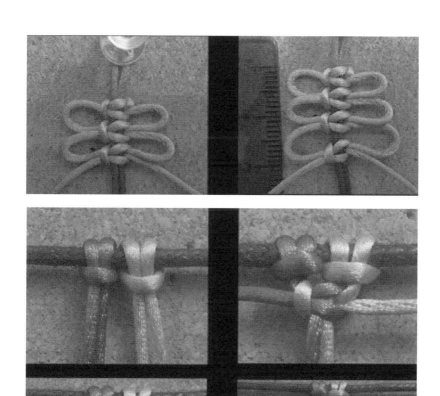

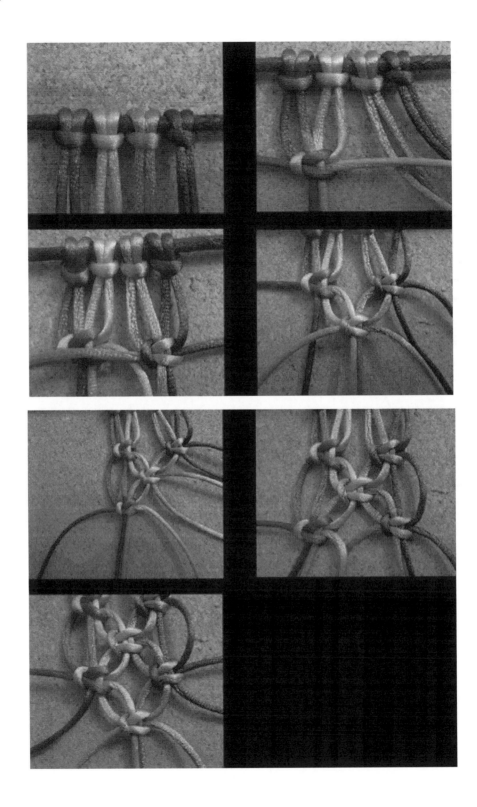

485

The Half Hitch Knot and Half Hitch Variations

The half hitch knot is another very common and versatile knot that is used in macramé. Like the square knot it is fairly easy to learn and can be used to create a variety of designs. Beads and other items can easily be added to either the central or knotting cords to embellish your designs.

Half hitch knots can be tied in two different ways. The knotting cord can be tied either over-under-over the holding cord or alternately it can be tied under-over-under the holding cord. I have included photographs showing both on the following pages. Either of these half hitch knots can be used to tie a variety of formations and I have included step by step photographs for four of these in the following part.

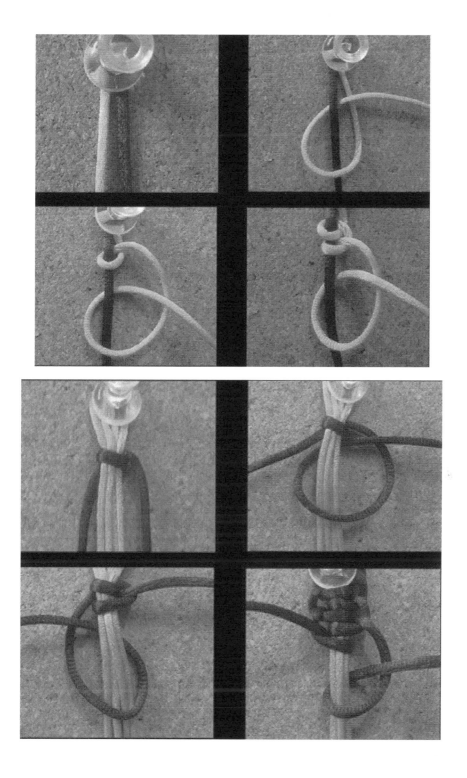

488

This is a vintage knot that can be used to create wide flat knotted pieces that would be suitable for bracelets, belts, bag straps, and similar. The width of the finished piece is based on the number of central cords used.

CHAPTER 9:

Panel Patterns

Designer Hat

T his Macramé Hat has a round top and a beautifully decorated brim with tiny triangles. It can also be used as a Macramé basket.

For this, it is recommended to use a material which is not extremely flexible, or it doesn't keep its shape. Bonnie Braid is used in the illustration given below.

A medium-sized hat with dimensions of 28 inches around with a 1.5-inch brim will be created here. If you want to make a smaller or larger hat, I have provided you with cord measurements.

It is a simple project for beginners.

Be sure to practice the decorative knots stated under before you attempt to make this personalized hat if you're new to Macramé.

Materials Required:

- 4mm Cord Material (114 yards)
- Fabric Glue
- Tape Measure
- Pins and Project Board

Knots used:

- Alternating Square Knots (ASK)
- Larks Head Knot
- Overhand Knot
- Double Half Hitch (DHH)

Step by Step Instructions:

1. For the hat created here, you will need to cut 56 cords, which should be 2 yards in length each. For a 24-inch hat cut one holding cord 36 inches long and 48 other strings, each of which must be 2 yards in length. For a 32-inch hat, you will need a total of 64 cords, 2.5 yards each. For a hat above or below these sizes, increase or decrease the size as needed (2 strings per inch). The number of cords you use should be multiples of 4. Fix the split ends of the cord with a tape. It would prevent the unraveling of the strings. Tie the holding string with your work station horizontally, and make sure it is stretched firmly. Fold in half one of the two-yard strings, and place it under the holding string, so that it lies near the center.

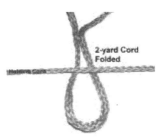

2. Place the ends over the holding cord to complete the formed Larks Head knot, going downward. Move them underneath the folded line. Stiffly close.

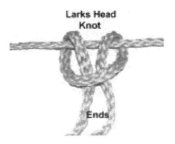

3. Attach each end of Half Hitch knot by leading the rope over and below the holding string. It will ride over the thread you're working with when you set it down.

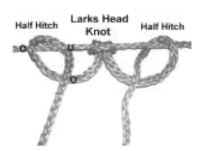

4. Repeat the steps from step 1 to 3, by wrapping the remaining strings to your holding string. Start working from the center and move to the ends. There must be an equivalent amount of strings in both directions.

5. For creating the edge for your Macramé Hat, chose any eight cords and marked them from cord 1 to 8 from left towards right. All the triangle designs are created using eight strings, so split them out now, before you start working on the triangles. Make a Square Knot with 2-4 strings. You only have one filler the string 3. Tightly firm it, so it sets against your mounted knots. Do it again with the strings 5, 6, and 7. This time the filler is cord 6.

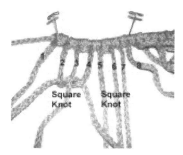

6. Now attach the other Square Knot under the first two, using strings 3 - 6 (two fillers – 4 and 5). Tighten the knots firmly, so it rests over the knots above it.

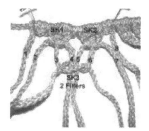

7. Move the cord number 1 with the left side of the three knots that forms a triangular shape. Lock it, so that it's tight since it is a holding string. Join the cords 2, 3, and 4 to it through the Double

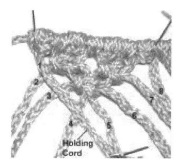

8. Move the string 8 along the right edge of the triangle, and fix it as well. Attach strings 5, 6, and 7 with it with a Double Half Hitch knot. Make sure not to attach the holding cord 1 with it, or the design will be unbalanced.

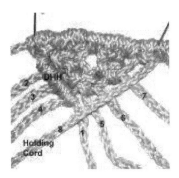

9. Make a cross using the firming string 1 and 8, and extent all the strings in a manner so it will be easier for you to see them. Attach a Square Knot using cords 1, 4, 5, and 8. Use cords 8 and 1 as the fillers. Firmly tie the knots, so that the knot stays below triangle level.

10. Repeat steps 5 to 9, to make additional triangle with the help of your next eight cords. Attach a Square Knot from the first line, with cords 6 and 7, and 2 and 3 from the second side. Tighten it so under each triangle it meets up with the Square Knot.

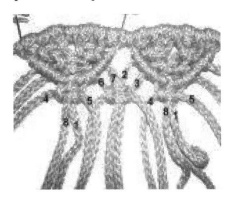

11. Repeat step from step no 5 to 10 with the help of remaining clusters of cords. When you reach the final triangle figure for your Macramé Hat, connect this triangle to the first triangle you created, to make a complete circle. Now begin turning upside down the brim of your Macramé Cap. Although actually the right side of the triangles is on the opposite side of the hat. Keep in mind that the brim which is created will be folded in a manner, so the orders are swapped. It can be also be seen in the picture attached below, which is showing the rear side of the triangles at the moment, where you will be doing your work.

Attach a Square Knot with the help of strings 2 and 3 from the first triangle that you created, with 6 and 7 from the last triangle. It is just what you have done in the previous step, and the only difference is that the cords come from each edge of the brim.

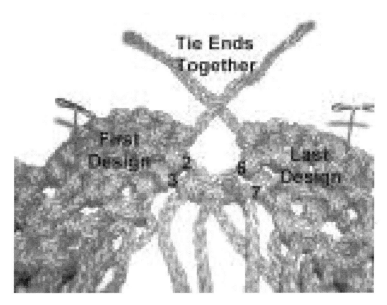

12. To create the top part, you will link a row of Alternating Square knots (ASK) using 4 cords per knot, two working cords, and two fillers. Starting at the place where the two ends were connected in phase 7 is easiest, then continuing around the entire route. To create the next row, alternate the strings. Keep the brim on the inner side while creating your hat. Mentally number each set with four cords. Strings No.1 and No.4 act as the working cords, while two and three are the filler cords. Combine 3 and 4 with 1 and 2 from next knot over to alternate for next lines. And the current knot lies between the two above.

13. Stop tying Alternating Square Knot when your Macramé hat is at least 7 inches in height which starts from the lower end of the brim, till the row of knots that you are currently working on. Keep in mind you'll cover the bottom, so you'll only have a couple more rows to add to the top.

14. Choose 12 cords that are coming from the three Alternating Square Knots. Visually mark each set with four cords as A, B, and C. Push all the four strings from the set B to the inside of the Macramé hat.

15. Use the cords 3 and 4 from set A (that is at the extreme left side), with strings No.1 and No.2 from your set C. With these four ropes, tie securely a Square Knot over the gap left by the strings you just put through. Tighten the knots firmly. So the top edge of your hat will appear more rounded.

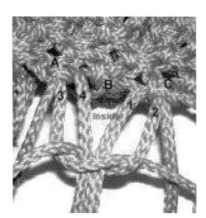

16. Repeat the previous step by dropping all the remaining knots by pushing the knots inside. This will fasten the top of the Macramé Hat. Do steps 3 and 4 two more times, until you've been all the way back? Move the remaining cords into the inside until you are done.

17. Take the right side of the hat up. Note, that the front of the triangles at the top is the bottom, and while you're focusing on these final stages, they can be seen around the lower lip. Tie two very

tight overhead knot using two cords at a time but from two different knots. Hook one knot, apply adhesive to the thread, then tie the knot next to the previous. Trim the excess cords after you tie the knots. As the strings are taped at the ends, you can simply cut them off to identify which cords are used. After you are done with tying all the knots, let the glue dry and cut off any extra material. Switch the Designer Hat's brim outwards, arrange it at the triangular tip.

Macramé Pillow

Now we will learn how to create this beautiful DIY Macramé Pillow. It's not as complicated as it looks– the toughest part is to cut the long cords.

Knots used:

- Lark Head Knot

- Square Knot

- Double Half Hitch Knot

Materials Needed:

- Macramé Cord

- Sewing Machine/Thread (optional)

- Dowel or Stick

- Scissors

- Pillow cover and insert

- Tape Measure

Step by Step Instructions:

You can start with your pillow cover you have for this pillow, or create a simple pillow cover for any pillow available. Don't just make it yet-see first Stage no 5. In the illustration below, the pillow cover is made of drop fabric. This ended up exactly identical to the rope, which looks impressive.

However, if you do want to see the Macramé show, pick a different color for your pillow cover.

The cover in the picture is 20 x 20 inches, for reference. You have to ensure that your Macramé pattern can cover your pillow-but if not. The best news is if required, it can be stretched out.

1. 12-foot string.

2. Using reverse lark's head knots tie all 16 cords to the dowel. You've learned how to tie a lark head knot to build the hat in the previous instructions.

3. For this cover, the pattern is the only rows of alternating square knots. Leave a little gap among each knot-around half of an inch as a reference. Having a little space makes the project run even quicker.

You have to keep making the alternating square knots till you get down to the 20 " edge. Measure using the tape to watch where you are.

Create two horizontal rows of (left-to-right, then right-to-left) double half-hitch knots until you touch down the bottom.

4. So, now that we're done with the design cut off the excess from the bottom but keep a piece of the fringe – about 5 inches or so. You may leave more or less, it's entirely up to you.

So, you are either going to remove your pattern from the rod or just cut it off.

5. Break it off. Here's how you stick the Macramé design to your pillow. Before you stitch it up, whether you're making a cover by yourself – you're necessarily going to line up the design to the facade of the cover, leaving the cut edges a little over the top hang.

Place the back part over the cover, and Macramé design-right sides are facing each other-essentially you make a sandwich, and the Macramé design is called the "meat."

So, now patch your pillow cover's top edge-go above the cords too! Then it takes some degree of finesse, however you can fix it. Pin it all down to hold it all together.

Shove the Macramé pattern within your pillow to stitch rest of your pillow cover and stitch the remaining seams as usual.

Take another length of the Macramé cord and tie an easy knot on the back to attach the rest of the cover. Loop this string from out and in of square knots. Not only does this help spread out your pattern.

Yet it must protect it down to the bottom too.

That is it! At the bottom edge of your pillow, the fringes will hang.

For A Ready Made Pillow Cover: You can open one of the joints and follow the instructions above or simply take the other piece of Macramé cord and thread it around the top. Then twist it backward. As mentioned above, you can also tie the sides.

Or, you could even hand stitch it to your pillow cover that certainly gives your sofa or easy chair a bit of an oomph. Yet this is sort of a novelty cushion – laying your head on it is kind of uncomfortable.

CHAPTER 10:

Macrame Project

Cross Choker

Step 1 - Fold over the first 1.5 inches if the shorter length of rattail cord. This will be used to create a loop as part of the bracelets fastening.

Step 2 - Fold the longer length of cord in half. Place the center point underneath the shorter cord and tie one square knot. These will be your knotting cords. This knot needs to be positioned so that it creates a loop in the end of the shorter cord that the disk bead can fit through with some pressure. If the bead slides through too easily there is a possibility that the bracelet could come unfastened.

Step 3 - Tie a further five square knots.

Pull each knot tight as these are holding the two lengths of cord together.

Step 4 - Continue tying square knots until you have a Sennett 5.5 inches long.

Step 5 - Thread one silver foil bead on to the central cord.

Step 6 - Bring the knotting cords around the bead and tie one square knot.

Step 7 - Now thread on one cross charm and push it up to the last square knot. Because of the hole positioning the cross will not lay flat

Step 8 - Tie another square knot around the cross top.

Step 9 - Continue with steps 5 - 8 until all the beads and crosses have been added.

Step 10 - Now tie another Sennett of square knots 5.5 inches long.

Step 11 - Leaving a 3mm tail cut of the excess knotting cords. Using the lighter gently melt the ends and press them on to the square knots.

Care needs to be taken with this step as the melted cord can get very hot and stick to skin and burn. It is best to use a needle or scissor point to press down the cord.

Step 12 - Thread the disk bead (or button) on to the remaining cord.

Step 13 - Leaving a 3mm gap tie an overhand knot to secure the bead.

Step 14 - Cut of the excess cord and heat the ends gently with the lighter to seal and prevent fraying.

Macramé Beaded Wave Bracelets

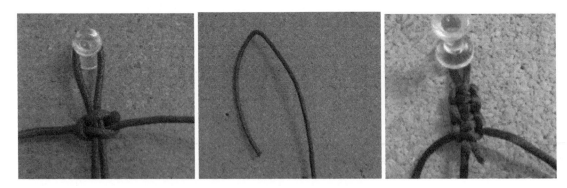

Step 1 - Fold over the first 2 inches of the shorter length of waxed cotton cord.

Step 2 - Fold one of the long lengths of waxed cord in half. Place the half-way point underneath the shorter cord and tie one square knot around both cords.

Position the knot so that the loop created is a tight fit for the 12mm bead/button to fit through.

Step 3 - Fold a second longer length of cord in half and tie one square knot as in step one, directing under the existing knot.

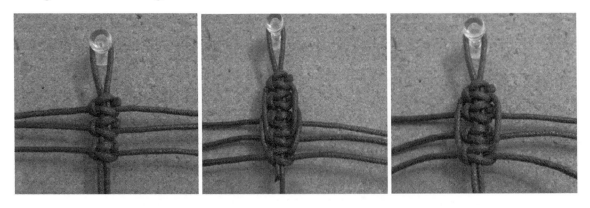

Step 4 - Repeat step 3 with the final length of waxed cord. Tighten each of these knots as they are holding the bracelets fastener secure and if they are loosed it may work itself undone with wear.

Step 5 - Arrange the cords so they are laying out to the sides of your central cord. Carry the first pair of cords over the others and tie one square knot underneath the set of three knots previously tied.

Step 6 - Repeat step 5 using the second pair of cords.

Step 7 - Finally repeat step 5 again with the third set of cords.

Step 8 - Thread one 8mm bead onto the central cord. Carry the first set of cords over the others and tie one square knot underneath the bead.

Step 9 - Carry the second set of cords over the others and tie one square knot underneath under the knot created in step 8.

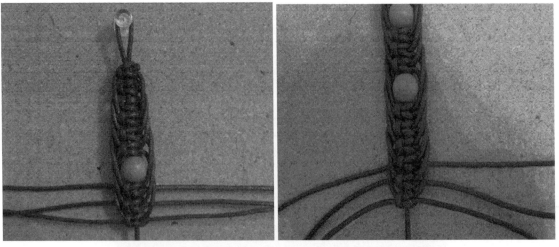

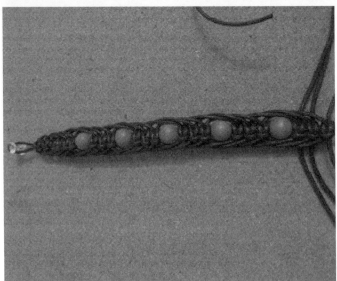

Step 10 - Repeat step 9 using the third set of cords.

Step 11 - Repeat steps 8 to 10 until you have added all five beads to the bracelet. Take care to always carry the cords over each other to keep the pattern continuous.

The bracelet length can be adjusted by adding or removing beads or by tying square knots at the beginning and end of the bracelet.

Step 12 - Repeat steps 5 - 7 so you have six square knots after the fifth bead.

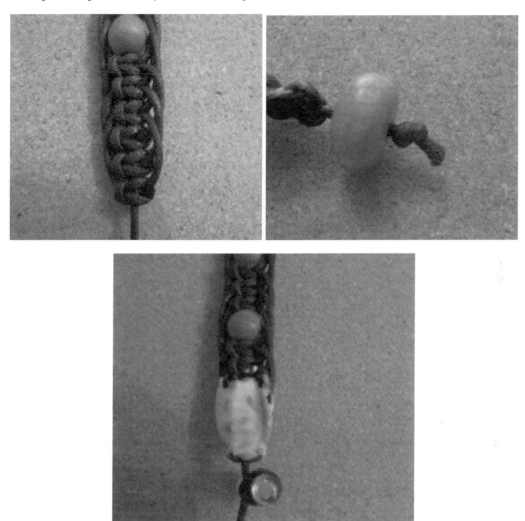

Step 13 - Pull the cords to tighten the final knots and then cut off the remaining cord.

Step 14 - Cover the cord ends and the surrounding area in PVA glue and allow to dry.

Step 15 - Thread the 12mm bead/button onto the central cord.

Rainbow Bows Macramé Bracelet

Step 1 - Fold over the first 3cm on the shorter cord and secure it to your macramé board (if using) or lay it flat in front of you.

Step 2 - Fold in half the longer length of cord and tie one square knot around the cords. These will be your knotting cords.

Position the knot so that the loop created is sized to fit the disk bead/button through snugly. This loop forms part of the bracelets fastener and if it is too big, the bracelet may come unfastened.

Step 3 - Tie a further four-square knot.

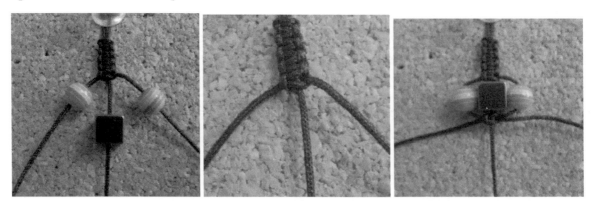

Step 4 - Very carefully trim off the short central cord.

Step 5 - Now begin added beads to the bracelet. To do this thread one hematite cube bead on to the central cord and one rainbow bead on to each of the knotting (side) cords.

Step 6 - Tie one square knot underneath the cube bead and maneuver the beads into place as you do.

Step 7 - Continue adding beads in this way (steps 5 and 6) until they all been knotted into the bracelet.

Take care to keep the rainbow beads all the same way up. So, if the first beads have the red stripe first, keep them all this way up as this will lead to a neater and more fluid finished look.

Step 8 - Tie four square knots so you have five in total.

Step 9 - Turn the bracelet over and trim of the excess knotting cords, leaving a 3mm tail.

Step 10 - Using the lighter gently melt the cord ends and press them against the back of the bracelet to seal.

Take care with this step as the cord can get very hot and burn. The point of the scissors can be used to press the ends down.

Step 11 - Thread the disk bead/button onto the central cord. Leave a 3mm gap between the bead and the square knots and tie one overhand knot to secure.

Step 12 -. Use the lighter to gently melt the cord ends and fuse them to the final square knot.

Take care completing this step as the cord will get hot and can stick to your stick and burn. Use the scissors or a needle to press the cords down.

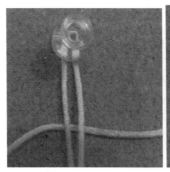  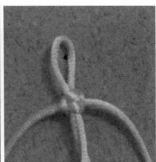

Beaded Half Macramé Bracelet

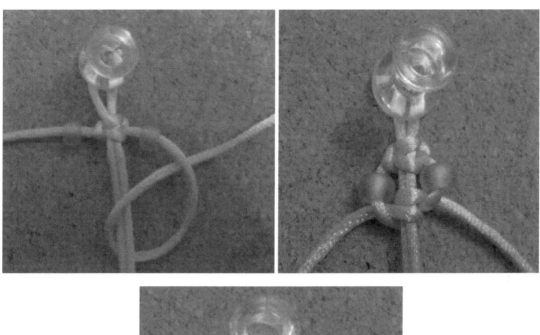

Step 1 - Gently melt the rattail cord ends. This stop fraying and makes it easier to thread the beads on.

Fold in half the 20-inch length of rattail and lay it flat in front of you. This will be your central cords.

Step 2 - Fold the long length of cord in half and place the center point underneath the shorter cord. This will be your knotting cords.

Step 3 - 1 cm from the top of the cord loop tie one square knot.

This knot needs to be placed so that the flat bead fits through the loop but is a tight fit.

Step 4 - Thread one frosted capri blue bead onto each of the yellow knotting cords and push them up to the square knot tied in step 3.

Step 5 - Using the right-side cord tie one half hitch knot and pull tight.

Step 6 - Now use the left side cord to tie one half hitch knot underneath the first.

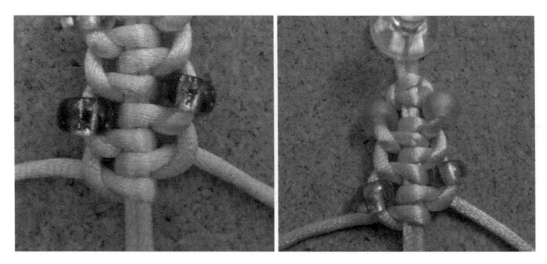

Step 7 - Tie one half hitch knot with each cord starting with the right side.

Step 8 - Thread one blue lined bead on to each cord.

Step 9 - Tie a set of half hitch knots, first using the right cord and then the left.

Step 10 - Tie one half hitch knot with each cord starting with the right side.

Step 11 - Repeat step 8 - 10, this time using the silver lined sapphire beads.

Step 12 - Finally repeat steps 8 - 10 using the frosted dark blue beads.

Continue adding beads in this way until all the beads have been added. The bracelet will measure approx. 7.5 inches long.

Bead order: Frosted cobalt blue, blue lined, silver lined sapphire and then frosted dark blue.

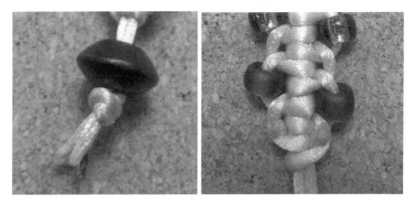

Step 13 - Trim the two knotting cords leaving a 3mm end.

Using the lighter gently melt the cord ends and fuse them to the back of the bracelet.

Do not put the cord into the flame or it will burn and discolor, just hold it close. The melted cord is very hot and can stick to your skin and burn so it is safer to use a needle, scissors point of like press them down on the bracelet.

Step 14 - Thread the flat bead onto the two central cords and leaving a 3mm gap between the bead and the final half hitch knot, secure it using an overhand knot.

Cut off the excess central cords and melt the end to prevent it fraying.

Modern Macramé Hanging Planter

Plant hangers are beautiful because they give your house or garden the feel of an airy, natural space. This one is perfect for condominiums or small apartments—and for those with minimalist, modern themes!

Plant Pot

Supplies:

- 50 ft. Par cord (Parachute Cord)

- 16 to 20 mm wooden beads

First, fold in half 4 strands of the cord and then loop so you could form a knot.

Now, divide the cords into groups of two and make sure to string 2 cords through one of the wooden beads you have on hand. String some more beads—at least 4 on each set of 2 grouped cords.

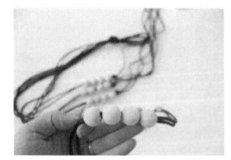

Then, measure every 27.5 inches and tie a knot at that point and repeat this process for every set of cords.

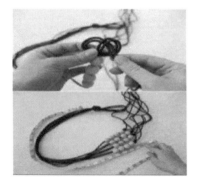

Look at the left set of the cord and tie it to the right string. Repeat on the four sets so that you could make at least 3" from the knot you have previously made.

Tie another four knots from the previous knot that you have made. Make them at least 4.5" each.

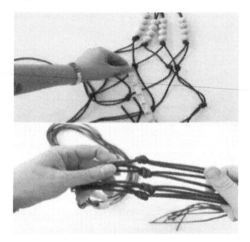

Group all the cords together and tie a knot to finish the planter. You will get something like the one shown below—and you could just add your very own planter to it!

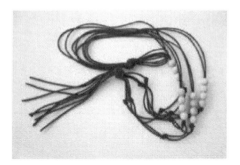

Mini Macramé Planters

Succulents are all the rage these days because they are just so cute and are decorative! What is more is that you can make a lot of them and place them around the house—that will give your place a unique look!

Supplies:

- Small container

- Garden soil/potting mix

- Succulents/miniature plants

- ¼ inch jump ring

- 8 yards embroidery thread or thin cord

Cut 36-inch of 8 lengths of cord. Make sure that 18 inches are already enough to cover enough half-hitches. If not, you can always add more. Let the thread loop over the ring and then tie a wrap knot that could hold all the cords together.

Create a half-twist knot by tying half of a square knot and repeating it multiple times with the rest of the cord.

Drop a quarter inch of the cord down and repeat step twice.

Arrange your planter and place it on the hanger that you have made.

Nail to the wall and enjoy seeing your mini planter!

CHAPTER 11:

Projects 2

Serenity Bracelet

(Note: if you are familiar with the flat knot, you can move right along into the pattern)

This novice bracelet offers plenty of practice using one of micro macramé's most used knots. You will also gain experience beading and equalizing tension. This bracelet features a button closure and the finished length is 7 inches.

Knots Used:

- Flat Knot (aka square knot)

- Overhand knot

Supplies:

- White C-Lon cord, 6 ½ ft, x 3

- 18 - Frosted Purple size 6 beads

- 36 - Purple seed beads, size 11

- 1 - 1 cm Purple and white focal bead

- 26 - Dark Purple size 6 beads

- 1 - 5 mm Purple button closure bead

(Note: the button bead needs to be able to fit onto all 6 cords)

Instructions:

Take all 3 cords and fold them in half. Find the center and place on your work surface as shown:

Now hold the cords and tie an overhand knot, loosely, at the center point. It should look like this:

1. We will now make a buttonhole closure. Just below the knot, take each outer cord and tie a flat knot (aka square knot). Continue tying flat knots until you have about 2 ½ cm.

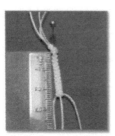

2. Undo your overhand knot and place the ends together in a horseshoe shape.

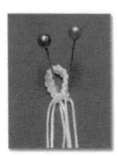

3. We now have all 6 cords together. Think of the cords as numbered 1 through 6 from left to right. Cords 2-5 will stay in the middle as filler cords. Find cord 1 and 6 and use these to tie flat knots around the filler cords. (Note: now you can pass your button bead through the opening to ensure a good fit. Add or subtract flat knots as needed to create a snug fit. This size should be fine for a 5mm bead). Continue to tie flat knots until you have 4 cm worth. (To increase bracelet length, add more flat knots here, and the equal amount in step 10).

4. Separate cords 1-4-1. Find the center 2 cords. Thread a size 6 frosted purple bead onto them, then tie a flat knot with cords 2 and 5.

5. We will now work with cords 1 and 6. With cord 1, thread on a seed bead, a dark purple size 6 bead and another seed bead. Repeat with cord 6, then separate the cords into 3-3. Tie a flat knot with the left 3 cords. Tie a flat knot with the right 3 cords.

6. Repeat step 4 and 5 three times.

7. Find the center 2 cords, hold together and thread on the 1cm focal bead. Take the cords out (2 and 5) and bead as follows: 2 size 6 dark purple beads, a frosted purple bead, 2 dark purple beads. Find cords 1 and 6 and bead as follows: 2 frosted purple beads, a seed bead, a dark purple bead, a seed bead, 2 frosted purple beads.

8. With cords 2 and 5, tie a flat knot around the center 2 cords. Place the center 4 cords together and tie a flat knot around them with outer cords 1 and 6.

9. Repeat steps 4 and 5 four times.

10. Repeat step 3.

11. Place your button bead on all 6 cords and tie an overhand knot tight against the bead. Glue well and trim the cords.

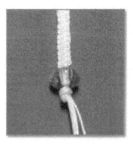

Lantern Bracelet

This pattern may look simply, but please don't try it if you are in a hurry. This one takes patience. Don't worry about getting your picot knots all the exact same shape. Have fun with it! The finished bracelet is 7 ¼ inches in length. If desired, add a picot knot and a spiral knot on each side of the center piece to lengthen it. This pattern has a jump ring closure.

Knots Used:

- Lark's Head Knot

- Spiral Knot

- Picot Knot

- Overhand Knot

Supplies:

- 3 strands of C-Lon cord (2 light brown and 1 medium brown) 63-inch lengths

- Fasteners (1 jump ring, 1 spring ring or lobster clasp)

- Glue - Beacon 527 muti-use

- 8 small beads (about 4mm) amber to gold colors

- 30 gold seed beads

- 3 beads (about 6 mm) amber color (mine are rectangular, but round or oval will work wonderfully also)

- Note: Bead size can vary slightly. Just be sure all beads you choose will slide onto 2 cords (except seed beads).

Instructions:

1. Find the center of your cord and attach it to the jump ring with a lark's head knot. Repeat with the 2 remaining strands. If you want the 2-tone effect, be sure your second color is NOT placed in the center, or it will only be a filler cord and you will end up with a 1 tone bracelet.

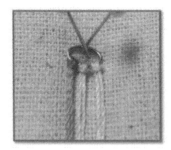

2. You now have 6 cords to work with. Think of them as numbered 1 thorough 6, from left to right. Move cords 1 and 6 apart from the rest. You will use these to work the spiral knot. All others are filler cords. Take cord number 1 tie a spiral knot. Always begin with the left cord. Tie 7 more spirals.

3. Place a 4mm bead on the center 2 cords. Leave cords 1 and 6 alone for now and work 1 flat knot using cords 2 and 5.

4. Now put cords 2 and 5 together with the center strands. Use 1 and 6 to tie a picot flat knot. If you don't like the look of your picot knot, loosen it up and try again. Gently tug the cords into place then lock in tightly with the spiral knot.

Notice here how I am holding the picot knot with my thumbs while pulling the cords tight with my fingers. If you look closely you may be able to see that I have a cord in each hand.

5. Tie 8 spiral knots (using left cord throughout pattern).

6. Place a 4mm bead on the center 2 cords. Leave cords 1 and 6 alone for now and work 1 flat knot using cords 2 and 5. Now put cords 2 and 5 together with the center strands. Use strands 1 and 6 to tie a picot flat knot.

7. Repeat steps 5 and 6 until you have 5 sets of spirals.

8. Place 5 seed beads on cords 1 and 6. Put cords 3 and 4 together and string on a 6 mm bead. Tie one flat knot with the outermost cords.

Repeat this step two more times.

Now repeat steps 5 and 6 until you have 5 sets of spirals from the center point. Thread on your clasp. Tie an overhand knot with each cord and glue well. Let dry completely. As this is the weakest point in the design, I advise trimming the excess cords and gluing again. Let dry.

Celtic Choker

Elegant loops allow the emerald and silver beads to stand out, making this a striking piece. The finished length is 12 inches. Be sure to use the ribbon clasp which gives multiple length options to the closure.

Knots Used:

- Lark's Head Knot

- Alternating Lark's Head Chain

Supplies:

- 3 strands of black C-Lon cord; two 7ft cords, one 4ft cord

- 18 - green beads (4mm)

- 7 - round silver beads (10 mm)

- Fasteners: Ribbon Clasps, silver

- Glue - Beacon 527 multi-use

Note: Bead size can vary slightly. Just be sure all beads you choose will slide onto 2 cords.

Instructions:

1. Optional – Find the center of your cord and attach it to the top of the ribbon clasp with a lark's head knot. I found it easier to thread the loose ends through and pull them down until my loop was near the opening, then push the cords through the loop. Repeat with the 2 remaining strands, putting the four-foot cord in the center. If this is problematic, you could cut all the cords to 7ft and not worry about placement. (If you really trust your glue, you can skip this step by gluing the cords into the clasp and going from there).

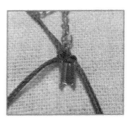

2. Lay all cords into the ribbon clasp. Add a generous dap of glue and use pliers to close the clasp.

3. You now have 6 cords to work with. Find the 4 ft cords and place them in the center. They will be the holding (or filler) cords throughout.

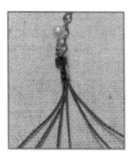

4. Begin your Alternating Lark's Head (ALH) chain, using the outmost right cord then the outermost left cord. Follow with the other right cord then the last left cord. For this first set, the pattern will be hard to see. You may need to tug gently on the cords to get a little slack in them.

5. Now slide a silver bead onto the center 2 cords.

6. The outer cords are now staggered on your holding cords. Continue with the ALH chain by knotting with the upper right cord…

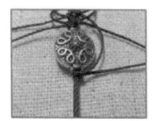

then tie a knot with the upper left cord.

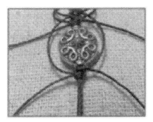

7. Finish your set of 4 knots, then add a green bead

8. Tie four ALH knots followed by a green bead until you have 3 green beads in the pattern. Then tie one more set of 4 ALH knots.

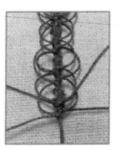

9. Slide on a silver bead and continue creating sequences of 3 green, 1 silver (always with 4 ALH knots between each). End with the 7th silver bead and 1 more set of 4 ALH knots, for a 12" necklace. (Use this to shorten or lengthen as you choose).

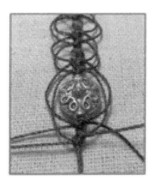

10. Lay all cords in the ribbon clasp and glue well.

11. Crimp shut and let dry completely. Trim excess cords.

CHAPTER 12:

Project 3

Macramé Skirt Hanger

What you need:

12 mm size beads

One 8-inch ring

One 2-inch ring

4mm cord

Instructions:

Cut 8 cords that are at least 8.5 yards long then cut a cord that is 36 inches long before cutting 4 more yards of cord.

Fold the 8.5 yard in half to start the top part of the thread. Let it pass through the ring and let some parts drape down before choosing two cords from outside the bundle. Make sure to match the ends and then try the square knot.

You should find the center and move 8 inches down from it and then stop when you reach 12 inches.

Wrap the center a couple of times and then pull the ends tightly until you build a sturdy bundle, and then tug on the ends so that the roll could get smaller.

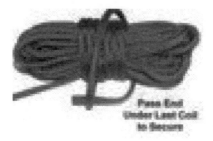

Make a total of four spirals that could at least be 20 inches and then manage the filler cords by adding a bead to them.

Attach the cords to the 8-inch ring by using double half-hitch stitches and then arrange the cords so they could be in four groups. Pull the stitches tightly so there is enough spacing and then mount all the cords to the ring in counterclockwise motion. To cover the ring, make sure to tie a half-hitch at each end.

Make alternating square knots just below the ring and divide into two groups of 40 strings each—it sounds like a lot, but it is what would naturally happen. Add some tape to the cords you have labeled 1 to 40 and then tie a half-square knot to the four injected threads. Add some beads, and then tie a knot again.

Add beads to cords 20 to 21 after using cords 19 to 22 and then make alternating square knots and then repeat on the cords on the back side. Add beads and make more alternating square knots, then add beads to cords 16 to 17 after using cords labeled 15 to 18. Tie the next row without adding any beads and then use cords 11 to 30. Work on cords 12 to 29 by adding beads to them and making use of alternating square knots. Repeat the 3rd row with no beads, and the 4th row with beads and choose four of your favorite cords to make fringes.

- **Macramé Speaker Hanger**

What you need:

Measuring tape

Fabric glue

Brass rings

50 yards paracord

Instructions:

Cut 16 cords that are 15 yards long, then cut 2 cords that are 2 yards long, and finally, cut 2 cords that are 60 inches long.

What you must do is wrap the two rings together using 2 cords and by tying with the crown knot. Make use of half hitch stitches to secure the wrap and then find the center of the cord. Make sure to secure them on the surface and to hold them close together. 8 of the two cords should then be lined up in a central manner so that they would be able to hold the speaker.

Now, go and bundle the long cords by wrapping and pulling them tightly together and letting the first end pass under the last coil. Wrap securely so it would not unravel.

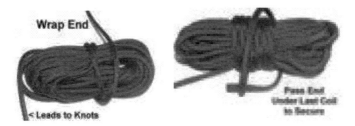

Make sure to pull more cords from the bundles and then tighten the wraps on the center with your working cords. Let the lower portion come together by using square knots and make sure that you go and tighten the first half of it. Tie the second half around the board and then turn the board around after you have let the rolled coils pass through at one end of the ring.

Use half-hitches to arrange the center and let the rolled bundles dangle on the other end of the ring. Fold the sennit so you could match it with the last couple of knots, and then wrap the scrap cord around it. Now, put the hanger horizontally on your workspace and secure with square knots.

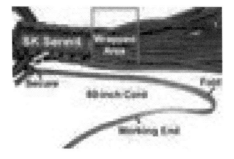

Let the working end pass through the middle of the bundle and then bring the working end around the bundle that you are using.

Let it pass over the front and under the cord's back and keep wrapping as firmly as you can until you see something that looks like a loop.

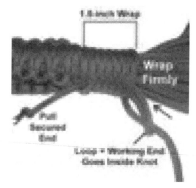

Take the pin away from the secured end and pull until you reach the knot inside. Make use of fabric glue to coat this with and trim the ends. Let flame pass through it to secure it, as well.

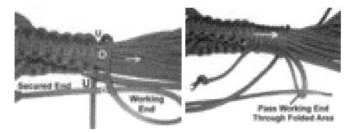

Tie 5 half knots to keep the hanger secure and start suspending on the wall or ceiling—whichever you prefer. Place some beads before tying the knot again, and then make use of fillers as working cords before firmly tightening the knot. Create 25 more square knots and push the knots up to eliminate spooling. Repeat process until your desired length.

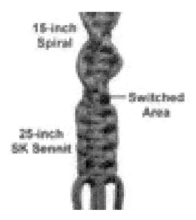

Finally, make a figure-eight knot and make sure to pull the end tightly before tying several more.

Macramé Tie-Dye Necklace

This one is knotted tightly, which gives it the effect that it is strong—but still elegant. This is a good project to craft—you would enjoy the act of making it, and wearing it, as well!

What you need:

1 pack laundry rope

Tulip One-Step Dye

Fabric glue

Candle

Jump rings

Lobster clasp

Instructions:

Tie the rope using crown knots

After tying, place the knotted rope inside the One-Step Dye pack (you could get this in most stores) and let it set and dry overnight.

Upon taking it out, leave it for a few hours and then secure the end of the knot with fabric glue mixed with a bit of water.

Trim the ends off and burn off the ends with wax from candle.

Add jump rings to the end and secure with lobster clasp.

Enjoy your tie-dye necklace!

Macramé Watch Strand

If you are looking for ways to spice up your wristwatch, well, now's your chance! Make use of this Macramé Watch Strand Pattern and you will get what you want!

What you need:

Jump rings

Closure

2mm Crimp ends (you can choose another size, depending on your preferences)

Embroidery or craft floss

Watch with posts

Instructions:

Choose your types of floss, as well as their colors. Take at least 10 long strands for each side of the watch.

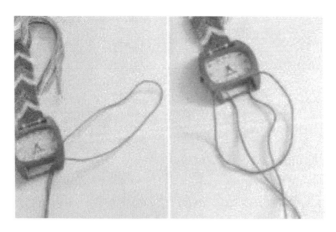

Lash each floss onto the bar/posts of the watch and thread like you would a regular Macramé bracelet or necklace.

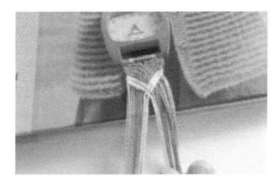

Braid the ends tightly if you want to make it more stylish and cut the ends. Burn with lighter to secure before placing jump rings and closure.

Use and enjoy!

Conclusion

The beauty of Macramé as a vintage art that has survived extinction for centuries and has continued to thrive as a technique of choice for making simple but sophisticated items is simply unrivalled. The simple fact that you have decided to read this manual means that you are well on your way to making something great. There is truly a certain, unequaled feeling of satisfaction that comes from crafting your own masterpiece, and by reading this book, you have taken the first step towards experiencing that feeling of euphoria.

As you have read this book, do not simply discard it. Keep it as a guide, and look out for more extensive materials online and offline to help you perfect your skills. This book explains basic knots and projects for beginners, but if you practice Macramé regularly, you wouldn't be a beginner for long. As stated earlier, Macramé can be very relaxing, and it is an amazing avenue to bring family and friends together. As you have learnt here, you can teach your loved ones some of these basic knots, and refer them to obtain their copy of this carefully prepared beginner's guide to Macramé.

The most important rule in Macramé is the maxim: "Practice makes perfect." If you cease to practice constantly, your skills are likely to deteriorate over time. So keep your skills sharp, exercise the creative parts of your brain, and keep creating mind-blowing handmade masterpieces. Jewelry and fashion accessories made with even the most basic Macramé knots are always a beauty to behold, hence they serve as perfect gifts for loved ones on special occasions. Presenting a Macramé bracelet to someone, for instance passes the message that you didn't just remember to get them a gift, you also treasure them so much that you chose to invest your time into crafting something unique specially for them too, and trust me, that is a very powerful message. However, the most beautiful thing about Macramé is perhaps the fact that it helps to create durable items. Hence you can keep a piece of decoration, or a fashion accessory you made for yourself for many years, enjoy the value and still feel nostalgic anytime you remember when you made it. It even feels better when you made that item with someone. This feature of durability also makes Macramé accessories incredibly perfect gifts.

Macramé can also serve as an avenue for you to begin your dream small business. After perfecting your Macramé skills, you can conveniently sell your items and get paid well for your products, especially if you can perfectly make items like bracelets that people buy a lot. You could even train people and start your own little company that makes bespoke Macramé fashion accessories. The opportunities that Macramé presents are truly endless.

Macramé can also serve as an avenue for you to begin your dream small business. After perfecting your Macramé skills, you can conveniently sell your items and get paid well for your products, especially if you can perfectly make items like bracelets that people buy a lot. You could even train people and start your own little company that makes bespoke Macramé fashion accessories. The opportunities that Macramé presents are truly endless.

There you have it, everything you need to know to get you started with your own macramé knots. This is going to show you just how easy it is to get started in this hobby, and once you get the hang of things, you are going to find that it is easier than ever to get started with your own projects.

Good luck and create to your heart's content.

So, stay sharp, keep practicing and keep getting better.

Welcome to a world of infinite possibilities!

Printed in Great Britain
by Amazon